CRUISE PORTS
NORTHEAST ASIA

A GUIDE TO PERFECT DAYS ON SHORE

Ray Bartlett, Andrew Bender, Jade Bremner, Stephanie
d'Arc Taylor, Dinah Gardner, Trent Holden, Craig
McLachlan, Rebecca Milner, Kate Morgan, MaSovaida
Morgan, Thomas O'Malley, Simon Richmond,
Phillip Tang, Benedict Walker

CHINA

RUSS

●Vladivostok

●BĚIJĪNG

NORTH
KOREA

●PYONGYANG

Sea of Japan
(East Sea)

KANAZA

KYOTO

●SEOUL

OSAKA p

SOUTH
KOREA

Yellow Sea
(West Sea)

●Gwangju

●Jeju-si

Matsuya

Shikoku ●

● Kyūshū

●Kagoshima

CHINA

East China Sea
(South Sea)

Okinawa
Islands

Naha●

Taiwan
Strait

TAIWAN

Statue, Ryōan-ji (p97), Kyoto
COWARDLION/SHUTTERSTOCK ©

Plan Your Trip
Northeast Asia's Top 16

SAKARIN SAWASDINAKA/SHUTTERSTOCK ©

Tokyo

Planet earth's unrivalled 24/7 megalopolis

Tokyo (p35) is one of the world's reigning cities of superlatives –
the dining, drinking and shopping are all top class. It's a city
always in flux, which is one of its enduring charms, forever sending
up breathtaking new structures and dreaming up new culinary
delights. It truly has something for everyone, whether your ideal
afternoon is spent in an art museum or racing through the streets
of Akihabara in a go-kart.

NIKADA/GETTY IMAGES ©

Shànghǎi

China's neon-lit beacon of change and modernity

Its sights set squarely on the not-too-distant future, Shànghǎi (p231) offers a taste of all the superlatives China can dare to dream up, from the world's highest observation deck to its fastest commercially operating train. Start with the Bund, Shànghǎi's iconic riverfront area, then head to the French Concession, where the Paris of the East turns on its European charms to maximum effect.
Above: The Bund (p234)

2

MAŠOVAIDA MORGAN/LONELY PLANET ©

Busan

Mountains, beaches, street food and a cosmopolitan vibe

South Korea's second-largest metropolis, Busan (p265) is one of the country's most enjoyable cities. Its top attraction is the atmospheric, waterside Jagalchi Fish Market, where you can buy and eat the freshest of seafood. Also don't miss walking the tranquil path to Beomeo-Sa temple, strolling the lanes of Gamcheon Culture Village, sampling the local dessert *sulbing* and knocking back shots of *soju*. Above: Jagalchi Fish Market (p270)

3

Kyoto

National treasures, historic temples and modern-day geisha

There are said to be more than 1000 Buddhist temples in Kyoto (p87). The city is a showroom for centuries of Japanese religious architecture, which produced both the glittering Kinkaku-ji (Golden Temple) and the stark Zen garden at Ryōan-ji. But don't equate religiosity with temperance here: Kyoto is also the city where geisha entertained in lantern-lit teahouses (and still do). Above: Kiyomizu-dera (p99)

Taipei

A multitude of influences make up one unique city

Surrounded by forested hills, within Taipei's (p219) city limits are world-class museums, historic temples and never-ending opportunities for snacking and shopping. Temples and markets dating back centuries coexist with Taipei's flashy modernity. Plus you'll find culinary influences from every corner of China, some of the best Japanese food outside Japan, Asia's best coffee and a night-market scene loaded with unique local snacks. Above: Chiang Kai-shek Memorial Hall (p222)

Osaka

The friendly metropolis of food and fun

Osaka (p115) is a city that packs more colour than most; its acres
of concrete are cloaked in dazzling neon billboards. The best way to
get under its skin is by chowing down on local cuisine and enjoying
a drink at an *izakaya* (pub restaurant) alongside locals. The city's
unofficial slogan is *kuidaore* ('eat until you drop'), and it seems that
everyone is always out for a good meal and a good time. It's the
perfect stop for your urban Japan fix. Above: Dōtombori (p124)

Hokkaidō

Pristine nature and outdoor adventures galore

Hokkaidō (p189), Japan's northernmost island, is an untamed landscape of mountains that is pockmarked with crystal-blue caldera lakes and sulphur-rich hot springs. This is 'big mountain and snow' country, where skiers carve snow drifts reaching several metres in depth. In the green season, hikers and cyclists are drawn to the island's wide open spaces and dramatic topography. This is a place of seasonal thrills galore: don't miss out. Above: Hakodate (p202)

7

NICEPIX/SHUTTERSTOCK ©

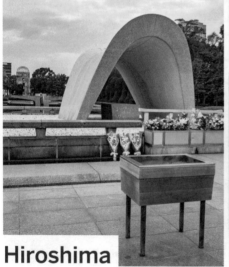

ITZAVU/SHUTTERSTOCK © ARCHITECT: KENZO TANGE

Hiroshima

GRANT M HENDERSON/SHUTTERSTOCK ©

Heartbreaking history with a message of hope

It's not until you visit the Peace Memorial Museum that the true extent of human tragedy wrought by the atomic bomb in 1945 becomes vividly clear. A visit here is a sobering history lesson and the park around the museum offers opportunities for reflection. But the city's (p153) spirit of determination – and its food – will ensure that you'll have good memories to take with you when you leave. Clockwise, this page: Atomic Bomb Dome (p158), Hiroshima-jō (p160), Peace Memorial Park (p156)

VASSAMON ANANSUKKASEM/SHUTTERSTOCK ©

Okinawa-hontō

Spectacular beaches, intriguing history and 'island time'

Originally settled by the Ryūkyū people, Okinawa-hontō (p207) offers a totally different experience from the rest of Japan. War memorials are clustered in the south of the island, while the bustling capital Naha offers the chance to sip fresh juice from the market, fill up on island delicacies, and gain insight into Okinawa's rich cultural heritage. Above: Tsuboya Pottery Street (p210)

9

ANDREAS H/SHUTTERSTOCK ©

Kanazawa

Feudal-era capital on the Sea of Japan coast

In its heyday, Kanazawa (p175) rivalled Kyoto as a centre for the arts. This artisan tradition is today evident in a number of shops and galleries. Kanazawa also has one of Japan's top gardens, Kenroku-en, an excellent art museum and a food culture that draws heavily from the seafood pulled from the ocean. Kanazawa has long flown under the radar, though that's changing. Go now, before everyone else catches on. Above: Kenroku-en (p178)

10

CJ NATTANAI/SHUTTERSTOCK ©

Jeju Island

Where volcanic scenery accompanies leisurely hikes

A volcanic landmass with spectacular craters and lava tubes, Jeju-do (p255) holds unique charms amid beautiful, accessible surroundings. The frequently dramatic landscape is best seen on foot – spending a day following all or part of a trail is a wonderful way to soak up Jeju's unique charms and beautiful surroundings. Jeju's separately developed island culture is revealed in its distinct cuisine and customs. Above: Seongsan Ilchul-bong (p260)

SANGA PARK/SHUTTERSTOCK ©

Nagasaki

WWII tragedy and a colourful trading history

History weighs heavily on Nagasaki (p165), the second Japanese city destroyed by an atomic bomb. But as Japan's only truly open port during the 200-year period of isolation in the 17th to 19th centuries, Nagasaki has a cosmopolitan legacy that lives on today in its food and architecture. As paradoxical as it may seem, Nagasaki is vibrant and charming, and it begs to be explored far beyond the bomb museums, monuments and memorials. Above: Dejima Wharf (p172)

PATARA/SHUTTERSTOCK ©

Yokohama

Sophisticated portside city

Japan's second-largest city and part of the Greater Tokyo Metropolitan Area along with Tokyo and Kawasaki, Yokohama (p65) is often overshadowed by the nation's capital. Come to sample craft beer, contemporary art and jazz tunes. The rejuvenated port area, fringed by amusement parks, museums and historic and contemporary architecture, generously repays a day's exploring.

Above: Yokohama Cosmoworld (p73)

13

FBDESIGNCENTER/SHUTTERSTOCK ©

Nagoya

Underestimated and underappreciated – a hidden gem

Although its GDP tops that of many small countries, Nagoya (p77) struggles to shake its reputation among Japanese (many of whom have never visited) as the nation's most boring metropolis. But those who visit discover a friendly city with fabulous shopping, food and parks. Hit Japan's first Legoland, explore the absorbing train and Toyota museums, and paint your own Noritake china keepsake. Above: Ōsu area (p80)

14

Kōbe

Historic naval gateway to Japan

Sandwiched between the sea and the mountains, in 1859 Kōbe (p131) became one of just five ports in Japan open to international trade. The legacy of this period lives on in modern Kōbe, a hub of international maritime travel and commerce to this day. Famous for its namesake top-grade beef, the city also boasts waterfalls, shopping, gardens, historic houses and fabulous views. Above: Kōbe port (p133)

15

Kōchi

A laid-back yet lively city

Home to one of Japan's most famous and best-preserved castles, Kōchi (p141) has a deserved reputation as a city that enjoys a good time. This smart, friendly and compact city is small (for a Japanese city), making its many interesting sights super accessible. It's home to an impressive pilgrimage temple, beautiful botanical gardens, a paper museum with occasional workshops, and a terrific Sunday market. Above: Kōchi-jō (p144)

16

Plan Your Trip
Need to Know

When to Go

Sapporo
GO Apr–Oct

Tokyo
GO any time

Busan
GO Oct–Jun

Kyoto
GO Mar–Jun or Sep–Nov

Shànghǎi
GO Mar–May
& Sep–Nov

Nagasaki
GO May–Oct

Naha
GO Mar–Nov

Taipei
GO any time

Warm to hot summers, mild winters
Warm to hot summers, cold winters
Dry climate

High Season (Apr–Aug)

o Golden Week (early May) and O-Bon (mid-August) in Japan: sights are packed and prices are sky-high.

o April brings cherry blossoms and crowds of admirers.

o Temperatures and humidity soar July through August – prepare for summer downpours.

Shoulder (Mar, Sep & Oct)

o In the north this is the optimal season, with fresh weather and clear skies.

o In autumn (roughly September through October) you can experience nature in all its russet shades.

Low Season (Nov–Feb)

o Crowds dwindle. Bitterly cold in Hokkaidō, cool and dry in the south.

o Many businesses close over the New Year period (end of December to early January).

Currencies

China: yuán (元; ¥); Japan: yen (¥); South Korea: Korean won (₩); Taiwan: New Taiwanese dollar (NT$)

Languages

China: Mandarin, Cantonese; Japan: Japanese; South Korea: Korean; Taiwan: Mandarin, Taiwanese

Visas

Visas on arrival in Japan, South Korea and Taiwan for most nationalities for stays of up to 90 days. Not needed for 72 hours or less in Shànghǎi.

Money

Credit cards are widely accepted in midrange and top-end restaurants and shops, though less so in Shànghǎi. ATMs are common, but not all accept foreign cards.

Mobile Phones

Different networks operate across the region. Prepaid SIM cards for unlocked smartphones are available at electronics stores.

Time

Japan and South Korea are nine hours ahead of GMT/UTC; China and Taiwan are eight hours ahead.

Costs for a Day in Port

Budget: Less than ¥5000

- Bowl of noodles: ¥750
- Public-transport pass: ¥600
- Temple or museum entry: ¥500

Midrange: ¥5000–10,000

- Lunch for two at a midrange eatery: ¥6000
- Gourmet coffee: ¥700
- Half-day organised tour: ¥5000

Top End: More than ¥10,000

- Lunch for two at a top-end restaurant: from ¥15,000
- Taxi between city sights: ¥2500
- Private, customised tours: from ¥10,000

Useful Websites

Lonely Planet (www.lonelyplanet.com) Destination information, hotel bookings, traveller forum and more.
Japan National Tourism Organization (www.jnto.go.jp) Official tourist site with planning tools and events calendar.
Cruise Critic (www.cruisecritic.com) Cruise forum, reviews and info on cruise deals.
Cruise Line (www.cruiseline.com) Ship reviews, deals and a cruise forum.

What to Pack

Wear slip-on shoes, as you'll be taking your shoes off a lot; during sandal season many locals will carry socks to slip into to avoid walking barefoot. You also may find yourself sitting on the floor, so dress comfortably for that. Neat, smart casual wear will fit right in; pack more formal attire for top-end bars and restaurants. Winters can be bitterly cold, especially in the north, and summers hot and humid. Dressing in layers is ideal.

An umbrella won't go astray in winter or summer, nor a good hat and sunscreen in summer.

Wi-Fi Access

- Wi-fi is often available in port, on buses and trains, and at major tourist sites, train stations, cafes and restaurants.
- South Korea has a particularly fast and widespread connection.
- Service in Japan and Taipei can be spotty and slow. Service in China is particularly frustrating. The Chinese authorities maintain strong controls on internet access; the list is constantly changing but sites and apps such as Facebook, Google-owned sites (YouTube, Google Maps, Gmail, Google Drive), WhatsApp and many international media outlets have been blocked in the past, so plan ahead.
- Wi-fi is generally unsecured, so take care what kind of information you enter if you're using a wireless connection.

Arriving in Northeast Asia

Kōbe Regular high-speed ferries connect Kansai International Airport (near Osaka) and Kōbe airport (adult/child ¥1850/930, 30 minutes). From here it's a short trip on the Portliner monorail to Kōbe Port Terminal.

Shànghǎi There's no direct public transport from Pǔdōng or Hóngqiáo airports to the cruise terminals. A private transfer company or taxi are your best bets. Times and prices vary, up to about ¥200 and a little over an hour to get from Pǔdōng airport to Shànghǎi Port International Cruise Terminal. A fun option is to take the maglev (www.smtdc.com) warp-speed train into the city centre, and a taxi or metro from there to your port.

Yokohama Regular JR Narita Express trains (adult/child ¥4290/2145, 80 minutes) run direct from Narita airport to Yokohama station. From here take the subway to Nihon-ōdōri station, from where it's a short walk to port. Friendly Airport Limousine (www.limousinebus.co.jp; adult/child ¥3600/1800) runs to Yokohama's waterfront.

For more on **getting around**, see p308

Plan Your Trip
Hot Spots for...

OPERATION SHOOTING/SHUTTERSTOCK ©

Regional Cuisine

Eating is one of the great pleasures of visiting Northeast Asia. Discover just how varied the cuisine is, from region to region and season to season.

Kyoto (p87)
Japan's ancient imperial capital is the birthplace of *kaiseki* (haute cuisine) and the tea ceremony.

Roan Kikunoi (p107) An experimental and creative approach to *kaiseki*.

Osaka (p115)
Colourful Osaka is Japan's capital of street food: fierce competition turns humble dishes to high art.

Wanaka Honten (p120) Top for *tako-yaki* (octopus dumplings, pictured above).

Taiwan (p219)
Taiwan is synonymous with night markets: sweet, savoury and fresh, the food is an explosion of flavours.

Miaokou Night Market (p228) Step into one of Taiwan's best night markets.

TRAVELLIGHT/SHUTTERSTOCK ©; ARCHITECT: XING TONGHE

Art & Architecture

The region's sublime artistic tradition transcends gallery walls, embodying its past and present.

Tokyo (p35)
Art museums, theatres and the creations of Japan's modern-day architects.

Tokyo National Museum (p38) The world's largest collection of Japanese art.

Shànghǎi (p231)
Shànghǎi: few cities in the world evoke so much history and mystique in name alone.

Shanghai Museum (pictured above; p242) Explores Chinese history through art.

Osaka (p115)
An urban sprawl that lacks Tokyo's grace but offers unexpected delights amid the chaos.

Abeno Harukas (p124) Japan's tallest building opened in 2014.

Outdoor Activities

Northeast Asia is a year-round destination for walkers keen for relaxed strolls or serious peaks. In winter, a day of skiing is a top option.

TORJRTRX/SHUTTERSTOCK ©

Fuji Five Lakes (p62)
Iconic Mt Fuji is the main draw, but the pretty lake district offers gentler hikes through the foothills, too.

Mt Fuji (pictured above; p62) Watch sunrise from Japan's highest summit.

Hokkaidō (p189)
Japan's northernmost island has become a playground for outdoor enthusiasts.

Kushiro-shitsugen (p196 An important habitat for the red-crowned crane.

Jeju Island (p255)
Amazing volcanic scenery accompanies leisurely hikes, topped off with spectacular views.

Sanbanggul-sa (p258) Take in the sea views from this cave temple.

Historic Sites

See the sights where the region's history – the samurai warrior, the wandering ascetic and the rice-paddy farmer – is brought to life.

KHONG KATESORN/SHUTTERSTOCK ®

Nara (p112)
The nation's first capital hosts Buddhist art, architecture and historical relics from the 8th century.

Tōdai-ji (pictured above; p112) Home of Nara's Daibutsu statue.

Hiroshima (p153)
This city has numerous monuments commemorating the day that changed history for Japan and the world.

Peace Memorial Museum (p159) Evocative account of the bomb's aftermath.

Okinawa-hontō (p207)
Today it feels like a tropical paradise, but this island saw tremendous carnage in WWII.

Okinawa Prefectural Peace Memorial Museum (p213) Details the US invasion.

Plan Your Trip
Month by Month

BY JENG/SHUTTERSTOCK ©

January

January is wet and cool in Taipei and Okinawa, and icy cold up in Hokkaidō. In Japan, many businesses close for the whole first week of the new year, and transport is busy.

February
❄ Yuki Matsuri

Two million visitors head to Sapporo's annual snow festival (www.snowfes.com) in early February. Highlights include an international snow-sculpture contest, ice slides and mazes for kids.

❄ Lunar New Year

Families gather in China, South Korea and Taiwan to greet the New Year together, feasting on traditional food and giving gifts. Expect parades, fireworks and lots of colour. Many businesses take a holiday in the days following.

❄ Lantern Festival

Music, street performers, light shows and floating lanterns fill this week-long event held at the end of the Lunar New Year in Taipei Expo Park. See www.taipeitravel. net/en for details.

March

Spring begins in fits and starts. The Japanese have a saying: *sankan-shion* – three days cold, four days warm.

April

Warmer weather and blossoming trees make April a favoured month, but places such as Kyoto and Jeju-do can be crowded.

❄ Cherry-Blossom Viewing

When the cherry blossoms burst into bloom, the Japanese hold rollicking *hanami* (blossom-viewing) parties. The blossoms are fickle and hard to time: on average, they hit their peak in Tokyo and Kyoto between 25 March and 7 April. In Taiwan they appear a little earlier – mid to late February.

May

May is lovely: it's warm and sunny in most places. On 1 May, the whole of China gears up for a hard-earned three-day holiday.

🎏 Sanja Matsuri

The grandest Tokyo festival of all, this three-day event, held over the third weekend of May, attracts around 1.5 million spectators to Asakusa, for a rowdy parade of *mikoshi* (portable shrines) carried by men and women in traditional dress.

🎏 Buddha's Birthday

Brings a kaleidoscope of light and colour, as rows of paper lanterns are strung down main thoroughfares and in temple courtyards across South Korea.

June

Through June and July the summer heat picks up and rains set in.

★ Best Festivals

Cherry-Blossom Viewing April
Gion Matsuri July
Lunar New Year February
Yuki Matsuri February
Dream Parade October

🎏 Hyakumangoku Matsuri

In early June, Kanazawa's biggest festival celebrates the city's 16th-century glory days with period-costume parades, cultural performances and more.

July

🎏 Gion Matsuri

Japan's most vaunted festival is held on 17 and 24 July in Kyoto, when huge, elaborate floats are paraded through the streets. Three evenings prior, locals stroll through street markets dressed in beautiful *yukata* (light cotton kimonos).

From left: Cherry blossoms, Tokyo; Gion Matsuri, Kyoto

🎣 Peiron Dragon-Boat Races

In late July, dragon-boat races are held in the harbour of Nagasaki, a tradition introduced from China in the 17th century.

🍷 Sapporo Summer Matsuri

The big names plus microbrewers set up outdoor beer gardens in Ōdōri-kōen from mid-July to mid-August. A whole month (www.sapporo-natsu.com) of beer drinking in the sun!

🎊 Minato Matsuri

Held around 'Ocean Day' (the third Monday in July), this street festival in Nagoya Port features a parade, dancing, fireworks and a water-logging contest dating back to the Edo period.

August

Hot, humid summer hits a peak – watch out for rainstorms. In Japan, three days in mid-August are set aside to honour the dead; public transport is hectic and shops may close.

🎊 Hakodate Port Festival

In early August, thousands of locals gather to perform traditional dances in the streets, including Hakodate's signature squid dance.

🎊 Peace Memorial Ceremony

On 6 August, a memorial service is held in Hiroshima for victims of the WWII atomic bombing of the city. Thousands of paper lanterns are floated down the river.

☆ World Cosplay Summit

Some 30 countries compete in early August (or late July) in Nagoya (www.world cosplaysummit.jp) to see who has the best *cosplayers* (manga and anime fans who dress up as their fave characters).

September

Days are still warm, hot even, though less humid – though the odd typhoon rolls through this time of year.

🎊 Kishiwada Danjiri Matsuri

Osaka's wildest festival, held over the third weekend in September, is a kind of running of the bulls except with *danjiri* (floats), many weighing more than 3000kg.

October

Autumn is a great time to visit; outdoors you'll enjoy a palate of rustic colours.

☆ Busan International Film Festival

South Korea's top international film festival (www.biff.kr), held in the architecturally stunning Busan Cinema Center, attracts stars from across Asia and beyond.

🎊 Ryūkyū-no-Saiten

Brings together more than a dozen festivals and special events celebrating Okinawan culture for three days at the end of the month.

🎊 Dream Parade

Dream Parade is Taipei's Mardi Gras. Not to be missed if you can help it!

🍷 Yokohama Oktoberfest

For two weeks in early October much beer drinking goes down during this event held in Yokohama's historic harbour district.

November

☆ China Shanghai International Arts Festival

A month-long program (www.artsbird.com) of cultural events in October and November, which includes the Shanghai Art Fair, a program of international music, dance, opera and acrobatics, and exhibitions of the Shanghai Biennale (www.shanghaibiennale.org).

December

December is cold across most of the region, although Taipei and Okinawa remain fairly mild.

🎊 Luminarie

Kōbe streets are lined with illuminated arches every year for this event (http://kobe-luminarie.jp) in early December, in memory of the victims of the 1995 Great Hanshin Earthquake.

Plan Your Trip
Get Inspired

LKUNL/SHUTTERSTOCK ©

Read

Shōgun (James Clavell; 1975) An historic tale based on the true story of a Brit who visited Japan in 1600.

Kyoto: A Cultural History (John Dougill; 2006) Touches on everything from courtly verse to Zen Buddhism to modern film.

Norwegian Wood (Murakami Haruki; 1987) Coming-of-age story set in 1960s Tokyo, by Japan's most popular living writer.

Shanghai: The Rise and Fall of a Decadent City 1842–1949 (Stella Dong; 2000) Rip-roaring profile of Shànghǎi's good-old, bad-old days.

Watch

Spirited Away (Miyazaki Hayao; 2001) Academy Award–winning animated feature, said to be inspired by Jiufen, near Taipei.

Eat Drink Man Woman (Ang Lee; 1994) A must-see for those interested in Taiwanese culture.

Train to Busan (Yeon Sang-ho; 2016) Just when you thought it was good to go 1st class: rail-roading apocalyptic zombie horror.

Your Name (Shinkai Makoto; 2016) Popular anime where a city boy and country girl swap places.

Shanghai Triad (Zhang Yimou; 1995) Stylish take on Shànghǎi's 1930s gangster scene.

Listen

Shimanchu nu Takara (Begin) Love song to Okinawa with *eisa* (Okinawan folk-style) chanting.

Hanamizuki (Hitoto Yō) Tender ode to love and loss and a perennial karaoke favourite.

Tokyo, Mon Amour (Pizzicato Five) Moody lounge track from the '90s Shibuya indie scene.

Love Yourself: Tear (BTS) The first-ever K-Pop album to take the number-one spot on the Billboard 200.

13 Classic Shanghai Pop Rock Songs (Top Floor Circus) This legendary outfit sang in Shanghainese and played anything from folk to punk.

Above: Arashiyama Bamboo Grove (p103), Kyoto

Plan Your Trip
Essential Northeast Asia

Activities

Many ports offer easy access to short walks; in Sapporo you can even zip up to the snowfields. Follow up with a massage, a spa or an onsen (hot-spring bath). Many believe the waters to have curative properties; at the very least, you will sleep very, very well after a soak.

Amusement parks are another regional highlight, from big international names (Disney and Lego), to homegrown ones.

Shopping

Tokyo is the fashion trendsetter for all of Japan; Osaka has a street-smart style of its own. Kyoto is the place to pick up traditional goods, such as anything tea related. Around the country are pottery towns (Naha is a highlight) and others famous for local crafts.

Shànghǎi shoppers buy up big-time. Whether you're after boutique threads, handmade ceramics or a period poster from the Mao era, Shànghǎi is an A to Z of shopping.

In South Korea, make-up and beauty products are particularly hot items. More unique mementos include pottery, tea, *soju* (local vodka), K-Pop branded food, Korean sweets and *hanbok* (traditional clothing).

Eating

As visitors to Northeast Asia quickly discover, people here are absolutely obsessed with food. Every region has its own proud specialities and traditions, and, unsurprisingly, sublime seafood is common across the ports. Seasonal cuisine is also a key feature, with each season bringing signature ingredients and dishes.

Lavish restaurants featuring Michelin stars, celebrity chefs and degustation menus abound, but just as satisfying are hole-in-the-wall dumpling joints (a Shànghǎi classic) and bustling markets (Taipei's are renowned). In Japan, look to food courts in department stores and train stations for easy options. Few sights lack an on-site cafe, kiosk or street stalls selling tasty snacks.

HENRY WESTHEIM PHOTOGRAPHY/ALAMY STOCK PHOTO ©

Drinking

Tea is a fundamental part of life in Northeast Asia. In Japan, *o-cha* (tea) means green tea and broadly speaking there are two kinds: *ryokucha* (steeped with leaves) and *matcha*, which is made by whisking dried and milled leaves with water until a cappuccino level of frothiness is achieved. Green tea is also popular in South Korea. Prized high-mountain oolong, found in Shànghǎi and Taipei, makes a great gift for the folks back home. A newer tradition is bubble tea – a mixture of tea, milk, flavouring, sugar and giant black tapioca balls.

Coffee culture has taken off and you won't have trouble finding a good coffee shop. For something harder, look for *nihonshū* (sake) and whisky in Japan, cocktails in Shànghǎi, *soju* in Korea and craft beers everywhere you go.

Entertainment

Many ships are greeted on arrival by dancers in gorgeous, traditional dress, a fantastic introduction to local traditions.

★ Best Markets

Tsukiji (p50), Tokyo

Nishiki (p98), Kyoto

Daichi Makishi Kōsetsu Ichiba (p214), Okinawa

Jagalchi Fish Market (p270), Busan

Miaokou Night Market (p228), Taipei

Hakodate Morning Market (p203), Hokkaidō

Sumo, steeped in ancient ritual, is Japan's national sport. Tournaments take place in January, May and September in Tokyo and in March in Osaka. A geisha performance in Kyoto is also worth seeking out. Cinema is booming in Busan; if you can't catch a movie while in port, check out the city on screen in *Black Panther* (2018) or *Train to Busan* (2016).

From left: Nishiki Market (p98), Kyoto; Yosakoi Yume Matsuri, Nagoya (p77)

Plan Your Trip
Choose Your Cruise

STOCKPHOTO MANIA/SHUTTERSTOCK ©

Matching your expectations, budget and travel style to the right cruise is the most important decision of the trip, so it pays to think carefully about what's important to you. There's a very wide range of trips, from floating cities with thousands of passengers to smaller, more intimate ships.

Narrow it Down

So many options! So many decisions! Things to consider:

Budget Check the small print about what's included in the price before you commit. Unless you're on a luxury cruise, you'll likely be paying extra for alcoholic beverages, shore excursions, wi-fi and tips. Then there's the spa, casino, gift shop and other money sinks to look out for.

Style A mass-market, upscale or specialist cruise? Do you prefer numerous formal evenings or would you rather keep things casual? What are your special interests?

Itinerary Where do you want to go and what ports of call appeal? Do you like the idea of days spent just at sea?

Size The megaships are geared for various budgets, so the important decision is how many people you want to sail with. On large ships, you can have 5000 potential new friends and the greatest range of shipboard diversions. Small ships, while sometimes exclusive and luxurious, are not always so, and usually lack the flashier amenities (such as climbing walls). They are, however, able to stop at smaller ports that can't cater for the larger vessels, and disembarking can be considerably quicker.

Demographics Different cruise lines, and even ships within cruise lines, tend to appeal to different groups. Although cruisers in general are often slightly older, some ships have quite a party reputation; others are known for their art auctions and old-timey music in the lounges.

Cabin Types

Some modern ships offer only exterior cabins with balcony, but typically you'll have a choice. It's worth looking at a map

KATHRYNHATASHITALEE/GETTY IMAGES ©

of the ship before you choose, as you may want to prioritise being near the pool, the bar, the lifts or a play area.

Interior cabins are generally compact, with little or no natural light, though some have interior windows. They are the cheapest category and will suit those who plan to spend most of their time in public areas.

Sea-view cabins offer a porthole or window but no exterior access. They are typically as compact as interior rooms or more so.

Balcony cabins give you some access to the outside. Balconies are often quite small but will have space for a couple of chairs and small table at least. This is generally the first category in which spending significant time in your room is appealing.

Suites are a significant upgrade in size and usually separate the sleeping and sitting areas.

Some ships have a few single cabins, but these get snapped up fast. Solo travellers will usually have to pay a hefty single

★ **Best Online Resources**
Cruise Critic (www.cruisecritic.com)
Cruise Line (www.cruiseline.com)
Cruise Mates (www.cruisemates.com)
Cruise Reviews (www.cruisereviews.com)

supplement at best, or pay the full rate for a double cabin at worst.

Bigger Ships

It's not so much about the destination as it is about the panoply of amenities on board. These aren't mere cruises – they're floating cities stocked with every entertainment option under the sun. The competition in this category is fierce. Some options:

Celebrity (www.celebritycruises.com) Family-friendly, upscale and laid-back cruises on large 2000-plus-passenger ships.

From left: Osaka (p115); Hiroshima Bay (p153)

Costa Cruises (www.costacruises.com) Costa is aimed at European travellers: bigger spas, smaller cabins and better coffee. Ships are huge.

Dream Cruise Line (www.dreamcruiseline.com) Asia-based cruise company with large, luxurious ships.

Holland America (www.hollandamerica.com) Offers a traditional cruising experience, generally to older passengers.

MSC Cruises (www.msccruises.com) Italian-inflected cruising on large, luxurious ships.

Norwegian Cruise Line (NCL; www.ncl.com) Offers 'freestyle cruising' on large ships; dress codes are relaxed and dining options are more flexible than on many other lines.

Princess (www.princess.com) Has large ships that offer a slightly older crowd a range of pampering activities while aboard.

Royal Caribbean (www.royalcaribbean.com) Has a huge fleet of megaships, aimed right at the middle of the market, with lots of activities for kids. Despite the name, it offers voyages to Asia as well.

Star Cruises (www.starcruises.com) Large ships sailing purely Asian itineraries; plenty of on-board entertainment.

Luxury & Smaller Vessels

These luxury lines promise a palpable uptick in service across the board. From small 100-person ships with sails to large 1000-person cruisers that feel more like floating five-star hotels, opulence and exclusivity are the major draws. Expect sweet suites and perks on board. Some luxury lines include the following:

Azamara Club Cruises (www.azamaraclub cruises.com) Specialises in destination immersion – longer calls and more overnights allow passengers more time to soak up the local atmosphere and to experience the nightlife.

Crystal Cruises (www.crystalcruises.com) Offers excellent service without stuffiness or dated formality. Also promotes social responsibility, encouraging passengers to participate in volunteering excursions on some trips.

SETSUKON/GETTY IMAGES ©

Cunard Line (www.cunard.com) Operating since the 19th century, the atmosphere on these ships is sophisticated. Attracts an older crowd.

Ponant (www.ponant.com) This French operator runs intimate trips with a social atmosphere.

Seabourn Cruise Line (www.seabourn.com) Competing in the ultra-luxury market, Seabourn's ships can dock in smaller ports. But you'll remember the on-board experience as much as the destinations.

Silversea Cruises (www.silversea.com) Expect formal service – couples in their forties and older dress for dinner.

Viking Cruises (www.vikingcruises.com) A fairly new operator that is growing rapidly. The cruises are designed for travellers with an interest in geography, culture and history.

Theme Cruises

Gardens, WWII, music, crafting, food, bridge... What these have in common is that they're all themes for cruises.

Cruise lines sell group space to promoters of theme cruises, but typically no theme is enough to fill an entire ship. Rather, a critical mass of people will occupy a block of cabins and have activities day and night just for them, including lectures, autograph sessions, costume balls and performances.

No theme or interest is too obscure or improbable. To find one, jump online and search your phrase with 'cruise'.

LGBT+ Cruises

One of the largest segments of special-interest cruises are those aimed at lesbian, bisexual, gay and transgender people. So popular are these cruises that often an entire ship will be devoted to catering for LGBT+ passengers. The following sites can help you find a cruise:

All Gay Cruises (www.cruisingwithpride.com)

Atlantis Events (www.atlantisevents.com)

Happy Gay Travel (www.happygaytravel.com)

From left: Cruise ship in port, Shànghǎi (p231); Ship send off, Yokohama (p65)

Plan Your Trip
Sustainable Cruising

ASIA/ALAMY STOCK PHOTO ©

From air and water pollution to the swamping of popular destinations by hordes of tourists, travelling on cruise ships isn't without significant impacts – choose your cruise line carefully.

Environmental Issues

Although all travel comes with an environmental cost, by their very size, cruise ships have an outsized effect. Among the main issues:

Air pollution According to UK-based Climate Care, a carbon-offsetting company, cruise ships emit more carbon per passenger than airplanes – nearly twice as much – and that's not factoring in the flights that most passengers take to get to their point of departure. Most ships burn low-grade bunker fuel, which contains more sulphur and particulates than higher-quality fuel.

Water pollution Cruise ships generate enormous amounts of sewage, solid waste and grey water, which often just gets dumped directly (or with minimal treatment) into the sea. Some countries are beginning to introduce legislation to curb this behaviour, but unfortunately legislation is lacking when it comes to international waters.

Cultural impact Although cruise lines generate money for their ports of call, thousands of people arriving at once can change the character of a town and may seem overwhelming to locals and noncruising travellers.

What You Can Do

The cruise industry notes that it complies with international regulations, and adapts to stricter regional laws as required. As consumer pressure grows, more ships are being equipped with new waste-water treatment facilities, LED lighting and solar panels. Some operators are also upping their game when it comes to recycling and waste management.

If you're planning a cruise, it's worth doing some research. Email the cruise lines and ask them about their environmental policies: waste-water treatment, recycling

IGOR GROCHEV/SHUTTERSTOCK ©

initiatives and whether they use alternative energy sources. Knowing that customers care about these matters has an impact on cruise-ship operations.

There are also organisations that review the environmental records of cruise lines and ships. These include the following:

Friends of the Earth (www.foe.org/projects/cruise-ships) Letter grades given to cruise lines and ships for environmental and human health impacts.

World Travel Awards (www.worldtravelawards.com) Annual awards for the 'World's Leading Green Cruise Line'.

On the Ship

- Ask about recycling facilities on the ship and use them.

- Conserve water and energy.

- Don't use sinks and toilets as rubbish bins – only flush away what you must.

- Never throw rubbish from the ship into the sea.

★ Most Sustainable Companies

According to Friends of the Earth, two of the most sustainable large cruise-ship companies running cruises in Asia are Holland America and Norwegian Cruise Line.

In Port

Skip bottled water Apart from in Shànghǎi, the water in Northeast Asia is generally safe to drink, so pack a reusable water bottle.

Ride the bus, train or tram Most cities in the region have excellent public-transport networks. Also take the opportunity to explore cities on foot.

Hire a bike Some ports have easily accessible rental or share bikes.

Say no to plastic Bring your own reusable bags to carry anything you buy. Avoid plastic straws.

Make a positive impact Support independently owned businesses and look for opportunities to interact with locals.

From left: Yamashita-kōen (p69), Yokohama; Cruising into port, Shànghǎi (p231)

Plan Your Trip
Family Time Ashore

TASCH/SHUTTERSTOCK ©

Safe, lively and full of mod cons, Northeast Asia is a great place to travel with kids. Pop culture, neon streetscapes and big-name amusement parks are easy wins; street markets, interactive museums and endless snack options sweeten the deal.

Practicalities

○ Be sure to bring any necessary medicines from home (prescription or over the counter), as pharmacies may not stock them.

○ A small fork and spoon can be handy, as not all restaurants have these on hand.

○ Baby food, nappies and milk powder are widely available in supermarkets.

○ Few restaurants have baby chairs.

○ Convenience stores stock sandwiches and other familiar foods – and the quality and range on offer is often eye-opening.

○ Lonely Planet's book *Travel with Children* prepares you for the joys and pitfalls of travelling with little ones.

Attitudes to Children

Children are adored and welcomed throughout the region, and people will go out of their way to help you if needed. In Shànghǎi and South Korea, children may find themselves the centre of attention and curiosity, which can be a great way to meet some locals, and can also be a little overwhelming. In Taipei and Japan, you may find local children are expected to be a bit quieter than you're used to back home.

Crowded trains and streets do make prams a challenge, and may be overwhelming for little ones; if possible avoid riding trains and subways during peak commuting hours in the larger cities (7am to 9am and 5pm to 7pm).

Breastfeeding is generally not done in public, though some mothers do (find a quiet corner and use a shawl).

ATKHARAT JARUSILAWONG/SHUTTERSTOCK ©

Top Stops for Kids

Shanghai Natural History Museum, Shànghǎi (p243) Kids will love this new-look museum, with its dinosaur fossils, taxidermied animals, live reptiles and butterfly house.

Universal Studios Japan, Osaka (p125) The Japanese version of the American theme park.

SCMAGLEV & Railway Park, Nagoya (p82) See an actual maglev (the world's fastest train) and test-ride a *shinkansen* simulator.

Miniatures Museum of Taiwan, Taipei (p224) Dozens of tiny creations, with so many details to discover, intrigue and delight.

Sapporo Teine, Sapporo (p200) Quality, family-friendly snowfields, just minutes from Sapporo. Ski or just throw snowballs.

★ Best Bites for Kids

Dumplings Shànghǎi

Bubble tea Taipei

Okonomiyaki Osaka and Hiroshima

Castella sponge cake Nagasaki

Ramen Sapporo

Cup Noodles Museum, Yokohama (p72) Make-your-own cup noodles. Who can resist?

Tokyo Disney Resort, Tokyo (p57) Visit the only-in-Japan Disney Sea park (along with classic Disney attractions).

Shànghǎi Disneyland, Shànghǎi (p243) Set to suck in Chinese tots and young kids nationwide, this is mainland China's first Disney Resort. Expect epic queues.

From left: Skiers at Sapporo Teine (p200), Hokkaidō; Shanghai Natural History Museum (p243)

Sensō-ji (p42)

Honkan (Japanese Gallery)

Tokyo National Museum

...u visit only one museum, make ...s one. Established in 1872, this ...ction of Japanese art covers ...t pottery, Buddhist sculpture, ...ai swords, colourful ukiyo-e ...block prints), gorgeous kimonos ...re.

For...

Miss

...e of weeks in spring and ...e back garden, home to five ...ouses, opens to the public.

Honkan (Japanese Gallery)

The museum is divided into several buildings, the most important of which is the Honkan (Japanese Gallery), which houses the collection of Japanese art. Visitors with only an hour or two should hone in on the galleries here. The building itself is in the Imperial Style of the 1930s, with art deco flourishes throughout. Allow two hours to take in the highlights, a half-day to do the Honkan in depth or a whole day to take in everything else as well.

Gallery of Hōryū-ji Treasures

Next on the priority list is the enchanting Gallery of Hōryū-ji Treasures, which displays masks, scrolls and gilt Buddhas from Hōryū-ji (in Nara Prefecture, dating from 607) in a spare, elegant, box-shaped contemporary building (1999) by Taniguchi

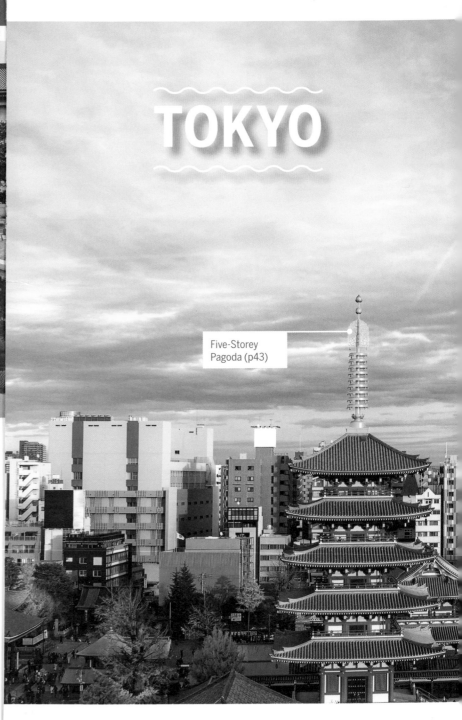

TOKYO

Five-Storey Pagoda (p43)

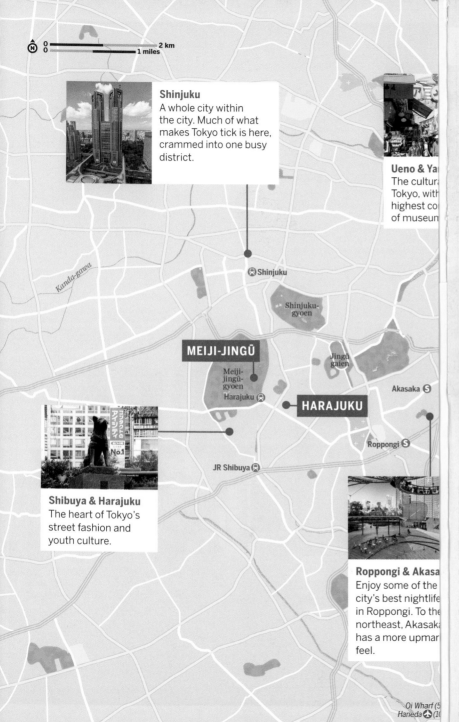

Shinjuku

A whole city within the city. Much of what makes Tokyo tick is here, crammed into one busy district.

Ueno & Ya[...]

The cultura[...] Tokyo, with[...] highest co[...] of museum[...]

MEIJI-JINGŪ

Meiji-jingū-gyoen

Harajuku

HARAJUKU

Jingū-gaien

Akasaka Ⓢ

Roppongi Ⓢ

Shinjuku-gyoen

🚉 Shinjuku

Kanda-gawa

JR Shibuya 🚉

Shibuya & Harajuku

The heart of Tokyo's street fashion and youth culture.

Roppongi & Akasa[...]

Enjoy some of the [...] city's best nightlife [...] in Roppongi. To the[...] northeast, Akasaka[...] has a more upmar[...] feel.

*Oi Wharf (5[...]
Haneda ✈ (10[...]*

Sensō-ji (p42)

Getting from the Port

○ Most cruise ships dock at Harumi Wharf. The Harumi-Futo bus stop is right at the port. Kachidoki Station on the Toei Oedo subway line is five minutes by bus or taxi or a 20-minute walk away.

○ Large ships dock at Oi Wharf, which is a five-minute walk to Yashio 2-chome bus stop. Shuttle buses run to Shinagawa JR train station.

○ Some larger ships dock at Ōsanbashi Pier in Yokohama (p67).

○ At the time of research Tokyo International Cruise Terminal Pier was under construction and due to be completed in time for the 2020 Olympics.

Fast Facts

Tourist information The[...] Metropolitan Governme[...] Tourist Information Ce[...] English-language info[...] publications.

Transport Tokyo's[...] system is the env[...] use to travellers [...] system, which [...] thanks to Eng[...]

Wi-fi The cit[...] of free hots[...] that says '[...]

Great [...]

☑ **Don't [...]**

For a coup[...] autumn, th[...] vintage teah[...]

Buddha statue

Explore Ashore

From Harumi Wharf take a bus to Yūra-kuchō station then a train to Ueno; it'll take about 45 minutes. From Oi Wharf take a bus to Shinagawa JR train station to connect to a train running to Ueno; allow an hour to get from the port to the museum.

❶ Need to Know

東京国立博物館, Tokyo Kokuritsu Hakubutsukan; Map p58; ☑03-3822-1111; www.tnm.jp; 13-9 Ueno-kōen, Taitō-ku; adult/child ¥620/free; ☺9.30am-5pm Tue-Thu, to 9pm Fri & Sat, to 6pm Sun; ☒JR lines to Ueno, Ueno-kōen exit

Yoshio. Nearby, to the west of the main gate, is the **Kuro-mon** (Black Gate), transported from the Edo-era mansion of a feudal lord. On weekends it opens for visitors to pass through.

Tōyōkan & Heiseikan

Visitors with more time can explore the three-storied Tōyōkan (Gallery of Asian Art), with its collection of Buddhist sculptures from around Asia and delicate Chinese ceramics. The Heiseikan, accessed via a passage on the 1st floor of the Honkan, houses the Japanese Archaeological Gallery, full of pottery, talismans and articles of daily life from Japan's palaeolithic and neolithic periods. Temporary exhibitions (which cost extra) are held on the 2nd floor of the Heiseikan; these can be fantastic, but

sometimes lack the English signage found throughout the rest of the museum.

Kuroda Memorial Hall

Kuroda Seiki (1866–1924) is considered the father of modern Western-style painting in Japan. The **Kuroda Memorial Hall** (黒田記念室; Map p58; ☑03-5777-8600; www.tobunken.go.jp/kuroda/index_e.html; 13-9 Ueno-kōen, Taitō-ku; ☺9.30am-5pm Tue-Sun; ☒JR lines to Ueno, Ueno-kōen exit) FREE, an annexe to the Tokyo National Museum, has some of his works, including key pieces such as *Maiko Girl* and *Wisdom, Impression and Sentiment*, a striking triptych of three nude women on canvases coated with ground gold.

Tokyo National Museum

HISTORIC HIGHLIGHTS

It would be a challenge to take in everything the sprawling Tokyo National Museum has to offer in a day. Fortunately, the Honkan (Japanese Gallery) is designed to give visitors a crash course in Japanese art history from the Jōmon era (13,000–300 BC) to the Edo era (AD 1603–1868). The works on display here are rotated regularly, to protect fragile ones and to create seasonal exhibitions, so you're always guaranteed to see something new.

Buy your ticket from outside the main gate then head straight to the Honkan with its sloping tile roof. Stow your coat in a locker and take the central staircase up to the 2nd floor, where the exhibitions are arranged chronologically. Allow two hours for this tour of the highlights.

The first room on your right starts from the beginning with **ancient Japanese art ❶**. Pick up a free copy of the brochure *Highlights of Japanese Art* at the entrance to the first room on your right. The exhibition starts here with the **Dawn of Japanese Art**, covering the most ancient periods of Japan's history.

Continue to the **National Treasure Gallery ❷**. 'National Treasure' is the highest distinction awarded to a work of art in Japan. Keep an eye out for more National Treasures, labelled in red, on display in other rooms throughout the museum.

Moving on, stop to admire the **courtly art gallery ❸**, the **samurai armour and swords ❹** and the *ukiyo-e and kimono* ❺.

Next, take the stairs down to the 1st floor, where each room is dedicated to a different decorative art, such as lacquerware or ceramics. Don't miss the excellent examples of **religious sculpture ❻**, and folk art and **Ainu and Ryūkyū cultural artefacts ❼**.

Finish your visit with a look inside the enchanting **Gallery of Hōryū-ji Treasures ❽**.

Ukiyo-e & Kimono (Room 10)
Chic silken kimono and lushly coloured *ukiyo-e* (woodblock prints) are two icons of the Edo-era (AD 1603–1868) *ukiyo* – the 'floating world', or world of fleeting beauty and pleasure.

TOKYO NATIONAL MUSEUM ©

Japanese Sculpture (Room 11)
Many of Japan's most famous sculptures, religious in nature, are locked away in temple reliquaries. This is a rare chance to see them up close.

MUSEUM GARDEN
Don't miss the garden if you visit in spring and autumn during the few weeks it's open to the public.

Heiseikan & Japanese Archaeology Gallery

Research & Information Centre

❽

Hyōkeikan

Kuro-mon

Main Gate

Gallery of Hōryū-ji Treasures
Surround yourself with miniature gilt Buddhas from Hōryū-ji, one of Japan's oldest Buddhist temples, founded in 607. Don't miss the graceful Pitcher with Dragon Head, a National Treasure.

TOKYO NATIONAL MUSEUM ©; PHOTO BY SATO AKIRA

Samurai Armour & Swords (Rooms 5 & 6)
Glistening swords, finely stitched armour and imposing helmets bring to life the samurai, those iconic warriors of Japan's medieval age.

Courtly Art (Room 3-2)
Literature works, calligraphy and narrative picture scrolls are displayed alongside decorative art objects, which allude to the life of elegance led by courtesans a thousand years ago.

Honkan (Japanese Gallery) 2nd Floor

National Treasure Gallery (Room 2)
A single, superlative work from the museum's collection of 88 National Treasures (perhaps a painted screen, or a gilded, hand-drawn sutra) is displayed in a serene, contemplative setting.

Honkan (Japanese Gallery) 1st Floor

GIFT SHOP

The museum gift shop, on the 1st floor of the Honkan, has an excellent collection of Japanese art books in English.

Museum Garden & Teahouses

Honkan (Japanese Gallery)

Tōyōkan (Gallery of Asian Art)

Dawn of Japanese Art (Room 1)
The rise of the imperial court and the introduction of Buddhism changed the Japanese aesthetic forever. These clay works from previous eras show what came before.

Ainu and Ryūkyū Collection (Room 16)
See artefacts from Japan's historical minorities – the indigenous Ainu of Hokkaidō and the former Ryūkyū Empire, now Okinawa.

RUDY BALASKO/SHUTTERSTOCK ©

Sensō-ji

According to legend, in AD 628, two fishermen brothers pulled out a golden image of Kannon (the bodhisattva of compassion) from the nearby Sumida-gawa. Sensō-ji, the capital's oldest temple, was built to enshrine it.

Great For...

☑ Don't Miss

Sensō-ji is home to many traditional festivals: ask for a list at a Tourist Information Center (p61).

Kaminari-mon

The temple precinct begins at the majestic Kaminari-mon (雷門), which means Thunder Gate. An enormous *chōchin* (lantern), which weighs 670kg, hangs from the centre. On either side are a pair of ferocious protective deities: Fūjin, the god of wind, on the right; and Raijin, the god of thunder, on the left. Kaminari-mon has burnt down countless times over the centuries; the current gate dates to 1970.

Nakamise-dōri Shopping Street

Beyond Kaminari-mon is the bustling shopping street, Nakamise-dōri. With its lines of souvenir stands it is very touristy, though that's nothing new: Sensō-ji has been Tokyo's top tourist sight for centuries, since travel was restricted to religious pilgrimages

Five-Storey Pagoda

MANUEL ASCANIO/SHUTTERSTOCK ©

Explore Ashore

From Oi Wharf take a bus to Shinagawa station, a train running to Ueno and then the Ginza line subway to Asakusa, which will take just over an hour. From Harumi Wharf take a bus to Ginza station, then a Ginza line subway to Asakusa; it'll take 50 minutes.

❶ Need to Know

浅草寺; Map p58; ☎03-3842-0181; www.senso-ji.jp; 2-3-1 Asakusa, Taitō-ku; admission free; ◷24hr; ⑤Ginza line to Asakusa, exit 1

during the feudal era. In addition to the usual T-shirts, you can find Edo-style crafts and oddities (such as wigs done up in traditional hairstyles). There are also numerous snack vendors serving up crunchy *sembei* (rice crackers) and *age-manju* (deep-fried *anko* – bean-paste – buns).

Hōzō-mon

At the end of Nakamise-dōri is Hōzō-mon (宝蔵門), another gate with fierce guardians. On its rear are a pair of 2500kg, 4.5m-tall *waraji* (straw sandals) crafted for Sensō-ji by some 800 villagers in northern Yamagata Prefecture.

These are meant to symbolise the Buddha's power, and it's believed that evil spirits will be scared off by the giant footwear.

Hondō

In front of the grand Hondō (Main Hall), with its dramatic sloping roof, is a large cauldron with smoking incense. The smoke is said to bestow health and you'll see people wafting it over their bodies. The current Hondō was constructed in 1958, replacing the one destroyed in WWII air raids. The style is similar to the previous one, though the roof tiles are now made of titanium.

The **Kannon image** (a tiny 6cm) is cloistered away from view deep inside the Hondō (and admittedly may not exist at all). Nonetheless, a steady stream of worshippers visits the temple to cast coins, pray and bow in a gesture of respect. Do feel free to join in.

Off the courtyard stands a 53m-high **Five-Storey Pagoda** (五重塔), a 1973 reconstruction of a pagoda built by Tokugawa Iemitsu. The current structure, renovated in 2017, is the second-highest pagoda in Japan.

Omikuji

Don't miss getting your fortune told by an *omikuji* (paper fortune). Drop ¥100 into the slots by the wooden drawers at either side of the approach to the Hondō, grab a silver canister and shake it. Extract a stick and note its number (in kanji). Replace the stick, find the matching drawer and withdraw a paper fortune (there's English on the back). If you pull out 大凶 (*dai-kyō*, great curse), never fear. Just tie the paper on the nearby rack, ask the gods for better luck, and try again!

Asakusa-jinja

On the east side of the temple complex is **Asakusa-jinja** (浅草神社; Map p58; ☎03-3844-1575; www.asakusajinja.jp; 2-3-1 Asakusa, Taitō-ku; ⊙9am-4.30pm; ⑤Ginza line to Asakusa, exit 1), built in honour of the brothers who discovered the Kannon statue that inspired the construction of Sensō-ji. (Historically, Japan's two religions, Buddhism and Shintō, were intertwined and it was not uncommon for temples to include shrines and vice versa.) This section of Sensō-ji survived WWII and Asakusa-jinja's current structure dates from 1649. Painted a deep shade of red, it is a rare example of early Edo architecture.

Next to the shrine is the temple complex's eastern gate, **Niten-mon** (二天門; Map p58; 2-3-1 Asakusa, Taitō-ku; ⑤Ginza line to Asakusa, exit 1), which has stood since 1618. Though it appears minor today, this gate was the point of entry for visitors arriving in Asakusa via boat – the main form of transport during the Edo period.

Edo-Tokyo Museum

What's Nearby?

The **Edo-Tokyo Museum** (江戸東京博物館; Map p58; 03-3626-9974; www.edo-tokyo-museum.or.jp; 1-4-1 Yokoami, Sumida-ku; adult/child ¥600/free; 9.30am-5.30pm, to 7.30pm Sat, closed Mon; JR Sōbu line to Ryōgoku, west exit) documents the city's transformation from tidal flatlands to feudal capital to modern metropolis via detailed scale re-creations of townscapes, villas and tenement homes, plus artefacts such as *ukiyo-e* and old maps. Reopened in March 2018 after a renovation, the museum also has interactive displays, multilingual touch-screen panels and audio guides. Still, the best way to tour the museum is with one of the gracious English-speaking volunteer guides, who can really bring the history to life.

The woodblock artist Hokusai Katsushika (1760–1849) was born and died close to the location of the **Sumida Hokusai Museum** (すみだ北斎美術館; Map p58; 03-5777-8600; http://hokusai-museum.jp; 2-7-2 Kamezawa, Sumida-ku; adult/child/student & senior ¥400/free/300; 9.30am-5.30pm Tue-Sun; Ōedo line to Ryōgoku, exit A4) , which opened in 2016 in a striking aluminium-clad building designed by Pritzker Prize–winning architect Sejima Kazuyo. The small permanent exhibition gives an overview of his life and work, mostly through replicas.

Tokyo Skytree (東京スカイツリー; Map p58; 0570-55-0102; www.tokyo-skytree.jp; 1-1-2 Oshiage, Sumida-ku; 350m/450m observation decks ¥2060/3090; 8am-10pm; Hanzōmon line to Oshiage, Tokyo Sky Tree exit) opened in May 2012 as the world's tallest 'free-standing tower' at 634m. Its silvery exterior of steel mesh morphs from a triangle at the base to a circle at 300m. There are two observation decks, at 350m and 450m. You can see more of the city during daylight hours – at peak visibility you can see up to 100km away, all the way to Mt Fuji – but it is at night that Tokyo appears truly beautiful.

★ Did You Know?

Tokyo Skytree employs an ancient construction technique used in pagodas: an independent *shimbashira* column that acts as a counterweight when the tower sways, cutting vibrations by 50%.

COWARDLION/SHUTTERSTOCK ©

✕ Take a Break

Dandelion Chocolate (Map p58; 03-5833-7270; http://dandelionchocolate.jp; 4-14-6 Kuramae, Taitō-ku; 10am-8pm; ; Asakusa line to Kuramae, exit A3) specialises in bean-to-bar, small-batch chocolate, made on the premises, but also has delicious drink and food offerings that are impossible to resist.

PIUS LEE/SHUTTERSTOCK ©

Shopping in Harajuku

Harajuku is the gathering point for Tokyo's eccentric fashion tribes: teens who hang out on Takeshita-dōri, polished divas who strut up and down Omote-sandō, and trendsetters and peacocks who haunt the side streets.

Great For...

☑ Don't Miss

The narrow streets on either side of Omote-sandō, known as Ura-Hara ('back' Harajuku).

Takeshita-dōri

Takeshita-dōri (竹下通り; Map p54; Jingūmae, Shibuya-ku; ℝJR Yamanote line to Harajuku, Takeshita exit) is Tokyo's famously outré fashion bazaar and a pilgrimage site for teens from all over Japan. Here trendy duds sit alongside the trappings of decades of fashion subcultures (plaid and safety pins for the punks; colourful tutus for the decora; Victorian dresses for the Gothic Lolitas).

Laforet

Laforet (ラフォーレ; Map p54; www.laforet. ne.jp; 1-11-6 Jingūmae, Shibuya-ku; ⊙11am-9pm; ℝJR Yamanote line to Harajuku, Omote-sandō exit) has been a beacon of cutting-edge Harajuku style for decades and lots of quirky, cult-favourite brands still cut their teeth here (you'll find some examples at the ground-floor boutique, Wall).

Explore Ashore

From Harumi Wharf take a bus to Hibiya station, then the Chiyoda line to Meiji-jingūmae subway station. From Oi Wharf take a bus to Shinagawa station, then take the JR Yamanote line to Harajuku. Both routes take 45 to 50 minutes.

ⓘ Need to Know

Trends move fast in Harajuku. To keep up, follow @TokyoFashion on Instagram.

KiddyLand

Multistorey toy emporium **KiddyLand** (キデイランド; Map p54; ☑03-3409-3431; www.kiddyland.co.jp; 6-1-9 Jingūmae, Shibuya-ku; ⊗11am-9pm Mon-Fri, 10.30am-9pm Sat & Sun; ℝJR Yamanote line to Harajuku, Omote-sandō exit) is packed to the rafters with character goods, including all your Studio Ghibli, Sanrio and Disney faves. It's not just for kids either; you'll spot plenty of adults on a nostalgia trip down the Hello Kitty aisle.

Cat Street

Had enough of crowded Harajuku? Exit, stage right, for **Cat Street** (キャットストリート; Map p54; ℝJR Yamanote line to Harajuku, Omote-sandō exit), a windy road closed to cars and lined with a mishmash of boutiques and more room to move.

House @Mikiri Hassin

Hidden deep in Ura-Hara (Harajuku's backstreet area), this **shop** (ハウス@ミキリハッシン; Map p54; ☑03-3486-7673; http://house.mikirihassin.co.jp; 5-42-1 Jingūmae, Shibuya-ku; ⊗noon-9pm Thu-Tue; ⑤Ginza line to Omote-sandō, exit A1) stocks an ever-changing selection of experimental Japanese fashion brands. Contrary to what the cool merch might suggest, the sales clerks are polite and friendly – grateful, perhaps, that you made the effort to find the place. Look for 'ハウス' spelled vertically in neon.

6% Doki Doki

Tucked away on an Ura-Hara backstreet in a bubblegum-pink building, **6% Doki Doki** (ロクパーセントドキドキ; Map p54; www.dokidoki6.com; 2nd fl, 4-28-16 Jingūmae, Shibuya-ku; ⊗noon-8pm; ℝJR Yamanote line to Harajuku, Omote-sandō exit) sells acid-bright accessories that are part raver, part schoolgirl and, according to the shop's name, 'six percent exciting'. It's 100% Harajuku.

COWARDLION/SHUTTERSTOCK ©

Meiji-jingū

Tokyo's largest and most famous Shintō shrine feels a world away from the city. The grounds are vast, enveloping the classic wooden shrine buildings and a landscaped garden in a thick coat of green.

Great For...

☑ Don't Miss

Meiji-jingū Gyoen when the irises bloom in June.

History

Meiji-jingū is dedicated to the Emperor Meiji and Empress Shōken, whose reign (1868–1912) coincided with Japan's transformation from isolationist, feudal state to modern nation.

The Gates

Several wooden *torii* (gates) mark the entrance to Meiji-jingū. The largest, created from a 1500-year-old Taiwanese cypress, stands 12m high. It's the custom to bow upon passing through a *torii*, which marks the boundary between the mundane world and the sacred one.

The Font

Before approaching the main shrine, visitors purify themselves by pouring water

Ladles at the font

VACANCYLIZM/SHUTTERSTOCK ©

⊚ *Meiji-jingū*

Meiji-jingū Gyoen

Yoyogi-kōen

Takeshita-dōri

Meiji-dōri

Harajuku Ⓡ

Ⓢ Meiji-jingūmae

⚓

Explore Ashore

From Harumi Wharf take a bus to Hibiya station, then the Chiyoda line to Meiji-jingūmae subway station (use exit 2). From Oi Wharf take a bus to Shinagawa station, then take the JR Yamanote line to Harajuku (take the Omote-sandō exit). Both routes take 45 to 50 minutes.

❶ Need to Know

明治神宮; Map p54; www.meijijingu.or.jp; 1-1 Yoyogi Kamizono-chō, Shibuya-ku; admission free; ⊙dawn-dusk; 🚃JR Yamanote line to Harajuku, Omote-sandō exit

over their hands at the *temizuya* (font). Dip the ladle in the water and first rinse your left hand then your right. Pour some water into your left hand and rinse your mouth, then rinse your left hand again. Make sure none of this water gets back into the font!

Main Shrine

Constructed in 1920 and destroyed in WWII air raids, the shrine was rebuilt in 1958; however, unlike so many of Japan's postwar reconstructions, Meiji-jingū has an authentic old-world feel. The main shrine is made of cypress from the Kiso region of Nagano. To make an offering, toss a ¥5 coin in the box, bow twice, clap your hands twice

and then bow again. To the right, you'll see kiosks selling *ema* (wooden plaques on which prayers are written) and *omamori* (charms).

Meiji-jingū Gyoen

The shrine itself occupies only a small fraction of the sprawling forested grounds, which contain some 120,000 trees collected from all over Japan. Along the path towards the main shrine is the entrance to **Meiji-jingū Gyoen** (明治神宮御苑, Inner Garden; Map p54; ¥500; ⊙9am-4.30pm, to 4pm Nov-Feb), a landscaped garden. It once belonged to a feudal estate; however, when the grounds passed into imperial hands, the emperor himself designed the iris garden to please the empress.

⊙ SIGHTS

◎ Ginza & Marunouchi

Tsukiji Market
Market

(場外市場, Jōgai Shijō; Map p52; www.tsukiji.
or.jp; 6-chōme Tsukiji, Chūō-ku; ⊘mostly 5am-
2pm; Ⓢ Hibiya line to Tsukiji, exit 1) Tokyo's
main wholesale market may have moved to
Toyosu (豊洲市場, Toyosu Shijō; www.shijou.
metro.tokyo.jp; 6-chōme Toyosu, Kōtō-ku; ⊘5am-
5pm Mon-Sat, closed some Wed; Ⓡ Yurikamome
line to Shijō-mae), but there are many reasons
to visit its old home. The tightly packed
rows of vendors (which once formed the
Outer Market) hawk market and culi-
nary-related goods, such as dried fish,
seaweed, kitchen knives, rubber boots and
crockery. It's also a fantastic place to eat,
with great street food and a huge concen-

teamLab Borderless

Art collective teamLab has created
60 artworks for this new **museum**
(☑03-6406-3949; https://borderless.
teamlab.art; 1-3-8 Aomi, Kōtō-ku; adult/
child ¥3200/1000; ⊘10am-7pm Mon-Thu &
Sun, to 9pm Fri & Sat, closed 2nd & 4th Tue;
[♿]; Ⓡ Yurikamome line to Aomi) that tests
the border between art and the viewer,
and many of them are interactive. Not
sure how? That's the point – go up to
the artworks, move and touch them (or
just stand still) and see how they react.
There is no suggested route; teamLab
Borderless is all about exploration. Buy
tickets in advance online.

Interactive exhibit

TEAMLAB BORDERLESS, ODAIBA, TOKYO ©

tration of small restaurants and cafes, most
specialising in seafood.

Imperial Palace
Palace

(皇居, Kōkyo; Map p52; ☑03-5223-8071;
http://sankan.kunaicho.go.jp; 1 Chiyoda, Chiyoda-ku; ⊘tours usually 10am & 1.30pm Tue-Sat;
Ⓢ Chiyoda line to Ōtemachi, exits C13b & C10)
🆓 The Imperial Palace occupies the
site of the original Edo-jō, the Tokugawa
shogunate's castle. In its heyday this was
the largest fortress in the world, though
little remains today apart from the moat
and stone walls. Most of the 3.4-sq-km
complex is off limits, as this is the emper-
or's home, but join one of the free tours
organised by the Imperial Household
Agency to see a small part of the inner
compound.

Intermediatheque
Museum

(インターメディアテク; Map p52; ☑03-5777-
8600; www.intermediatheque.jp; 2nd & 3rd fl, JP
Tower, 2-7-2 Marunouchi, Chiyoda-ku; ⊘11am-
6pm, to 8pm Fri & Sat, usually closed Sun & Mon;
Ⓡ JR Yamanote line to Tokyo, Marunouchi exit)
🆓 Dedicated to interdisciplinary experi-
mentation, Intermediatheque cherry-picks
from the vast collection of the University
of Tokyo (Tōdai) to craft a fascinating, contemporary museum experience. Go from
viewing the best ornithological taxidermy
collection in Japan to a giant pop art print
or the beautifully encased skeleton of a
dinosaur. A handsome Tōdai lecture hall
is reconstituted as a forum for events,
including playing 1920s jazz recordings on
a gramophone or old movie screenings.

Hama-rikyū Onshi-teien
Gardens

(浜離宮恩賜庭園, Detached Palace Garden;
Map p52; ☑03-3541-0200; www.tokyo-park.
or.jp/teien; 1-1 Hama-rikyū-teien, Chūō-ku; adult/
child ¥300/free; ⊘9am-5pm; Ⓢ Ōedo line to
Shiodome, exit A1) This beautiful garden, one
of Tokyo's finest, is all that remains of a
shogunate palace that was also an outer
fort for Edo Castle. The main features are a
large duck pond with an island that's home
to a functioning tea pavilion, **Nakajima
no Ochaya** (中島の御茶屋; tea ¥510 or ¥720;

⊘9am-4.30pm), as well as three other tea-houses and wonderfully manicured trees (black pine, Japanese apricot, hydrangeas etc), some hundreds of years old.

◎ Roppongi & Akasaka

National Art Center Tokyo　Museum

(国立新美術館; Map p54; ☑03-5777-8600; www.nact.jp; 7-22-1 Roppongi, Minato-ku; admission varies; ⊘10am-6pm Wed, Thu, Sun & Mon, to 8pm Fri & Sat; Ⓢ Chiyoda line to Nogizaka, exit 6) Designed by Kurokawa Kishō, this architectural beauty has no permanent collection, but boasts the country's largest exhibition space for visiting shows, which have included Renoir and Modigliani. A visit here is recommended to admire the building's awesome undulating glass facade, its cafes atop giant inverted cones and the great gift shop, **Souvenir from Tokyo** (スーベニアフロムトーキョー; ☑03-6812 9933; www.souvenirfromtokyo.jp; ⊘10am-6pm Sat-Mon, Wed & Thu, to 8pm Fri) in the basement.

21_21 Design Sight　Museum

(21_21デザインサイト; Map p54; ☑03-3475-2121; www.2121designsight.jp; Tokyo Midtown, 9-7-6 Akasaka, Minato-ku; adult/child ¥1100/free; ⊘11am-7pm Wed-Mon; Ⓢ Ōedo line to Roppongi, exit 8) An exhibition and discussion space dedicated to all forms of design, the 21_21 Design Sight is a beacon for local art enthusiasts, whether they be designers or onlookers. The striking concrete and glass building, bursting out of the ground at sharp angles, was designed by Pritzker Prize–winning architect Andō Tadao.

◎ Shibuya & Harajuku

Shibuya Crossing　Street

(渋谷スクランブル交差点, Shibuya Scramble; Map p54; ℝ JR Yamanote line to Shibuya, Hachikō exit) Rumoured to be the busiest intersection in the world (and definitely in Japan), Shibuya Crossing is like a giant beating heart, sending people in all directions with every pulsing light change. Nowhere else says 'Welcome to Tokyo' better than this. Hundreds of people – and at peak times upwards of 3000 people –

Ghibli Museum, Mitaka

Master animator Miyazaki Hayao's Studio Ghibli (pronounced 'jiburi') is responsible for some of the best-loved films in Japan – and the world. Miyazaki designed the **Ghibli Museum, Mitaka** (ジブリ美術館; www.ghibli-museum.jp; 1-1-83 Shimo-Renjaku, Mitaka-shi; adult ¥1000, child ¥100-700; ⊘10am-6pm Wed-Mon; ℝ JR Chūō-Sōbu line to Mitaka, south exit) and the end result is faithful to the dreamy, vaguely steampunk atmosphere that makes his animations so enticing.

Looking like it was plucked from the pages of a fairy tale, the museum houses a whimsical workshop filled with books and artworks that inspired Miyazaki, oodles of original sketches and models, vintage animation tech and, of course, a hundreds-strong cast of your favourite characters and critters.

A highlight is a giant, plush replica of the cat bus from the classic *My Neighbor Totoro* (1988) that kids can climb on. There's also a small theatre where original animated shorts – only seen here! – are screened (you'll get a ticket when you enter). The film changes monthly to keep fans coming back.

Museum tickets are like gold and go quick, especially during holiday periods. With luck, there'll be a date and time-slot that suits your plans: changes aren't possible and you can't just show up. Order up to four months in advance from select travel agencies, or up to a month ahead using Lawson Ticket; see the museum website for info.

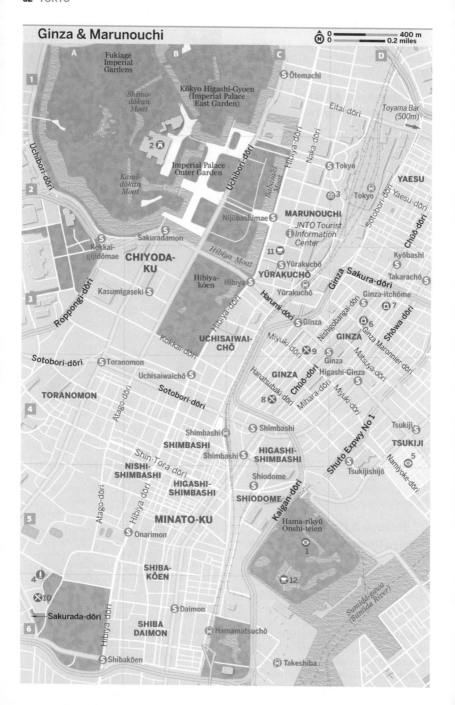

Ginza & Marunouchi

Ⓝ 0 ———— 400 m
0 ———— 0.2 miles

A **B** **C** **D**

1

Fukiage Imperial Gardens

Ⓢ Ōtemachi

Shimo-dōkan Moat

Kōkyo Higashi-Gyoen (Imperial Palace East Garden)

Eitai-dōri

Toyama Bar (500m) →

Uchibori-dōri

2🏛

Imperial Palace Outer Garden

Kami-dōkan Moat

Uchibori-dōri

Babasaki Moat

Naka-dōri

Ⓢ Tokyo

YAESU

Ⓢ Tokyo

🏛**3**

2

Uchibori-dōri

Nijūbashimae Ⓢ

MARUNOUCHI

JNTO Tourist ⓘ Information Center

Sotobori-dōri

Yaesu-dōri

Chūō-dōri

Ⓢ Sakuradamon

CHIYODA-KU

Hibiya Moat

11 Ⓢ

Kyōbashi Ⓢ

Ⓢ Yūrakuchō

YŪRAKUCHŌ

Ginza Sakura-dōri

Takarachō Ⓢ

Ⓢ Kokkai-gijidōmae

Hibiya-kōen

Hibiya Ⓢ

Yūrakuchō

Ginza-itchōme 🏛 7

3

Roppongi-dōri

Kasumigaseki Ⓢ

Hibiya-dōri

Harumi-dōri

Ⓢ Ginza

Nishigobangai-dōri

🏛6

GINZA

Shōwa-dōri

Kokkai-dōri

UCHISAIWAI-CHŌ

Miyuki-dōri 9

Ⓢ Ginza

Higashi-Ginza Ⓢ

Ginza Maronnier-dōri

Matsuya-dōri

4

Sotobori-dōri Ⓢ Toranomon

Atago-dōri

Uchisaiwaichō Ⓢ

Sotobori-dōri

Hanatsubaki-dōri

GINZA

8 🍴

Chūō-dōri

Mihara-dōri

Miyuki-dōri

Tsukiji Ⓢ

TSUKIJI

TORANOMON

Ⓢ Shimbashi

5

Shimbashi 🚇

SHIMBASHI

HIGASHI-SHIMBASHI

Shuto Expwy No 1

Namiyoke-dōri

Shin-Tora-dōri

Shimbashi Ⓢ

Tsukijishijō

NISHI-SHIMBASHI

HIGASHI-SHIMBASHI

Shiodome Ⓢ

5

Atago-dōri

Hibiya-dōri

MINATO-KU

SHIODOME

Kaigan-dōri

Ⓢ Onarimon

Hama-rikyū Onshi-teien

◎ 1

SHIBA-KŌEN

4 ⓘ

🍴10

12

6

— Sakurada-dōri

Sakurada-dōri

Hibiya-dōri

Ⓢ Daimon

SHIBA DAIMON

Sumida-gawa (Sumida River)

Ⓢ Shibakōen

🚉 Hamamatsuchō

🚉 Takeshiba

Ginza & Marunouchi

cross at a time, coming from all directions at once, dodging each other with a practised, nonchalant agility.

Yoyogi-kōen
Park

(代々木公園; Map p54; www.yoyogipark. info; Yoyogi-kamizono-chō, Shibuya-ku; 🚃JR Yamanote line to Harajuku, Omote-sandō exit) If it's a sunny and warm weekend afternoon, you can count on there being a crowd lazing around the large grassy expanse that is Yoyogi-kōen. You'll usually find revellers and noisemakers of all stripes, from hula-hoopers to African drum circles to retro greasers dancing around a boom box. It's an excellent place for a picnic and probably the only place in the city where you can reasonably toss a Frisbee without fear of hitting someone.

Ukiyo-e Ōta Memorial Museum of Art
Museum

(浮世絵太田記念美術館; Map p54; 🕿03-3403-0880; www.ukiyoe-ota-muse.jp; 1-10-10 Jingūmae, Shibuya-ku; adult ¥700-1000, child free; ⏰10.30am-5.30pm Tue-Sun; 🚃JR Yamanote line to Harajuku, Omote-sandō exit) This small museum (where you swap your shoes for slippers) is the best place in Tokyo to see *ukiyo-e*. Each month it presents a seasonal, thematic exhibition (with English curation notes), drawing from the truly impressive collection of Ōta Seizo, the former head of the Toho Life Insurance Company. Most exhibitions include a few works by masters such as Hokusai and Hiroshige. The museum closes the last few days of the month (between exhibitions).

Nezu Museum
Museum

(根津美術館; Map p54; 🕿03-3400-2536; www. nezu-muse.or.jp; 6-5-1 Minami-Aoyama, Minato-ku; adult/child ¥1100/free, special exhibitions extra ¥200; ⏰10am-5pm Tue-Sun; 🚇Ginza line to Omote-sandō, exit A5) Nezu Museum offers a striking blend of old and new: a renowned collection of Japanese, Chinese and Korean antiquities in a gallery space designed by contemporary architect Kuma Kengo. Select items from the extensive collection are displayed in seasonal exhibitions. The English explanations are usually pretty good. Behind the galleries is a woodsy strolling garden laced with stone paths and studded with teahouses and sculptures.

Omote-sandō
Street

(表参道; Map p54; 🚇Ginza line to Omote-sandō, exits A3 & B4, 🚃JR Yamanote line to Harajuku, Omote-sandō exit) This broad, tree-lined boulevard is lined with boutiques from the top European fashion houses. More interesting are the buildings themselves, designed by some of the biggest names in Japanese architecture. There's no better (or more convenient) place to gain an overview of Japan's current sense of design. Highlights include the Dior boutique by SANAA (Nishizawa Ryue and Sejima Kazuyo) and the Tod's boutique by Itō Toyō.

◎ Shinjuku

Tokyo Metropolitan Government Building
Observatory

(東京都庁, Tokyo Tochō; www.metro.tokyo.jp/english/offices; 2-8-1 Nishi-Shinjuku, Shinjuku-ku; ⏰observatories 9.30am-11pm; 🚇Ōedo

Roppongi, Harajuku & Shibuya

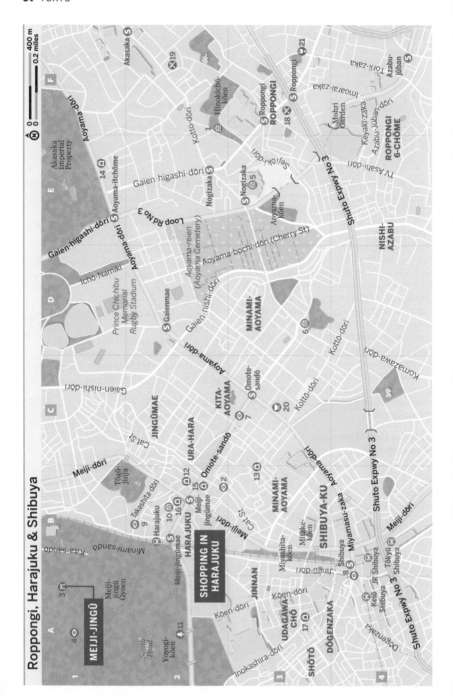

MEIJI-JINGŪ

SHOPPING IN HARAJUKU

0 400 m
0 0.2 miles

Akasaka Imperial Property

Aoyama-dōri

Akasaka Ⓢ

Ⓧ19

Ⓢ21
Ⓢ Roppongi

Ⓢ Roppongi
ROPPONGI
Ⓧ18 Ⓢ

Hinokichō-kōen

Kotto-dōri

Mohri Garden

Imoarai-zaka

Azabu-jūban Ⓢ

Keyaki-zaka

Azabu-jūban-dōri

Torii-zaka

ROPPONGI 6-CHŌME

TV Asahi-dōri

Seijōki-dōri

Nogizaka

Ⓢ Nogizaka

🏛5

Aoyama-kōen

Gaien-higashi-dōri

Ⓢ 14🏛

Aoyama-itchōme

Aoyama-dōri

Ⓢ Gaien-higashi-dōri

Ⓢ Aoyama-itchōme

Loop Rd No 3

Aoyama-reien (Aoyama Cemetery)

Aoyama-bochi-dōri (Cherry St)

NISHI-AZABU

Shuto Expwy No 3

Ichō-Namiki

Prince Chichibu Memorial Rugby Stadium

Ⓢ Gaienmae

Gaien-nishi-dōri

MINAMI-AOYAMA

🏛6

Kottō-dōri

Komazawa-dōri

Gaien-nishi-dōri

Aoyama-dōri

JINGŪMAE

Cat St

KITA-AOYAMA

Ⓢ Omote-sandō

Ⓢ7

🏤20

Kottō-dōri

Kottō-dōri

Aoyama-dōri

Shuto Expwy No 3

URA-HARA

Omote-sandō

🏢12

🏢15

Ⓢ Meiji-jingūmae

🏢16

Omote-sandō

Ⓢ2

13🏢

MINAMI-AOYAMA

Meiji-dōri

Cat St

SHIBUYA-KU

Aoyama-dōri

Shuto Expwy No 3

Togō-jinja

Takeshita-dōri

🚇 Harajuku

🏢10

Ⓢ9

HARAJUKU

🚇 Meiji-jingūmae

Meiji-dōri

Miyashita-kōen

Miyake-kōen

Miyamasu-zaka

🚇 Shibuya

Shibuya

Tōkyū 🚇 Shibuya

Meiji-dōri

Keiō JR Shibuya Shibuya

Shuto Expwy No 3

Minami-sandō

Kita-sandō

Meiji-jingū Gyoen

3🏛

South Pond

4Ⓢ

Yoyogi-kōen

🏛11

JINNAN

Jingū-dōri

Kōen-dōri

UDAGAWA-CHŌ

17🏢

SHŌTŌ

Kōen-dōri

DŌGENZAKA

Inokashira-dōri

Dōgenzaka

Roppongi, Harajuku & Shibuya

line to Tochōmae, exit A4) FREE Tokyo's city hall – a landmark building designed by Tange Kenzō – has observatories atop both the south and north towers of Building 1 (the views are virtually the same). On a clear day (morning is best), you may catch a glimpse of Mt Fuji beyond the urban sprawl to the west. Direct-access elevators are on the ground floor.

Golden Gai   Area
(ゴールデン街; http://goldengai.jp; 1-1 Kabukichō, Shinjuku-ku; ⓡJR Yamanote line to Shinjuku, east exit) Golden Gai – a Shinjuku institution for over half a century – is a collection of tiny bars, often literally no bigger than a closet and seating maybe a dozen. Each is as unique and eccentric as the 'master' or 'mama' who runs it. In a sense, Golden Gai, which has a strong visual appeal, with its low-slung wooden buildings, is their work of art. It's more than just a place to drink.

⊜ COURSES

Wanariya   Traditional Craft
(和なり屋; Map p58; ☑03-5603-9169; www.wanariya.jp; 1-8-10 Senzoku, Taitō-ku; indigo dyeing/weaving from ¥1920/1980; ⊙10am-7pm irregular holidays; ⓢHibiya line to Iriya, exit 1) A young and friendly team runs this indigo-dyeing and traditional *hataori* (hand-loom-weaving) workshop. In under an hour you can learn to dye a T-shirt or a tote bag

or weave a pair of coasters. It's a fantastic opportunity to make your own souvenirs. Book at least three days in advance.

Kitchen Kujo Tokyo   Cooking
(Map p58; ☑03-5832-9452; www.kujo.tokyo; 1-2-10 Yanaka, Taitō-ku; classes ¥6000-12,000; ⊙classes 10.30am or 1.30pm, bar 6-10.30pm Mon-Sat; ⓢChiyoda line to Nezu, exit 2) The Kobayashi family and their translator and ramen chef Jun offer an interesting variety of cooking and culture classes at this handy studio devoted to cooking with organic products. Learn how to make tofu, miso, vegan ramen and curry rice with guest instructor Curryman (who dresses in a wacky costume). Also available are calligraphy, tea-ceremony and yoga classes.

⊕ SHOPPING

Ginza, home to high-end department stores and boutiques, has long been Tokyo's premier shopping district, though Harajuku (p46) – popular with younger shoppers – puts up a good fight for the title. Shibuya is another trendy district, while Asakusa is good for traditional crafts.

Japan Traditional
Crafts Aoyama Square   Arts & Crafts
(伝統工芸 青山スクエア; Map p54; ☑03-5785-1301; www.kougeihin.jp; 8-1-22 Akasaka, Minato-ku; ⊙11am-7pm; ⓢGinza line to

Spa LaQua

One of Tokyo's few true onsen, this chic **spa complex** (スパ ラクーア; ☎03-5800-9999; www.laqua.jp; 5th-9th fl, Tokyo Dome City, 1-1-1 Kasuga, Bunkyō-ku; weekday/weekend ¥2850/3174; ⏰11am-9am; ⑤Marunouchi line to Kōrakuen, exit 2), renovated in 2017, relies on natural hot-spring water from 1700m below ground. There are indoor and outdoor baths, saunas and a bunch of add-on options, such as *akasuri* (Korean-style whole-body exfoliation). It's a fascinating introduction to Japanese health and beauty rituals.

An extra ¥865 gives you access to the Healing Baden area, with even more varieties of saunas and a lounge area styled like a Balinese resort. Here, men and women can hang out together (everyone gets a pair of rental pyjamas). There are lounging areas too, with reclining chairs.

NED SNOWMAN/SHUTTERSTOCK ©

Aoyama-itchōme, exit 4) Supported by the Japanese Ministry of Economy, Trade and Industry, this is as much a showroom as a shop, exhibiting a broad range of traditional crafts from around Japan, including lacquerwork boxes, woodwork, cut glass, textiles and pottery. There are some exquisite heirloom pieces here, but also beautiful items at reasonable prices.

Itōya   Arts & Crafts

(伊東屋; Map p52; ☎03-3561-8311; www.ito-ya. co.jp; 2-7-15 Ginza, Chūō-ku; ⏰10.30am-8pm Mon-Sat, to 7pm Sun; ⑤Ginza line to Ginza, exit A13) Explore the nine floors (plus several more in the nearby annex) of stationery at this famed, century-old Ginza establishment. There are everyday items (such as notebooks and greeting cards) and luxuries (fountain pens and Italian leather agendas). You'll also find *washi* (handmade paper), *tenugui* (beautifully hand-dyed thin cotton towels) and *furoshiki* (wrapping cloths).

Okuno Building   Arts & Crafts

(奥野ビル; Map p52; 1-9-8 Ginza, Chūō-ku; ⏰most galleries noon-7pm; ⑤Yūrakuchō line to Ginza-itchōme, exit 10) This 1932 apartment block (cutting edge for its time) is a retro time capsule, its seven floors packed with some 40 tiny boutiques and gallery spaces. Climbing up and down the Escher-like staircases, or using the antique elevator, you'll come across mini-exhibitions that change weekly.

Tokyu Hands   Department Store

(東急ハンズ; Map p54; http://shibuya.tokyu -hands.co.jp; 12-18 Udagawa-chō, Shibuya-ku; ⏰10am-9pm; ⑱JR Yamanote line to Shibuya, Hachikō exit) This DIY and *zakka* (miscellaneous things) store has eight fascinating floors of everything you didn't know you needed – reflexology slippers, bee-venom face masks and cartoon-character-shaped rice-ball moulds, for example. Most stuff is inexpensive, making it perfect for souvenir- and gift-hunting. Warning: you could lose hours in here.

Beams Japan   Fashion & Accessories

(ビームス・ジャパン; www.beams.co.jp; 3-32-6 Shinjuku, Shinjuku-ku; ⏰11am-8pm; ⑱JR Yamanote line to Shinjuku, east exit) Beams, a national chain of trendsetting boutiques, is a Japanese cultural institution and this multistorey Shinjuku branch has a particular audience in mind: you, the traveller. It's full of the latest Japanese streetwear labels, traditional fashions with cool modern twists, artisan crafts, pop art and more – all contenders for that perfect only-in-Tokyo souvenir. Set your budget before you enter.

Marugoto Nippon　　Food & Drinks

(まるごとにっぽん; Map p58; ☑03-3845-0510; www.marugotonippon.com; 2-6-7 Asakusa, Taitō-ku; ⊙10am-8pm; Ⓢ Ginza line to Tawaramachi, exit 3) Think of this as a minimall, showcasing the best of Japan's speciality food and drink (ground floor) and arts and crafts (2nd floor). The 3rd floor showcases the products and attractions of different Japanese regions on a regularly changing basis.

🍴 EATING

Honmura-An　　Soba ¥

(本むら庵; Map p54; ☑03-5772-6657; www.honmuraantokyo.com; 7-14-18 Roppongi, Minato-ku; noodles from ¥900, set meals lunch/dinner ¥1600/7400; ⊙noon-2.30pm & 5.30-10pm Tue-Sun, closed 1st & 3rd Tue of month; 🛜; Ⓢ Hibiya line to Roppongi, exit 4) This fabled soba shop, once located in Manhattan, now serves its handmade buckwheat noodles at this rustically contemporary noodle shop on a Roppongi side street. The noodles' delicate flavour is best appreciated when served on a bamboo mat, with tempura or with dainty slices of *kamo* (duck).

Innsyoutei　　Japanese ¥

(韻松亭; Map p58; ☑03-3821-8126; www.innsyoutei.jp; 4-59 Ueno-kōen, Taitō-ku; lunch/dinner from ¥1680/5500; ⊙restaurant 11am-3pm & 5-9.30pm, tearoom 3-5pm; Ⓡ JR lines to Ueno, Ueno-kōen exit) In a gorgeous wooden building dating to 1875, Innsyoutei (pronounced 'inshotei' and meaning 'rhyme of the pine cottage') has long been a favourite spot for fancy *kaiseki*-style meals while visiting **Ueno-kōen** (上野公園; Map p58; www.ueno-bunka.jp). Without a booking (essential for dinner) you'll have a long wait but it's worth it. Lunchtime *bentō* (boxed meals) offer beautifully presented morsels and are great value.

Hantei　　Japanese ¥¥

(はん亭; Map p58; ☑03-3287-9000; www.hantei.co.jp; 2-12-15 Nezu, Bunkyō-ku; lunch/dinner from ¥3200/3000; ⊙noon-3pm & 5-10pm Tue-Sun; Ⓢ Chiyoda line to Nezu, exit 2) Housed

 Fun for Young & Old

In need of amusement-park thrills? The latest virtual-reality gaming? Brownie points with the kids?

Tokyo Joypolis (東京ジョイポリス; http://tokyo-joypolis.com; 3rd-5th fl, DECKS Tokyo Beach, 1-6-1 Daiba, Minato-ku; adult/child ¥800/500, all-rides passport ¥4300/3300, passport after 5pm ¥3300/2300; ⊙10am-10pm; Ⓡ Yurikamome line to Odaiba Kaihin-kōen, north exit) is an indoor amusement park stacked with virtual-reality attractions and thrill rides.

Sky Circus (スカイサーカス; ☑03-3989-3457; www.skycircus.jp; Sunshine 60, 3-1-1 Higashi-Ikebukuro, Toshima-ku; observatory ticket adult/child ¥1200/600, attractions extra; ⊙10am-10pm; Ⓡ JR Yamanote line to Ikebukuro, east exit) is a giddying exploration of VR-tech to send you bouncing, flying and zooming around the 'future' city.

Tokyo Disney Resort (東京ディズニーリゾート; ☑domestic calls 0570-00-8632, from overseas +81-45-330-5211; www.tokyodisneyresort.jp; 1-1 Maihama, Urayasushi, Chiba-ken; 1-day ticket for 1 park adult/child ¥7400/4800, after 6pm ¥4200; ⊙varies by season; Ⓡ JR Keiyō line to Maihama, south exit) was one of the first Disney parks outside the US, and is still a great day or weekend out.

Tokyo Joypolis

in a beautifully maintained, century-old traditional wooden building, Hantei is a local landmark. Delectable skewers of seasonal *kushiage* (fried meat, fish and vegetables)

Ueno & Asakusa

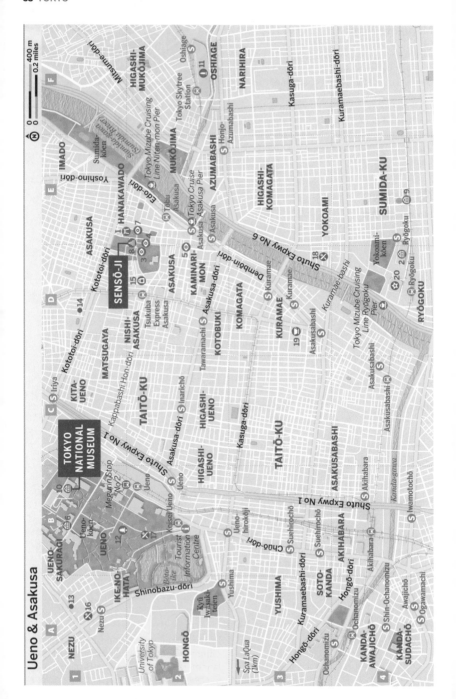

0 ___ 400 m
0 ___ 0.2 miles

NEZU

UENO-SAKURAGI

TOKYO NATIONAL MUSEUM

University of Tokyo

HONGŌ

IKENO-HATA

UENO

Shinobazu-dōri

Kyū Iwasaki-tei Teien

Spa LaQua (1km)

YUSHIMA

Ueno-hirokōji

Chūō-dōri

Suehirochō

SOTO-KANDA

AKIHABARA

Hongō-dōri

Ochanomizu

KANDA-AWAJICHŌ

Shin-Ochanomizu

Awajichō

Ogawamachi

KANDA-SUDACHŌ

Kuramaebashi-dōri

Kanda-gawa

Iwamotochō

Akihabara

ASAKUSABASHI

Asakusabashi

TAITŌ-KU

HIGASHI-UENO

Kasuga-dōri

Asakusa-dōri

Inarichō

Tawaramachi

KOTOBUKI

KOMAGATA

KURAMAE

Kuramae

Dembōin-dōri

KAMINARI-MON

ASAKUSA

SENSŌ-JI

NISHI-ASAKUSA

Tsukuba Express Asakusa

Kototoi-dōri

MATSUGAYA

KITA-UENO

Iriya

Kappabashi Hon-dōri

Shuto Expwy No 1

Megurin Stop No 2

Keisei Ueno

Tourist Information Centre

Ueno-kōen

Shuto Expwy No 1

Kuramae

Asakusa

Edo-dōri

Yoshino-dōri

IMADO

HANAKAWADO

Kototoi-dōri

ASAKUSA

Sumida-kōen

Sumida River (Sumida-gawa)

Tobu Asakusa

Tokyo Cruise Asakusa Pier

AZUMABASHI

MUKŌJIMA

Tokyo Mizube Cruising Line Niten-mon Pier

HIGASHI-MUKŌJIMA

Tokyo Skytree Station

Oshiage

OSHIAGE

NARIHIRA

Honjo-Azumabashi

Kasuga-dōri

HIGASHI-KOMAGATA

SUMIDA-KU

YOKOAMI

Kuramae-bashi

Shuto Expwy No 6

Tokyo Mizube Cruising Line Ryōgoku Pier

Asakusabashi

Yokoami-kōen

Ryōgoku

RYŌGOKU

Ryōgoku

Kuramaebashi-dōri

Mitsume-dōri

Ueno & Asakusa

are served with small, refreshing side dishes. Lunch includes eight or 12 sticks and dinner starts with six, after which you can order additional rounds (three/six skewers ¥800/1600).

Kappō Yoshiba   Japanese ¥¥
(割烹吉葉; Map p58; ☑03-3623-4480; www.kapou-yoshiba.jp; 2-14-5 Yokoami, Sumida-ku; dishes ¥650-7800; ⊙11.30am-2pm & 5-10pm Mon-Sat; ⑤Ōedo line to Ryōgoku, exit 1) The former Miyagino sumo stable is the location for this one-of-a-kind restaurant that has preserved the dōyō (practice ring) as its centrepiece. Playing up to its sumo roots, you can order the protein-packed stew chanko-nabe (for two people from ¥5200), but Yoshiba's real strength is its sushi, freshly prepared in jumbo portions.

Kikunoi   Kaiseki ¥¥¥
(菊乃井; Map p54; ☑03-3568-6055; www.kikunoi.jp; 6-13-8 Akasaka, Minato-ku; lunch/dinner course from ¥11,900/16,000; ⊙noon-12.30pm Tue-Sat, 5-7.30pm Mon-Sat; ⑤Chiyoda line to Akasaka, exit 7) Exquisitely prepared seasonal dishes are as beautiful as they are delicious at this Tokyo outpost of one of Kyoto's most acclaimed kaiseki (Japanese haute cuisine) restaurants. Kikunoi's third-generation chef, Murata Yoshihiro, has written a book on kaiseki (translated into English) that the staff helpfully use to explain the dishes you are served.

Tofuya-Ukai   Kaiseki ¥¥¥
(とうふ屋うかい; Map p52; ☑03-3436-1028; www.ukai.co.jp/english/shiba; 4-4-13 Shiba-kōen, Minato-ku; set meals lunch/dinner from ¥5940/10,800; ⊙11.45am-3pm & 5-7.30pm Mon-Fri, 11am-7.30pm Sat & Sun; ☑; ⑤Ōedo line to Akabanebashi, exit 8) One of Tokyo's most gracious restaurants is located in a former sake brewery (moved from northern Japan), with an exquisite traditional garden in the shadow of Tokyo Tower (東京タワー). Seasonal preparations of tofu and accompanying dishes are served in the refined kaiseki style. Make reservations well in advance. Vegetarians should advise staff when they book, and last orders for weekday lunch is 3pm, for dinner 7.30pm.

Kyūbey   Sushi ¥¥¥
(久兵衛; Map p52; ☑03-3571-6523; www.kyubey.jp; 8-7-6 Ginza, Chūō-ku; set meals lunch/dinner from ¥4400/11,000; ⊙11.30am-2pm & 5-10pm Mon-Sat; ⑤Ginza line to Shimbashi, exit 3) Since 1935, Kyūbey's quality and presentation have won it a moneyed and celebrity clientele. Despite the cachet, this is a relaxed restaurant. The friendly owner, Imada-san, speaks excellent English as do some of his team of talented chefs, who will make and serve your sushi, piece by piece. The ¥8000 lunchtime omakase (chef's choice) is great value.

Tempura Kondō — Tempura ¥¥¥

(てんぷら近藤; Map p52; ☑03-5568-0923; 9th fl, Sakaguchi Bldg, 5-5-13 Ginza, Chūō-ku; lunch/dinner course from ¥6500/11,000; ⊘noon-3pm & 5-10pm Mon-Sat; ⑤Ginza line to Ginza, exit B5) Nobody in Tokyo does tempura vegetables like chef Kondō Fumio. The carrots are julienned to a fine floss, the corn is pert and juicy, and the sweet potato is comfort food at its finest. Courses include seafood, too. Lunch at noon or 1.30pm; last dinner booking at 8pm. Reserve ahead.

🍷 DRINKING

Sakurai Japanese Tea Experience — Teahouse

(櫻井焙茶研究所; Map p54; ☑03-6451-1539; www.sakurai-tea.jp; 5th fl, Spiral Bldg, 5-6-23 Minami-Aoyama, Minato-ku; tea from ¥1400, course from ¥4800; ⊘11am-11pm; ⑤Ginza line to Omote-sandō, exit B1) Tea master (and former bartender) Sakurai Shinya's contemporary take on the tea ceremony is a must for anyone hoping to be better acquainted with Japan's signature brew. The course includes several varieties – you might be surprised how different tea can taste – paired with small bites, including some beautiful traditional sweets. Reservations recommended.

Purchase loose tea and beautiful teapots and cups at the attached shop (open until 8pm)

Chashitsu Kaboku — Teahouse

(茶室 嘉木; Map p52; ☑03-6212-0202; www.ippodo-tea.co.jp; 3-1-1 Marunouchi, Chiyoda-ku; tea set ¥1080-2600; ⊘11am-7pm; ◉JR Yamanote line to Yurakuchō, Tokyo International Forum exit) Run by famed Kyoto tea producer Ippōdō – which celebrated 300 years of business in 2017 – this teahouse is a fantastic place to experience the myriad pleasures of *ocha* (green tea). It's also one of the few places that serves *koicha* (thick tea), which is even thicker than ordinary *matcha* (powdered green tea). Sets are accompanied by a pretty, seasonal *wagashi*.

Toyama Bar — Bar

(トヤマバー; ☑03-6262-2723; www.toyama-kan.jp; 1-2-6 Nihombashi-muromachi, Chūō-ku; ⊘11am-9pm; ⑤Ginza line to Mitsukoshimae, exit B5) This slick counter bar offers a selection of sakes from 17 different Toyama breweries. A set of three 30mL cups costs a bargain ¥700 (90mL cups from ¥700 each). English tasting notes are available. It's part of the Nihonbashi Toyama-kan (日本橋とやま館), which promotes goods produced in Japan's northern Toyama Prefecture. Pick up a bottle of anything you like at the attached shop.

Two Dogs Taproom — Craft Beer

(Map p54; ☑03-5413-0333; www.twodogs-tokyo.com; 3-15-24 Roppongi, Minato-ku; ⊘11.30am-2.30pm Mon-Fri, 5-11pm Sun & Mon, until midnight Tue & Wed, until 2am Thu-Sat; ⑤Hibiya line to Roppongi, exit 3) There are 24 taps devoted to Japanese and international craft beers, including its own Roppongi Pale Ale, at this convivial pub just off the main Roppongi drag. Work your way through a few jars to wash down the tasty and decent-sized pizzas.

🎭 ENTERTAINMENT

Ryōgoku Kokugikan — Spectator Sport

(両国国技館, Ryōgoku Sumo Stadium; Map p58; ☑03-3623-5111; www.sumo.or.jp; 1-3-28 Yokoami, Sumida-ku; tickets ¥3800-11,700; ◉JR Sōbu line to Ryōgoku, west exit) If you're in town when a tournament is on, don't miss the chance to catch the big boys of Japanese wrestling in action at the country's largest sumo stadium. The key spectacle is at around 3.45pm, when the *makuuchi* (top division) wrestlers in elaborately decorated aprons parade into the ring. Tickets can be bought online one month before the tournament opens.

ℹ️ INFORMATION

DANGERS & ANNOYANCES

The biggest threat to travellers in Tokyo is the city's general aura of safety; keep up the same level of caution and common sense that you would back home.

○ Drink-spiking continues to be a problem in Roppongi (resulting in robbery, extortion and, in extreme cases, physical assault). This is most often the case when touts are involved; never follow a tout into a bar, anywhere.

○ Men are likely to be solicited in Roppongi and neighbourhoods that are considered red-light districts, including Kabukichō (in Shinjuku) and Dōgenzaka (in Shibuya). Women – particularly solo women – are likely to be harassed in these districts.

TOURIST INFORMATION

Tokyo Metropolitan Government Building Tourist Information Center (☑03-5321-3077; info@tokyo-tourism.jp; 1st fl, 2-8-1 Nishi-Shinjuku, Shinjuku-ku; ☺9.30am-6.30pm; ⑤Ōedo line to Tochōmae, exit A4) Has English-language information and publications. There are additional branches in **Keisei Ueno Station** (Map p58; ☑03-3836-3471; 1-60 Ueno-kōen, Taitō-ku; ☺9.30am-6.30pm; ☎; ℝJR & Keisei lines to Ueno, Ikenohata exit) and on the 3rd floor of the **Shinjuku Bus Terminal** (☑03-6274-8192; 5-24-55 Sendagaya, Shibuya-ku; ☺6.30am-11pm; ℝJR Yamanote line to Shinjuku, new south exit).

GETTING AROUND

TRAIN & SUBWAY

Tokyo's extensive rail network includes JR lines, a subway system and private commuter lines that depart in every direction for the suburbs, like spokes on a wheel. Journeys that require transfers between lines run by different operators cost more than journeys that use only one operator's lines. Major transit hubs include Tokyo, Shinagawa, Shibuya, Shinjuku, Ikebukuro and Ueno Stations. Trains arrive and depart precisely on time and are generally clean and pleasant, though they get uncomfortably crowded during rush hours.

Tokyo has 13 subway lines, nine of which are operated by **Tokyo Metro** (www.tokyometro.jp)

and four by **Toei** (www.kotsu.metro.tokyo.jp). The lines are colour-coded, making navigation fairly simple. Unfortunately a transfer ticket is required to change between the two; a Pasmo or Suica card makes this process seamless, but either way a journey involving more than one operator comes out costing slightly more. Rides on Tokyo Metro cost ¥170 to ¥240 (¥90 to ¥120 for children) and on Toei ¥180 to ¥320 (¥90 to ¥160 for children), depending on how far you travel.

KEY ROUTES

Ginza subway line Shibuya to Asakusa, via Ginza and Ueno. Colour-coded orange.

Hibiya subway line Naka-Meguro to Ebisu, Roppongi, Ginza, Akihabara and Ueno. Colour-coded grey.

JR Yamanote line Loop line stopping at many sightseeing destinations, such as Shibuya, Harajuku, Shinjuku, Tokyo and Ueno. Colour-coded light green.

JR Chūō line Express between Tokyo Station and Shinjuku, and onwards to points west. Colour-coded reddish-orange.

JR Sōbu line Runs across the city centre connecting Shinjuku with Iidabashi, Ryōgoku and Akihabara. Colour-coded yellow.

Yurikamome line Elevated train running from Shimbashi to points around Tokyo Bay.

TAXI

Taxis only make economic sense for short distances or groups of four.

○ Fares start at ¥410 for the first 1km, then rise by ¥80 for every 237m you travel or for every 90 seconds spent in traffic.

○ There's a surcharge of 20% between 10pm and 5am.

○ Drivers rarely speak English, though most taxis have navigation systems. Have your destination written down in Japanese, or better yet, a business card with an address.

○ Taxis take credit cards and IC passes.

Mt Fuji views from Kawaguchi-ko

Mt Fuji

Of all Japan's iconic images, Mt Fuji (富士山; 3776m) is the real deal. Admiration for the mountain appears in Japan's earliest recorded literature, dating from the 8th century.

Great For...

☑ Don't Miss

The famous mountain view from Motosu-ko.

Japan's highest and most famous peak is the big draw of the Fuji Five Lakes (富士五湖) region, but even without climbing Fuji-san, it's still worth coming here to enjoy the great outdoors around the volcano's northern foothills, and to admire the mountain photogenically reflected in the lakes. Culture buffs can also delve into the fascinating history of Mt Fuji worship at several sites.

Yamanaka-ko is the easternmost lake, followed by Kawaguchi-ko, Sai-ko, Shōji-ko and Motosu-ko.

Fuji-Spotting

Mt Fuji has many different personalities depending on the season. Winter and spring months are your best bet for seeing it in all its clichéd glory; although even during these times the snowcapped peak may be

Ashino-ko

AFLO CO., LTD/ALAMY STOCK PHOTO ©

⚓ Explore Ashore

Cruise ships dock in Shimizu, 90km southwest of Kawaguchi-ko. The quickest and easiest way to get there (or to other great mountain-view locations) is by taxi, which takes about 1¾ hours.

❶ Need to Know

Most visitors head straight for Mt Fuji as soon as they step off the ship so as to make the most of their time. If you have any extra time in port it's worthwhile exploring beautiful Shimizu.

Panorama-dai The end of this hiking trail (パノラマ台) rewards you with a magnificent front-on view of the mountain.

Kōyō-dai Mt Fuji can be seen from this **lookout** (adult/child ¥200/150), particularly stunning in the autumn colours.

Sightseeing Bus

The **Fuji Lakes Sightseeing Bus** (adult/child ¥1500/750) has three looping routes that start and finish at Kawaguchi-ko Station, with numbered stops for all the sightseeing spots around the western lakes. It's a hop-on, hop-off service with buses every 15 to 30 minutes (seasonal). Pick up the excellent map and timetable from Kawaguchi-ko Station, where patient English-speaking staff can answer all sightseeing bus-related queries.

The red line follows Kawaguchi-ko's northern shore and western area, the green line goes around Sai-ko and Aoki-gahara, and the blue line travels around Shōji-ko to the eastern end of Motosu-ko.

visible only in the morning before it retreats behind its cloud curtain. Its elusiveness, however, is part of the appeal, making sightings all the more special. Here are some of our top spots for viewing, both in the immediate and greater areas:

Kawaguchi-ko On the north side of the lake, where Fuji looms large over its shimmering reflection.

Motosu-ko The famous view depicted on the ¥1000 bill can be seen from the northwest side of the lake.

Hakone The mountain soars in the background of Ashino-ko and the red *torii* (shrine gate) rising from the water.

Izu Peninsula Journey along the west coast to catch glimpses of Fuji and the ocean, bathed in glorious sunsets.

Yokohama at a Glance

Just a 30-minute train ride south of central Tokyo, Yokohama (横浜) has an appealing flavour and history all its own. Locals are likely to cite the uncrowded, walkable streets or neighbourhood atmosphere as the main draw, but for visitors its appeal lies in the breezy bay front, creative arts scene, multiple microbreweries, jazz clubs and great international dining.

With a Day in Port

Start your day seeing an exhibition at **Yokohama Museum of Art** (p72), then stop in at the **Cup Noodles Museum** (p72) on the way to **Chinatown** (p68). Explore some of the area's 600 shops before ending the day at **NYK Hikawa Maru** (p72).

Best Places for...

Okonomiyaki Colombus Okonomiyaki (p74)

Tea Bashamichi Jyuban-Kan (p75)

Beer Kirin Beer Yokohama Factory (p74)

Travel with children Yokohama Cosmoworld (p73)

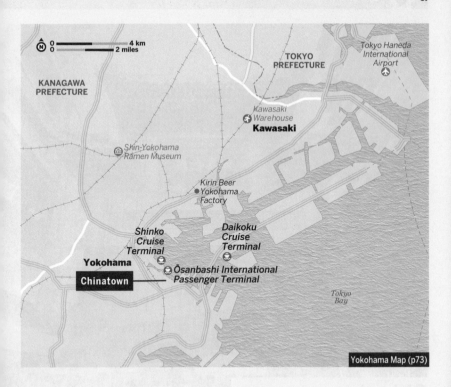

KANAGAWA
PREFECTURE

TOKYO
PREFECTURE

Tokyo Haneda
International
Airport

Kawasaki
Warehouse
Kawasaki

Shin-Yokohama
Rāmen Museum

Kirin Beer
Yokohama
Factory

*Shinko
Cruise
Terminal*

*Daikoku
Cruise
Terminal*

Yokohama

*Ōsanbashi International
Passenger Terminal*

Chinatown

Tokyo
Bay

0 ——— 4 km
0 ——— 2 miles

Yokohama Map (p73)

Getting from the Port

Ships visiting Yokohama dock at
**Ōsanbashi International Passenger
Terminal** (大さん橋国際客船ターミナル;
www.osanbashi.jp; 1-1-4 Kaigan-dōri, Naka-ku).
It's an easy walk to many highlights and
Nihon-ōdōri station is nearby.

At the time of research two new
cruise ports were about to open:
Daikoko Cruise Terminal (northeast of
Ōsanbashi) and Shinko Cruise Terminal
(west of Ōsanbashi).

Fast Facts

Tourist information See www.yoko
hamajapan.com and www.yokohama
seasider.com.

Transport Trains are the most convenient way to get around, but there is an
extensive bus network.

DKOIICH/SHUTTERSTOCK ©

Chinatown

Yokohama's frenetic Chinatown packs some 600 speciality shops and restaurants within a space of several blocks, marked by 10 elaborately painted gates. It's very touristy, but fun to visit for a meal or stroll.

Great For...

☑ **Don't Miss**

The delicious food in the area.

Kantei-byō

Chinatown's heart is **Kantei-byō** (関帝廟; 140 Yamashita-chō; ⊘9am-7pm; ⑤Motomachi-Chūkagai) FREE , an elaborately decorated shrine dedicated to Guan Yu, an adopted deity of business. This incarnation (the fourth) was built in 1990.

Masan-no-mise Ryūsen

The walls at cheerful little canteen **Masan-no-mise Ryūsen** (馬さんの店龍仙; ☎045-651-0758; www.ma-fam.com; 218-5 Yamashita-chō, Naka-ku; dishes from ¥700; ⊘7am-2am; ⓇIshikawachō) are literally wallpapered with appetizing photos of the stir-fries, dumplings, noodle soups and salads on offer. It has two other branches in Chinatown.

Yamashita-kōen

DIGIPUB/GETTY IMAGES ©

Explore Ashore

While Motomachi-Chūkagai station is nearby, it's only a 15-minute walk from Ōsanbashi pier.

❶ Need to Know

The most convenient subway for the area is Motomachi-Chūkagai, with an information center (p75) just a few blocks away.

Manchinrō Honten

The palatial Cantonese restaurant **Manchinrō Honten** (萬珍樓本店; ☑045-681-4004; www.manchinro.com; 153 Yamashita-chō, Naka-ku; lunch/dinner set menus from ¥2800/ 6000; ☺11am-10pm; ☒Motomachi-Chūkagai) is one of Chinatown's oldest (1892) and most respected. It serves a great selection of dim sum from 11am to 4pm, all in opulent surrounds, though it's a rather more formal affair for dinner. Book ahead on weekends.

What's Nearby?

Yamashita-kōen (山下公園周辺; 279 Yamashitachō; ☒Motomachi-Chūkagai) is an elegant bayside park that is ideal for strolling and ship-spotting. Moored at the eastern end is the 1930s passenger liner *Hikawa Maru* (p72).

At the **Yokohama Archives of History** (横浜開港資料館; ☑045-201-2100; www. kaikou.city.yokohama.jp; 3 Nihon-ōdōri, Naka-ku; adult/child ¥200/100; ☺9.30am-5pm Tue-Sun; ☒Nihon-ōdōri), displays in English chronicle the saga of Japan's opening up at the Yokohama port following the arrival of Commodore Matthew Perry and his persuasively well-armed steamships. It's located inside the former British consulate.

Yokohama Port Heritage Walk

This historic ramble takes in the sights along the edge of the harbour.

Start Kanagawa Prefectural Museum of Cultural History
Distance 2km
Duration 1½ hours

2 With its neoclassical colonnade, the **NYK Maritime Museum** (1936) served as a suitably bling HQ for Nippon Yusen Kaisha, one of the oldest shipping companies in the world.

3 The old **Yokohama Customs building** (1934) has a mosque-styled dome topping the tower.

1 The grand, domed **Kanagawa Prefectural Museum of Cultural History** (p72) was designed by a Japanese architect in neo-baroque style, a marker of Yokohama's newfound wealth and Western sensibilities after a few decades of global trade.

500 m
0.25 miles

Take a Break ...
Zō-no-hana Terrace (p75) is a promenade pitstop for drinks and snacks.

6 Yamashita Rinko Line Promenade, a raised scenic walkway, has views of the cruise ships docked at the stylish Ōsanbashi pier.

4 The leafy former British Consulate, now the **Yokohama Archives of History** (p69), was where Japan and the US signed the first of the 'unequal' trade treaties in 1854.

Yokohama-wan

Nihon-ōdōri

Yamashita-kōen

CHINATOWN

FINISH

Classic Photo Step back in time as you explore this vintage liner.

5 All-white **Kaigan Church** (1872) was the first Protestant church in Japan, established by an American missionary.

MOTOMACHI Motomachi-Chūkagai

7 NYK Hikawa Maru (p72) is a luxury liner that once conveyed Japanese passengers to Seattle in the 1930s, bringing back jazz and other Western cultural influences.

7 MARU/SHUTTERSTOCK © 6 COWARDLION/SHUTTERSTOCK © 7 SIRASTOCK/SHUTTERSTOCK ©

◎ SIGHTS

Yokohama Museum of Art   Gallery
(横浜美術館; ☎045-221-0300; www.yaf.or.jp/
yma; 3-4-1 Minato Mirai, Nishi-ku; adult/child
¥500/free; ☺10am-6pm, closed Thu; ⑤Minato
Mirai) The focus of the Yokohama Trien-
nale (2020, 2023), this museum hosts
exhibitions that swing between safe-bet
shows with European headliners to more
daring contemporary Japanese and up-
and-coming Southeast Asian artists. There
are also permanent works, including by
Picasso, Miró and Dalí, in the catalogue.

Cup Noodles Museum   Museum
(☎045-345-0918; www.cupnoodles-museum.
jp; 2-3-4 Shinkō, Naka-ku; adult/child ¥500/free;
☺10am-6pm, closed Tue; ♿; ⑤Bashamichi)
Dedicated to the 1956 invention of instant
ramen by Momofuku Ando (the 'cup' came
in 1971), this impressively slick attraction
has a host of wacky exhibits that drive
home the message to go against the grain,
be creative and 'Never give up!'. The highlight is the chance to design your own Cup
Noodle (additional ¥300) to take away.

NYK Hikawa Maru   Museum
(氷川丸; www.nyk.com; Yamashita-kōen, Naka-
ku; adult/child ¥300/100; ☺10am-5pm Tue-Sun;
⑤Motomachi-Chūkagai) Moored at the
eastern end of Yamashita-kōen, this 1930s
luxury liner has stories to tell from its days
conveying well-heeled Japanese passengers to Seattle, and later as a hospital ship
in WWII. Inside you can see cabins (one of
the staterooms was used by Charlie Chaplin), lounges, the engine room and bridge.

Shin-Yokohama Rāmen Museum   Museum
(新横浜ラーメン博物館; ☎045-471-0503;
www.raumen.co.jp; 2-14-21 Shin-Yokohama,
Kohoku-ku; adult/child ¥310/100, dishes around
¥900; ☺11am-10pm Mon-Sat, from 10.30am Sun;
⑤Shin-Yokohama) Nine ramen restaurants
from around Japan were hand-picked to
sell their wares in this theme-park-style
replica of a 1958 *shitamachi* (downtown
district) that's lit to feel like perpetual,
festive night-time. It's a short walk from

Shin-Yokohama station – ask for directions
at the station's information centre.

Nippon Maru Sailing Ship   Museum
(日本丸; ship & museum adult/child ¥600/300;
☺10am-5pm Tue-Sun; ⑤Sakuragichō) This
magnificent, four-masted barque (built in
1930 as a training ship for naval cadets)
sits in a wet dock adjacent to the **Yokohama Port Museum** (横浜みなと博物
館; ☎045-221-0280; www.nippon-maru.or.jp;
2-1-1 Minato Mirai, Nishi-ku; museum adult/child
¥400/200; ☺10am-5pm Tue-Sun), and is fascinating to board and explore. Tickets also
include entry to the museum building.

Hara Model Railway Museum   Museum
(原鉄道模型博物館; www.hara-mrm.com;
2nd fl, Yokohama Mitsui Bldg, 1-1-2 Takashima,
Nishi-ku; adult/child ¥1000/500; ☺10am-5pm
Wed-Mon; ⑤Shin-takashima) Hara Nobutaro
(1919–2014) was Japan's pre-eminent train-
spotter, taking the pastime to a delightfully
surprising level of obsessiveness as this
superb personal collection of model trains
and other railway-associated memorabilia
shows.

Kanagawa Prefectural Museum of Cultural History   Museum
(神奈川県立歴史博物館; http://ch.kanaga-
wa-museum.jp/english; 5-60 Minaminaka-dori,
Naka-ku; adult/child ¥300/100; ☺9.30am-
4.30pm Tue-Sun; ⑤Bashamichi) Housed in the
grand former Yokohama Specie Bank building (c1904) is this rather scholarly history
museum charting the course of Kanagawa
Prefecture from neolithic times through to
the opening up of the city's port.

◎ ACTIVITIES

Kawasaki Warehouse   Amusement Park
(アミューズメントパーク ウェアハウス
川崎店, Anata no Warehouse; 3-7 Nisshin-cho,
Kawasaki; ☺9am-11.45pm, from 7am Sat & Sun;
⑤Kawasaki) **FREE** If you check out just one
video-game arcade in Japan, make it this
cyber-punk styled 'warehouse' designed

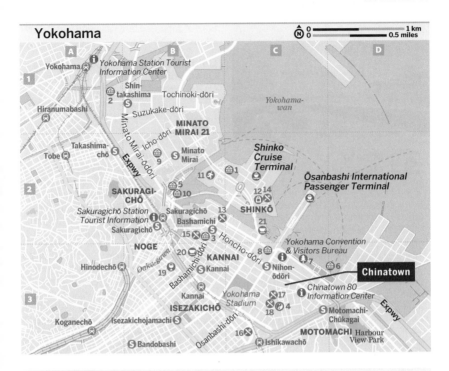

Yokohama

🔵 **Sights**

1 Cup Noodles Museum	C2
2 Hara Model Railway Museum	A1
3 Kanagawa Prefectural Museum of Cultural History	B2
4 Kantei-byō	C3
5 Nippon Maru Sailing Ship	B2
6 NYK Hikawa Maru	D3
7 Yamashita-kōen	C3
8 Yokohama Archives of History	C3
9 Yokohama Museum of Art	B2
10 Yokohama Port Museum	B2

🟠 **Activities, Courses & Tours**

11 Yokohama Cosmoworld	B2

🔴 **Shopping**

12 Akarenga Sōko	C2

⚫ **Eating**

13 Araiya	B2
14 Bills	C2
15 Charcoal Grill Green	B2
16 Colombus Okonomiyaki	C3
17 Manchinrō Honten	C3
18 Masan-no-mise Ryūsen	C3

🟢 **Drinking & Nightlife**

19 Antenna America	B3
20 Bashamichi Jyuban-Kan	B3
21 Zō-no-hana Terrace	C2

to resemble Kowloon Walled City. Step through the smoking, hissing entranceway and up the escalators to find arcade machines galore, as well as crane games, slots, and even pool and table tennis. The arcade is 500m southwest of Kawasaki station. Adults only.

Yokohama Cosmoworld
Amusement Park

(横浜コスモワールド; www.cosmoworld. jp; 2-8-1 Shinkō, Naka-ku; admission free, rides ¥100-800; ⏰11am-9pm Mon-Wed & Fri, to 10pm Sat & Sun; Ⓢ Minato Mirai) Perfect for children, this compact amusement park is home to

 Minato Mirai 21

Over the last three decades Yokohama's former shipping docks have been transformed into this planned city of tomorrow ('Minato Mirai' means 'port future'). There are plenty of recreation areas, including the old **Akarenga Sōkō** (横浜赤レンガ倉庫; www.yokohama-akarenga.jp; 1-1 Shinkō, Naka-ku; ⊙11am-8pm; ⑤Bashamichi) red-brick warehouses, transformed into a shopping, dining and events space; and a series of breezy **promenades** connecting the area's main attractions.

Nippon Maru ship (p72)
PICTURE CELLS/SHUTTERSTOCK ©

one of the world's tallest Ferris wheels, the 112.5m Cosmo Clock 21 (tickets ¥800).

⊙ TOURS

Kirin Beer Yokohama Factory Tours
(キリンビール 横浜工場; ☑045-503-8250; 1-17-1 Namamugi, Tsurumi-ku; ⊙10am-5pm Tue-Sun; ◪Namamugi) FREE Even teetotallers will be charmed by this hi-tech romp through one of the major breweries for Kirin beer. The free tour (in Japanese, but with translation cards) takes an hour to explain the stages of beer production with the help of touch screens and 3D goggles, finishing with a tasting of three beers. Reserve in advance (English spoken).

⊗ EATING

Feast on culinary variety in cosmopolitan Yokohama: Texas-style barbecue joints, Cantonese dim sum, and the full smorgasbord of Japanese fare including local takes on ramen and sukiyaki.

Colombus Okonomiyaki   Okonomiyaki ¥
(お好み焼きころんぶす; ☑045-633-2748; 1-3-7 Matsukage-chō, Naka-ku; mains ¥890-1120; ⊙11.30am-3pm & 5-10pm Mon-Thu, 11.30am-3pm & 5-11pm Fri, 11.30am-11pm Sat, 3-10pm Sun; ◪Ishikawachō) Friendly staff grill up a wide range of *okonomiyaki* (savoury pancakes) at your table, with prawn, squid, pork or veg (the English menu has some cute manga to help). It's a two-minute walk from the Ishikawachō Station. Turn right from the north exit, left at the first traffic lights and Colombus is 40m on your right.

Charcoal Grill Green   Grill ¥¥
(チャコールグリル グリーン 馬車道; ☑045-263-8976; www.greenyokohama.com; 6-79 Benten-dōri, Naka-ku; mains from ¥1380; ⊙11.30am-2pm & 5pm-midnight; ⑤Bashamichi) Char is the star at this hip grill restaurant and bar that serves pink-centred steaks and smoky chicken to go with craft beers on tap and a decent wine list. The lunch specials are a great deal.

Bills   International ¥¥
(ビルズ; ☑045-650-1266; www.bills-jp.net; Akarenga Sōkō Bldg 2, 1-1-2 Shinkō, Naka-ku; mains ¥1420-2200; ⊙9am-11pm Mon-Fri, from 8am Sat & Sun; ✍; ⑤Bashamichi) Popular for brunch, the zesty fusion food here comes from the cookbooks of Australian celebrity chef Bill Granger. Try his signature ricotta hotcakes, the berry pancakes, or go for the 'full Aussie' breakfast blowout. There are a couple of vegan options on the breakfast and dinner menus.

Araiya   Japanese ¥¥¥
(荒井屋; ☑045-226-5003; www.araiya.co.jp; 4-23 Kaigan-dōri, Naka-ku; set lunch/dinner from ¥1540/2970; ⊙11am-2.30pm & 5-10pm; ⑤Bashamichi) Yokohama has its own version of the beef hotpot dish sukiyaki, called *gyū-nabe*. This elegant restaurant, established in 1895, is the place to sample it.

🍺 DRINKING

Antenna America   Craft Beer

(アンテナアメリカ; ☑45-315-5228; www.
antenna-america.com; 5th fl, 5-4-6 Yoshida-machi,
Naka-ku; ⏱3-11pm Mon-Fri, from 11am Sat & Sun;
🚉Kannai) Sup imported cans of American
craft beer for just ¥500 at this showroom-
turned-bar attached to a beer distribution
company. Staff know their hops and the
selection is impressive; the decor less so. A
tiny kitchen turns out respectable fish tacos.

Bashamichi Jyuban-Kan   Cafe

(馬車道十番館; ☑045-651-2621; www.yoko
hama-jyubankan.co.jp; 5-67 Tokiwa-chō, Naka-ku;
⏱10am-10pm; Ⓢ Bashamichi) Soak up the
old Yokohama vibes at this former trading
company building turned cafe-bar and
French restaurant. You can join the well-to-
do regulars for tea and pastries at dainty
tables, or seek out the clubby little bar up
the wooden staircase past old photographs
of the port area.

Zō-no-hana Terrace   Cafe

(象の鼻テラス; ☑045-661-0602; www.zouno
hana.com; 1 Kaigan-dōri, Naka-ku; dishes ¥750;
⏱10am-6pm; ♿; Ⓢ Nihon-ōdōri) There's a liter-
al elephant in the room at this bright bayside cafe space (elephant is *zō* in Japanese),
a welcome promenade pit stop for bottled
beer, coffee, ice cream and light snacks.

ℹ️ INFORMATION

The following all have an English speaker.

Chinatown 80 Information Center (横浜中華
街インフォメーションセンター; ☑045-681-
6022; 80 Yamashita-chō; ⏱10am-8pm Sun-Thu,
to 9pm Fri & Sat; 🚉Motomachi-Chūkagai) A few
blocks from Motomachi-Chūkagai Station.

Sakuragichō Station Tourist Information
(☑045-211-0111; ⏱9am-6pm; 🚉Sakuragichō)
Outside the south exit of Sakuragichō Station.

Yokohama Convention & Visitors Bureau
(☑045-221-2111; www.yokohamajapan.com; 1st fl,
Sangyō-Bōeki Center, 2 Yamashita-chō, Naka-ku;
⏱9am-5pm Mon-Fri; 🚉Nihon-ōdōri) A 10-minute
walk from Nihon-ōdōri Station.

📖 Yokohama's History

Up until the mid-19th century, Yokohama was an unassuming fishing village.
Things started to change rapidly,
however, in 1853, when the American
fleet under Commodore Matthew Perry
arrived off the coast to persuade Japan
to open to foreign trade.

From 1858, when it was designated an
international port, through to the early
20th century, Yokohama served as a
gateway for foreign influence and ideas.
Among the city's firsts in Japan: a daily
newspaper, gas lamps and a train terminus (connected to Shimbashi in Tokyo).

The Great Kantō Earthquake of 1923
destroyed much of the city, but the
rubble was used to reclaim more land,
including Yamashita-kōen. The city
was devastated yet again in WWII air
raids. Despite all this, central Yokohama
retains some rather fine early 20th-
century buildings.

Yokohama Station Tourist Information Center
(☑045-441-7300; ⏱9am-7pm) It's in the east–
west corridor at Yokohama Station.

ℹ️ GETTING AROUND

BUS

Although trains are more convenient, Yokohama
has an extensive bus network. The cute,
red-coloured Akai-kutsu ('red shoe') bus loops
every 20 minutes from 10am to around 7pm
through the major tourist spots (adult/child
¥220/110 per ride).

SUBWAY & TRAIN

The Yokohama City blue line (*shiei chikatetsu*)
connects Yokohama with Shin-Yokohama (¥240,
11 minutes), Sakuragichō (¥210, four minutes)
and Kannai (¥210, six minutes). JR trains
connect Yokohama with Shin-Yokohama (¥170, 14
minutes), Sakuragichō (¥140, four minutes) and
Kannai (¥140, five minutes).

NAGOYA

In This Chapter

Nagoya at a Glance

Affable Nagoya (名古屋), birthplace of Toyota and pachinko (a pinball-style game), is a manufacturing powerhouse. But its manufacturing roots don't mean that Nagoya is a city of factories: well-maintained parks and green spaces prevail in the inner wards. Nagoya has cosmopolitan aspects, including some fantastic museums, significant temples and excellent shopping, and Nagoyans are vivacious and unpretentious.

With a Day in Port

Explore the streets surrounding **Ōsu Kannon** (p80) for a sampler of Nagoya's culture, shopping and cuisine. Swap ships for trains at **SCMAGLEV & Railway Park** (p82) or cars at **Toyota Commemorative Museum of Industry & Technology** (p82), and imagine life as a shogun at reconstructed **Nagoya-jō** (p83).

Best Places for...

Local cuisine Misen (p85)

Shopping Komehyō (p81)

Souvenir crafting Noritake Garden (p83)

A restorative drink Smash Head (p81)

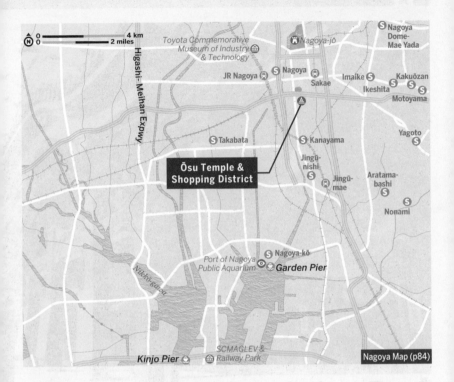

Ōsu Temple & Shopping District

Port of Nagoya Public Aquarium

Garden Pier

Kinjo Pier

SCMAGLEV & Railway Park

Nagoya Map (p84)

Getting from the Port

Both Garden and Kinjo Piers have nearby train stations, making city access straightforward. Allow about half an hour from either pier to Nagoya Station.

To get from Garden Pier to Kinjo Pier, home of Legoland and the SCMAGLEV & Railway Park (p82), you can make a bus and subway trip to Kinjofuto Station, or stick to the water with Nagoya Cruise (http://cruise-nagoya.jp).

Fast Facts

Money Look for Japan Post ATMs at Garden Pier and Nagoya Station.

Tourist information There's a small information kiosk at Garden Pier.

Wi-fi Free wi-fi is available at all subway stations, at Jetty mall (Garden Pier), Makers Pier centre (Kinjo Pier) and at the port building at Garden Pier.

Ōsu Kannon

DAVID QUIKLEY/SHUTTERSTOCK ©

Ōsu Temple & Shopping District

The area between Ōsu Kannon and Kamimaezu Stations, crammed with retailers, eateries and street vendors, has a delightfully young and alternative vibe. Patient shoppers can be rewarded with funky vintage threads and offbeat souvenirs. Take a break with a visit to Ōsu Kannon temple.

Great For...

☑ Don't Miss

Ōsu Kannon hosts a colourful antique market on the 18th and 28th of each month.

Exploring the Neighbourhood

From Kamimaezu Station, take exit 9 and walk north two blocks. Turn left on to Ban-shoji street (万松寺通), a covered shopping arcade that becomes Ōsu Kannon street and continues on to Ōsu Kannon temple. The streets either side are alive with activity. Along Akamon-dōri, Banshō-ji-dōri and Niomon-dōri are hundreds of funky vintage boutiques and discount clothing retailers. East of Ōsu, Otsu-dōri has a proliferation of manga (Japanese comic) shops.

Ōsu Kannon

The much-visited, workaday **Ōsu Kannon** (大須観音; ☎052-231-6525; www.osu-kannon. jp; 2-21-47 Osu, Naka-ku; ☺24hr; ⑤Ōsu Kannon, exit 2) temple traces its roots back to 1333. Devoted to the Buddha of Compassion, the temple was moved to its present location

Explore Ashore

Travel to Õsu Kannon from Garden Pier takes about half an hour on the subway; take the Meiko line to Kanayama, then change to the Meijo line for Kamimaezu. It takes another 20 minutes or so from Kinjo Pier.

❶ Need to Know

For cheap eats, head to the shopfronts of the Õsu Shopping Arcade, where street vendors hawk everything from kebabs to crêpes and pizza.

2-20-25 Õsu; ⏰10.30am-7.30pm Thu-Tue; ⓢÕsu Kannon, exit 2), Japan's largest discounter of secondhand, well...everything. Housed over seven floors in the main building, clothes, jewellery and accessories are of excellent quality and are sold at reasonable prices. With patience, you can find some real bargains, especially at 'yen=g' on the 7th floor, where clothing is sold by weight.

Local Lunch Specials

Yabaton Honten (矢場とん本店; ☎052-252-8810; http://english.yabaton.com; 3-6-18 Õsu; dishes from ¥1200; ⏰11am-9pm; ⓢYaba-chō, exit 4) has been the place to try Nagoya's famed *miso-katsu* (a type of *tonkatsu* – deep-fried pork cutlet) since 1947. Signature dishes include *waraji-tonkatsu* (schnitzel-style flattened, breaded pork) and *teppan-tonkatsu* (breaded pork cutlet with miso on a sizzling plate of cabbage). Look for the massive pig over the door, just south of the overpass. It's next to McDonald's.

in 1610, although the current buildings date from 1970. The library inside holds the oldest known handwritten copy of the *Kojiki* – the ancient mythological history of Japan.

Drink Break

Through the passageway to the left of the main Õsu Kannon temple building you'll find the motorcycle- and Vespa-repair shop-pub **Smash Head** (スマッシュヘッド; ☎052-201-2790; http://smashhead.main.jp; 2-21-90 Õsu; ⏰11.30am-9pm Wed-Sun, to 3.30pm Mon; ⓢÕsu Kannon, exit 2). Guinness and Corona are the beers of choice, the patrons are cool and the bacon cheeseburgers cost ¥1100.

Komehyō

Just a couple of hundred metres west of the temple, enjoy the genius of **Komehyō** (コメ兵; ☎052-242-0088; www.en.komehyo.co.jp;

⊙ SIGHTS

SCMAGLEV & Railway Park   Museum

(JR リニア・鉄道館, JR Rinia Tetsudō-kan; ☎050-3772-3910; http://museum.jr-central.co.jp; 3-2-2 Kinjo-futo, Minato-ku; adult/child ¥1000/200, shinkansen-driving simulator ¥500; ⊙10am-5.30pm Wed-Mon; P; ℝJR Aonami line to Kinjofuto) Trainspotters will be in heaven at this fantastic hands-on museum. Featuring an actual maglev (the world's fastest train – 581km/h), *shinkansen* (bullet trains), historical rolling stock and rail simulators, the massive museum offers a fascinating insight into Japanese postwar history through the development of a railroad like no other. The 'hangar' is a short walk from Kinjo Pier, on the Taiko-dōri side of JR Nagoya Station.

The *shinkansen*-driving-simulator tickets are assigned on a lottery basis. You must apply to the lottery on the day you wish to drive the simulator, and wait for the results.

Toyota Commemorative Museum of Industry & Technology   Museum

(トヨタテクノミュージアム産業技術記念館, Toyota Techno-museum Zangyō Gijutsu Kinenkan; ☎052-551-6115; www.tcmit.org; 4-1-35 Noritake-shinmachi; adult/child ¥500/200; ⊙9.30am-4.30pm Tue-Sun; ℝMeitetsu Nagoya line to Sako) The world's largest car manufacturer had humble beginnings in the weaving industry. This museum occupies the site of Toyota's original weaving plant. Car enthusiasts will find things textile heavy before warming to the 7900-sq-metre automotive and robotics pavilion. Science-minded folk will enjoy the countless hands-on exhibits. Displays are bilingual and there's an English-language audio tour available.

Don't confuse this museum with the **Toyota Exhibition Hall** (トヨタ会館, Toyota Kaikan; ☎museum 0565-29-3345, tours 0565-29-3355; www.toyota.co.jp/en/about_toyota/facility/toyota_kaikan; 1 Toyota-chō; ⊙9.30am-5pm Mon-Sat, tours 11am; ℝAichi Kanjō line to Mikawa Toyota) FREE and factory tours – the hall is about two hours out of town; tours need to be booked at least two weeks in advance.

Toyota Commemorative Museum of Industry & Technology

PICNOTE/SHUTTERSTOCK ©

Nagoya-jō — Castle

(名古屋城; ☏052-231-1700; www.nagoyajo.
city.nagoya.jp; 1-1 Honmaru; adult/child ¥500/
free; ⊗9am-4.30pm; ⑤Shiyakusho, exit 7) The
original structure, built between 1610 and
1614 by Tokugawa Ieyasu for his ninth son,
was levelled in WWII. Today's castle is a
concrete replica (with elevator) completed
in 1959. Renovations are ongoing. On the
roof, look for the 3m-long gilded *shachi-
hoko* (legendary creatures possessing a
tiger's head and a carp's body). Inside, find
treasures, an armour collection and the his-
tories of the Oda, Toyotomi and Tokugawa
families. Free English tours run every day at
1pm from the castle's east gate.

The beautiful year-round garden,
Ninomaru-en (二の丸園) has a number of
pretty teahouses.

Port of Nagoya Public Aquarium — Aquarium

(名古屋港水族館, Nagoya-ko Suizoku-kan;
☏052-654-7080; www.nagoyaaqua.com/english;
1-3 Minato-machi, Minato-ku; adult/child/student
¥2000/500/1000; ⊗9.30am-5.30pm Tue-Sun;
⑤Nagoya-ko) Among Nagoya's most well-
known attractions, this port-side aquarium
features one of the largest outdoor tanks
in the world, and the permanently moored
Fuji Icebreaker ship, now an **Antarctic
Museum**. The dolphin shows may concern
some visitors: there's increasing evidence
to suggest that it's harmful and stressful to
keep cetaceans (Nagoya's aquarium has
both dolphins and orcas) in captivity.

Noritake Garden — Gardens

(ノリタケの森, Noritake no Mori; ☏052-561-
7290; www.noritake.co.jp/eng; 3-1-36 Noritake-shinmachi; ⊗10am-6pm; ⑤Kamejima)
Pottery fans will enjoy a stroll around
Noritake Garden, the 1904 factory grounds
of one of Japan's best-known porcelain
makers, featuring remnants of early kilns
and the pleasant **Noritake Gallery** (ノリ
タケの森ギャラリー; ☏052-562-9811; www.
noritake.co.jp/eng/mori/look/gallery; 3-1-36
Noritake-shinmachi; ⊗10am-6pm; ⑤Kamejima) FREE. Glaze your own porcelain dish
(from ¥1800 plus shipping) in the **Craft**

Legoland

Nagoya is home to Japan's only **Legoland** (https://www.legoland.jp/en/)
theme park. It's handily located a short
walk away from Kinjo Pier (about 1km).
Allow about 45 minutes for the bus and
subway trip from Garden Pier, or try for
a boat trip with Nagoya Cruise (http://
cruise-nagoya.jp). The park features
seven different themed areas, rides,
shows and (naturally) many, many
pieces of Lego.

Garden Pier is home to its own small
theme park, **Sea Train Land** (http://
www.senyo.co.jp/seatrainland/attrac
tion.html).

BLANSCAPE/SHUTTERSTOCK ©

Centre & Museum (ノリタケクラフトセン
ター; ☏052-561-7114; www.noritake.co.jp/eng/
mori/look/museum; 3-1-36 Noritake-shinmachi;
adult/child ¥500/free; ⊗10am-5pm; ⑤Kamejima), which demonstrates the production
process. The 'Box Outlet Shop', ironically,
has unboxed wares at discounted prices.
English signs throughout.

🔒 SHOPPING

Nagoya's manufacturing roots make it a
great place to shop. Look for **Jetty** shopping mall at Garden Pier and **Makers Pier**
(http://www.makerspier.com/en) at Kinjo.
The areas of Meieki and Sakae are home to
gargantuan malls and department stores,
good for clothing, crafts and food, and the
streets around Ōsu Kannon (p80) are filled
with retail opportunities.

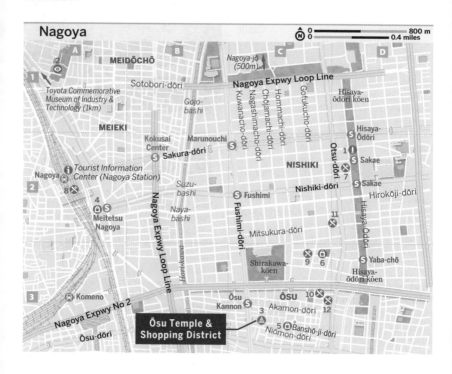

Nagoya

Kintetsu   Department Store
(近鉄; ☎052-582-3411; 1-2-2 Meieki; ⊙10am-7pm; Ⓡ Kintetsu Nagoya) The Nagoya HQ of this Osaka-based railway and department-store chain.

Loft Department Store   Department Store
(ロフト; ☎052-219-3000; 3-18-1 Sakae, Nadya Park; ⊙10am-8pm; Ⓢ Yaba-chō, exit 5 or 6) One

of Japan's coolest department stores has a definite design bent. You can't miss the yellow-and-black livery.

🍴 EATING

Nagoya is a fantastic place to experience Japan's passion for food, with many local specialities.

Misen   Taiwanese ¥

(味仙; ☎052-238-7357; www.misen.ne.jp; 3-6-3
Ōsu, Naka-ku; dishes ¥480-1500; ⊗11.30am-2pm
& 5pm-1am Sun-Thu, to 2am Fri & Sat; ❀♪; ⑤Yaba-chō, exit 4) Folks line up for opening time
at this jolly place, where the *Taiwan rāmen*
(台湾ラーメン; a spicy concoction of
ground meat, chilli, garlic and green onion,
served over noodles in broth) induces
rapture. It may be Taiwanese, but locals will
tell you: 'this is real Nagoya food'.

Love Pacific Cafe   Vegan ¥

(ラブ・パシフィックカフェ; ☎052-252-8429;
www.pacifit.jp/lovecafe.html; 3-23-38 Sakae;
items from ¥600; ⊗11.30am-5pm Tue-Sun; ♪;
⑤Yaba-chō, exit 4) Lovers of wholesome,
delicious, healthy foods are in for a treat at
this trendy, friendly vegan cafe preparing
lunch sets and cafe items that are free of
dairy, egg and white sugars. The changing
menu usually features a choice of two
soups, access to the organic salad bar
and a main: the tofu teriyaki burgers are
delicious.

Chomoranmen   Ramen ¥

(ちょもらん麺; ☎052-963-5121; 3-15-10
Nishiki; items ¥650-1100; ⊗11.30am-12.30am;
⑤Sakae, exit 3) Opposite the Nagoya TV
Tower, these cheap, chunky handmade
ramen bowls will fill you up. The walls are
covered with photos of famous patrons.
Someone will be happy to help you with
the vending machine used to take orders if
you get stuck.

Suzunami Honten   Seafood ¥¥

(鈴波本店; ☎052-261-1300; www.suzunami.
co.jp/shop/shop_honten.html; 3-7-23 Sakae,
Naka-ku; lunch sets ¥1300; ⊗11am-2.30pm;
❀) Delightfully traditional but not overly
formal, this Nagoyan *kappo* institution
specialises in simple grilled fish lunches
served with miso soup, rice and pickles,
and finished off with *umeshu* (plum wine).
You'll likely have a short wait for a table.

Din Tai Fung   Taiwanese ¥¥

(鼎泰豐; ☎052-533-6030; http://d.rt-c.co.jp/
nagoya; 12F Takashimaya Department Store, 1-1-4
Meieki; items from ¥600; ⊗11am-11pm; 🚇JR
Nagoya, Sakura-dōri exit) The Nagoya branch of
this globally acclaimed Taiwanese chain, located in the Takashimaya department store
at Nagoya Station, is likely to please with its
literally 'mouth-watering' *xiao long bao* soup
dumplings *(shōronpō)* and an extensive
menu of dim-sum delights. Best for duos
and groups of friends: the more the merrier.

 INFORMATION

Tourist Information Center – Nagoya Station
(名古屋駅観光案内所; ☎052-541-4301; 1-1-14
Meieki; ⊗9am-7pm; 🚇JR Nagoya)

ⓘ **GETTING AROUND**

Nagoya has an excellent subway system with six
lines, clearly signposted in English and Japanese.
Fares are ¥200 to ¥330 depending on distance.
One-day passes, available at ticket machines,
include subway transport and discounted admission to many attractions.

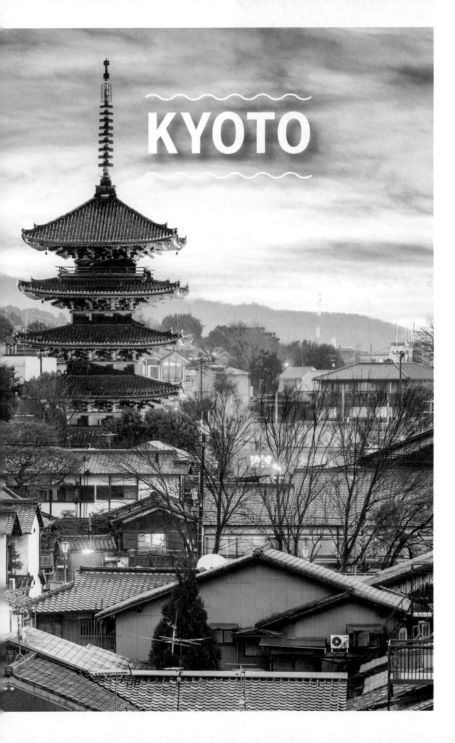

KYOTO

Kyoto at a Glance

Kyoto is old Japan writ large: quiet temples, sublime gardens, colourful shrines and geisha scurrying to secret liaisons. With 17 Unesco World Heritage Sites, and more than 1000 Buddhist temples and 400 Shintō shrines, it is one of the world's most culturally rich cities. But Kyoto is not just about sightseeing. While the rest of Japan has adopted modernity with abandon, the old ways are still clinging on in Kyoto. Visit an old shōtengai (market street) and admire the ancient speciality shops, including tofu sellers, washi (Japanese handmade paper) stores and tea merchants.

With a Day in Port

Start your Kyoto experience with a visit to **Fushimi Inari-Taisha** (p90), where you'll be entranced by the hypnotic arcades of *torii* (gates) at this sprawling Shintō shrine. Nearby is **Tōfuku-ji** (p91), a beautiful temple complex. Here you can meander through the expansive grounds and wander among the superb structures. In the afternoon take a taxi to downtown, hitting the excellent **Nishiki Market** (p98), craft shops and department stores. End with a stroll through the historic geisha district of **Gion** (p94).

Best Places for...

Kaiseki Kitcho Arashiyama (p109)

Sushi Chidoritei (p108)

Soba noodles Honke Owariya (p106)

Coffee Weekenders Coffee (p109)

Matcha Kaboku Tearoom (p110)

Previous page: Views across Higashiyama (p99)
SEAN PAVONE/SHUTTERSTOCK ©

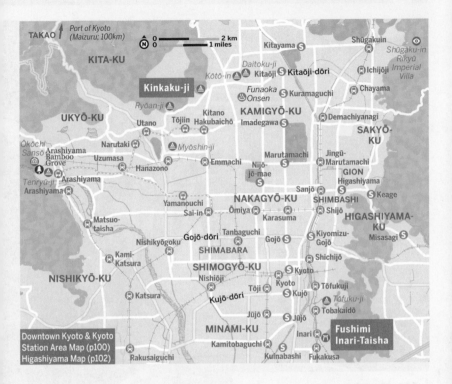

TAKAO ↑ Port of Kyoto
(Maizuru; 100km)

Ⓝ 0 ——— 2 km
0 ——— 1 miles

KITA-KU

Kitayama Ⓢ
Shūgakuin Ⓡ
Shūgaku-in Rikyū Imperial Villa

Daitoku-ji ⚪⚫ Kitaōji Ⓢ Kitaōji-dōri
Kōtō-in ⚪⚫
Ⓡ Ichijōji

Kinkaku-ji ⚫

Funaoka Ⓢ Kuramaguchi
♨Onsen
Ⓡ Chayama

Ryōan-ji ⚫

UKYŌ-KU

Utano
Kitano Hakubaichō
Tōjiin Ⓡ
Imadegawa Ⓢ
KAMIGYŌ-KU
Ⓡ Demachiyanagi

SAKYŌ-KU

Okōchi
Sansō Arashiyama
⚪⚫ Bamboo Grove
Narutaki Ⓡ
Ⓡ Myōshin-ji
Marutamachi Ⓢ
Jingū-
Marutamachi
GION
Higashiyama

Uzumasa
Hanazono
Ⓡ Emmachi
Nijō-jō-mae Ⓢ

Tenryū-ji ⚫
Arashiyama Ⓡ
Arashiyama
Ⓡ

Sanjō Ⓢ
Ⓢ Keage

Matsuo-
taisha Ⓡ
Yamanouchi Ⓡ
NAKAGYŌ-KU
SHIMBASHI
HIGASHIYAMA-KU

Sai-in Ⓡ
Ōmiya Ⓡ
Karasuma
Ⓢ Shijō
Misasagi Ⓢ

Nishikyōgoku Ⓡ
Gojō-dōri Tanbaguchi
Gojō Ⓢ
Ⓡ Kiyomizu-Gojō

Kami-
Katsura Ⓡ
SHIMABARA
Ⓡ Shichijō

NISHIKYŌ-KU
SHIMOGYŌ-KU
Ⓢ Kyoto

Nishiōji Ⓡ
Kyoto
Ⓡ Tōfukuji

Ⓡ Katsura
Tōji Ⓡ
Ⓢ Kujō
Tōfuku-ji

Kujō-dōri
Ⓡ Tobakaidō

Jūjō Ⓡ
Ⓢ Jūjō

MINAMI-KU

Inari Ⓡ Ⓢ
Fushimi Inari-Taisha

Downtown Kyoto & Kyoto
Station Area Map (p100)
Higashiyama Map (p102)

Rakusaiguchi Ⓡ
Kamitobaguchi Ⓡ Ⓢ
Kuinabashi Fukakusa

Getting from the Port

The Port of Kyoto, located at Maizuru, is approximately 90 minutes away by train or taxi from Kyoto. If getting the train into Kyoto, it's about a 10-minute taxi ride (¥775) from the port to Nishi-Maizuru Station. From here, take the Ltd Express train on the JR Hashidate line into Kyoto Station (around ¥2630), the main train station in the city. Train tickets are available at station ticket offices.

Fast Facts

Tourist information For bus and city maps and transport info, visit Kyoto Tourist Information Center (p110).

Transport Kyoto is a compact city with an excellent public transport system. It has two efficient subway lines, operating from 5.30am to 11.30pm. Minimum adult fare is ¥210 (children ¥110).

Wi-fi You'll find a couple of computer terminals with internet at Kyoto Tourist Information Center (p110). If you want constant access to wi-fi when you're out and about, your best bet is either renting a portable device or buying a data-only SIM for an unlocked smartphone.

Torii (gates)

TAKASHI IMAGES/SHUTTERSTOCK ©

Fushimi Inari-Taisha

With seemingly endless arcades of vermilion torii across a thickly wooded mountain, this vast complex is a world unto itself. One of the most impressive and memorable sights in all of Kyoto.

Great For...

☑ **Don't Miss**

The classic photo op from inside the tunnel of *torii*.

History

Fushimi Inari-Taisha was dedicated to the gods of rice and sake by the Hata family in the 8th century. As the role of agriculture diminished, deities were enrolled to ensure prosperity in business. Nowadays the shrine is one of Japan's most popular, and is the head shrine for some 40,000 Inari shrines scattered the length and breadth of the country.

Messenger of Inari

As you explore the shrine, you will come across hundreds of stone foxes. The fox is considered the messenger of Inari, the god of cereals, and the stone foxes, too, are often referred to as 'Inari'. The key often seen in the fox's mouth is for the rice granary. On an incidental note, the Japanese traditionally see the fox as a sacred,

Tōfuku-ji

PICACCH/GETTY IMAGES ©

Explore Ashore

From the port in Maizuru, it's 90 minutes by train or taxi into Kyoto. If travelling by train, once at Kyoto Station, hop on the JR Nara Line to Inari Station (five minutes). From here it's about a five-minute walk to the shrine. Expect to spend a few hours or more here, especially if you want to explore the pathway up the mountain.

❶ Need to Know

伏見稲荷大社; 68 Yabunouchi-chō, Fukakusa, Fushimi-ku; admission free; ⊙dawn-dusk; 🚉JR Nara line to Inari or Keihan line to Fushimi-Inari

somewhat mysterious figure capable of 'possessing' humans – the favoured point of entry is under the fingernails.

Hiking the Grounds

A pathway wanders 4km up the mountain and is lined with dozens of atmospheric subshrines. The walk around the upper precincts is a pleasant day hike. It also makes for a very eerie stroll in the late afternoon and early evening, when the various graveyards and miniature shrines along the path take on a mysterious air. It's best to go with a friend at this time.

What's Nearby?

Home to a spectacular garden, several superb structures and beautiful precincts, **Tōfuku-ji** (東福寺; ☎075-561-0087; www.

tofukuji.jp; 15-778 Honmahi, Higashiyama-ku; Hōjō garden ¥400, Tsūten-kyō bridge ¥400; ⊙9am-4pm; 🚉Keihan line to Tōfukuji or JR Nara line to Tōfukuji) is one of the best temples in Kyoto. It is linked to Fushimi Inari-Taisha by the Keihan and JR train lines. The present temple complex includes 24 subtemples. The huge **San-mon** is the oldest Zen main gate in Japan, the **Hōjō** (Abbot's Hall) was reconstructed in 1890, and the gardens were laid out in 1938.

The northern garden has stones and moss neatly arranged in a checkerboard pattern. From a viewing platform at the back of the gardens you can observe the **Tsūten-kyō** (Bridge to Heaven), which spans a valley filled with maples.

Maiko in Gion (p94)

Kyoto's Geisha Culture

Though dressed in the finest silks and often astonishingly beautiful, geisha are first and foremost accomplished musicians and dancers. These now-rare creatures – seemingly lifted from another world – still entertain in Kyoto today.

Great For...

☑ **Don't Miss**

A stroll through atmospheric Gion.

Geiko & Maiko

The word geisha literally means 'arts person'; in Kyoto the term used is *geiko* – 'child of the arts'. It is the *maiko* (apprentice *geiko*) who are spotted on city streets in ornate dress, long trailing obi and towering wooden clogs, their faces painted with thick white make-up, leaving only a suggestive forked tongue of bare flesh on the nape of the neck. As geisha grow older their make-up becomes increasingly natural; by then their artistic accomplishments need no fine casing. At their peak in the 1920s, there were around 80,000 geisha in Japan. Today there are approximately 1000 (including apprentices), with nearly half working in Kyoto.

Life of a Geisha Then & Now

Prior to the mid-20th century, a young girl might arrive at an *okiya* (geisha living

Geiko entering a teahouse

KEKYALYAYNEN/SHUTTERSTOCK ©

Explore Ashore

From the port in Maizuru, the quickest way to reach the Gion district is by taxi, which will take you about 90 minutes. Allow a few hours to wander around and be sure to veer off the main drag, where you'll escape the crowds and see some of the area's impossibly atmospheric backstreets.

❶ Need to Know

Gion (p94), on the Kamo-gawa's east bank, is Kyoto's most-famous geisha district.

quarters) to work as a maid. Should she show promise, the owner of the *okiya* would send her to begin training at the *kaburenjo* (school for geisha arts) at around age six. She would continue maid duty, waiting on the senior geisha of the house, while honing her skills and eventually specialising in one of the arts, such as playing the *shamisen* (three-stringed instrument resembling a lute or a banjo) or dance.

Geisha were often indebted to the *okiya* who covered their board and training. Given the lack of bargaining chips that have been afforded women in history, there is no doubt that many geisha of the past, at some point in their careers, engaged in compensated relationships; this would be with a *danna* (a patron) with whom the geisha would enter a contractual relationship not unlike a marriage (and one that

could be terminated). A wealthy *danna* could help a woman fulfil her debt to the *okiya* or help her start her own. Other geisha married, which required them to leave the profession; some were adopted by the *okiya* and inherited the role of house mother; still others worked into old age.

Today's geisha begin their training no earlier than their teens – perhaps after being inspired by a school trip to Kyoto – while completing their compulsory education (in Japan, until age 15). Then they'll leave home for an *okiya* (they do still exist) and start work as an apprentice. While in the past a *maiko* would never be seen out and about in anything but finery, today's apprentices act much like ordinary teens in their downtime. For some, the magic is in the *maiko* stage and they never proceed to become geisha; those who do live largely normal lives, free to live where they choose, date as they like and change professions when they please.

Hanamachi

Traditionally, the districts where geisha were licensed to entertain in *ochaya* (teahouses) were called *hanamachi*, which means 'flower town'. Of the five that remain in Kyoto, **Gion** (祇園周辺; Map p102; Higashi-yama-ku; [S]Tōzai line to Sanjō, [R]Keihan line to Gion-Shijō) is the grandest. Many of Kyoto's most upmarket restaurants and exclusive hostess bars are here.

On the other side of the river, **Ponto-chō** (先斗町; Map p100; Ponto-chō, Nakagyō-ku; [S]Tōzai line to Sanjo-Keihan or Kyoto-Shiyakusho-mae, [R]Keihan line to Sanjo, Hankyū line to Kawaramachi) has a different feel, with very narrow lanes. Not much to look at by day, the street comes alive at night, with wonderful lanterns, traditional wooden exteriors, and elegant Kyotoites disappearing into the doorways of elite old restaurants and bars.

Experiencing Geisha Culture

Modern *maiko* and geisha entertain their clients in exclusive restaurants, banquet halls and traditional *ochaya* much like they did a century ago. This world is largely off limits to travellers, as a personal connection is required to get a foot in the door, though some tour operators can act as mediator. Of course, these experiences can cost hundreds of dollars (if not more).

Ryokan Gion Hatanaka offers a rare chance to witness geisha perform and then interact with them. If your cruise schedule allows, the inn's **Kyoto Cuisine & Maiko Evening** (ぎおん畑中; Map p102; ☎075-541-5315; www.kyoto-maiko.jp; 505 Gion-machi, Minami-gawa, Higashiyama-ku; per person ¥19,000; ⏰6-8pm Mon, Wed, Fri & Sat; 🚌Kyoto City bus 206 to Gion or Chionin-mae, [R]Keihan line to Gion-Shijō) is an evening of elegant Kyoto *kaiseki* (haute cuisine) food and personal entertainment by both Kyoto *geiko* and *maiko*.

Performance at Kamogawa Odori

Geisha Dances

An excellent way to experience geisha culture is to see one of Kyoto's *odori* (annual public dance performances), a city tradition for over a century. Get tickets as early as you can.

Miyako Odori is held throughout April, usually at Gion Kōbu Kaburen-jō Theatre. See p110 for more.

Gion Odori (祇園をどり; Map p102; ☎075-561-0224; Gion, Higashiyama-ku; with/without tea ¥4500/4000; ☺shows 1.30pm & 4pm; ☒Kyoto City bus 206 to Gion) is held from 1 to 10 November, at the Gion Kaikan Theatre (祇園会館).

Kyō Odori (京おどり; Map p102; ☎075-561-1151; Miyagawachō Kaburenjo, 4-306 Miyaga-wasuji, Higashiyama-ku; with/without tea from ¥2800/2200; ☺shows 1pm, 2.45pm & 4.30pm; ☒Keihan line to Gion-Shijō) takes place from the first to the third Sunday in April at the Miyagawa-chō Kaburen-jō Theatre (宮川町歌舞練場).

Kamogawa Odori (鴨川をどり; Map p100; ☎075-221-2025; Ponto-chō, Sanjō-sagaru, Nakagyō-ku; seat ¥2300, special seat with/without tea ¥4800/4200; ☺shows 12.30pm, 2.20pm & 4.10pm; ⓢTōzai line to Kyoto-Shiyakusho-mae) is held from 1 to 24 May at Ponto-chō Kaburen-jō Theatre.

Maiko Makeover

Ever wondered how you might look as a *maiko*? Give it a try at **Maika** (舞香; Map p102; ☎075-551-1661; www.maica.tv; 297 Miyagawa suji 4-chōme, Higashiyama-ku; maiko/geisha from ¥6500/8000; ☒Keihan line to Gion-Shijo or Kiyomizu-Gojo) in Gion. The basic treatment includes full make-up and formal kimono. If you don't mind spending some extra yen, it's possible to head out in costume for a stroll through Gion (and be stared at like never before!). The process takes about an hour. Call to reserve at least one day in advance.

Photographing Geisha

A photo of a *maiko* is a much-coveted Kyoto souvenir; however, bear in mind that these are young women – many of whom are minors – on their way to work. Be respectful and let them pass.

DANITA DELIMONT/ALAMY STOCK PHOTO ©

★ Top Tip

Check with the Kyoto Tourist Information Center (p110) for events with local geisha.

MARCOCIANNAREL/SHUTTERSTOCK ©

Kinkaku-ji

Kyoto's famed 'Golden Pavilion', Kinkaku-ji is one of Japan's best-known sights. The main hall, covered in brilliant gold leaf, shining above its reflecting pond, is truly spectacular.

Great For...

☑ Don't Miss

The mirror-like reflection of the temple in the Kyō-ko pond is extremely photogenic.

History

Originally built in 1397 as a retirement villa for shogun Ashikaga Yoshimitsu, whose son converted Kinkaku-ji to a Buddhist temple in compliance with his wishes. In 1950 a young monk consummated his obsession with the temple by burning it to the ground. The monk's story is fictionalised in Mishima Yukio's 1956 novel *The Temple of the Golden Pavilion*. In 1955 a full reconstruction was completed, following the original design but extending the gold-foil covering to the lower floors.

The Pavilion & Grounds

The three-storey pavilion, covered in bright gold leaf with a bronze phoenix on top of the roof, is naturally the highlight. But there's more to this temple than its shiny main hall. Don't miss the Ryūmon-taki

Ryōan-ji

WAYNE EASTEP/GETTY IMAGES ©

Kinkaku-ji ⚓

⚓ *Ryōan-ji*

Utano · Ryōanji Tōjiin · Kitano
· · · Myōshinji · Hakubaichō
Narutaki · Omura-
· Ninnaji ⚓*Myōshin-ji*

⚓

Explore Ashore

From the port, it's quickest to get here by taxi, or take the train from Nishi-Maizuru Station to Kyoto Station. From here, catch the Kyoto City bus 205 to Kinkakuji-michi. It's about a 10-minute walk to Kinkaku-ji. You'll need at least a few hours to explore the famed 'Golden Pavilion' and the expansive grounds.

❶ Need to Know

金閣寺; 1 Kinkakuji-chō, Kita-ku; adult/child ¥400/300; ⊙9am-5pm; 🚍Kyoto City bus 205 from Kyoto Station to Kinkakuji-michi; 🚍Kyoto City bus 12 from Sanjō-Keihan to Kinkakuji-michi

waterfall and Rigyo-seki stone, which looks like a carp attempting to swim up the falls. Nearby, there is a small gathering of stone Jizō figures onto which people throw coins and make wishes. The quaint teahouse Sekka-tei embodies the spirit of *wabi-sabi* (rustic simplicity) of the Japanese tea-ceremony ethic.

What's Nearby?

You've probably seen a picture of the rock garden here – it's one of the symbols of Kyoto and one of Japan's better-known sights. **Ryōan-ji** (龍安寺; www.ryoanji.jp; 13 Goryōnoshitamachi, Ryōan-ji, Ukyō-ku; adult/child ¥500/300; ⊙8am-5pm Mar-Nov, 8.30am-4.30pm Dec-Feb; 🚍Kyoto City bus 59 from Sanjō-Keihan to Ryoanji-mae) belongs to the Rinzai school and was founded in 1450. The garden, with an austere collection of 15

carefully placed rocks apparently adrift in a sea of sand, is enclosed by an earthen wall. The designer, who remains unknown to this day, provided no explanation.

An early-morning visit on a weekday is probably your best hope of seeing the garden free from the ever-present crowds.

Myōshin-ji (妙心寺; www.myoshinji.or.jp; 1 Myoshin-ji-chō, Hanazono, Ukyō-ku; main temple free, other areas of complex adult/child ¥500/100; ⊙9.10-11.40am & 1-4.40pm, to 3.40pm Nov-Feb; 🚍Kyoto City bus 10 from Sanjo-Keihan to Myōshin-ji Kita-mon-mae) is a separate world within Kyoto, a walled-off complex of temples and subtemples that invites lazy strolling. The subtemple of **Taizō-in** contains one of the city's more interesting gardens. Myōshin-ji dates to 1342 and belongs to the Rinzai school.

SIGHTS

With over 1000 Buddhist temples and 400 Shintō shrines scattered over the city and into the hills, it's not hard to guess what most of your sightseeing time will be spent doing. The Southern and Northern Higashiyama areas are where the majority of the big-hitting temples lie. Downtown Kyoto is the hotspot for shopping and dining, but it does have a few worthy sights, including the impressive Nijō-jō and the famous food market, Nishiki. Around Kyoto Station and South Kyoto, there are a few good temples and the famous Fushimi Inari-Taisha (p90) shrine.

◉ Downtown Kyoto

Nijō-jō
Castle

(二条城; Map p100; 541 Nijōjō-chō, Nijō-dōri, Horikawa nishi-iru, Nakagyō-ku; adult/child ¥600/200; ⊙8.45am-5pm, last entry 4pm, closed Tue Dec, Jan, Jul & Aug; ⑤Tōzai line to Nijō-jō-mae, ⑤JR line to Nijō) The military might of Japan's great warlord generals, the Tokugawa shoguns, is amply demonstrated by the imposing stone walls and ramparts of their great castle, Nijō-jō, which dominates a large part of northwest Kyoto. Hidden behind these you will find a superb palace surrounded by beautiful gardens. Avoid crowds by visiting just after opening or shortly before closing.

Nishiki Market
Market

(錦市場; Map p100; Nishikikōji-dōri, btwn Teramachi & Takakura, Nakagyō-ku; ⊙9am-5pm; ⑤Karasuma line to Shijō, ⑤Hankyū line to Karasuma or Kawaramachi) Head to the covered Nishiki Market to check out the weird and wonderful foods that go into Kyoto cuisine. It's in the centre of town, one block north of (and parallel to) Shijō-dōri, running west off Teramachi covered arcade. Wander past stalls selling everything from barrels of *tsukemono* (pickled vegetables) and cute Japanese sweets to wasabi salt and fresh sashimi skewers. Drop into Aritsugu (p105) here for some of the best Japanese chef's knives money can buy.

Daitoku-ji
Buddhist Temple

(大徳寺; 53 Daitokuji-chō, Murasakino, Kita-ku; ⑤Kyoto City bus 205 or 206 to Daitokuji-mae, ⑤Karasuma line to Kitaōji) For anyone with the slightest fondness for Japanese gardens, don't miss this network of lanes dotted with atmospheric Zen temples. Daitoku-ji, the main temple here, serves as headquarters for the Rinzai Daitoku-ji school of Zen Buddhism. It's not usually open to the public but there are several subtemples with superb, carefully raked *karen-sensui* (dry landscape) gardens well worth making the trip for. Highlights include Daisen-in, Kōtō-in, Ryōgen-in and Zuihō-in.

Kōtō-in
Buddhist Temple

(高桐院; 73-1 Daitokuji-chō, Murasakino, Kita-ku; ¥400; ⊙9am-4.30pm; ⑤Kyoto City bus 205 or 206 to Daitokuji-mae, ⑤Karasuma line to Kitaōji) On the far western edge of the Daitoku-ji complex, the sublime garden of this subtemple is one of the best in Kyoto and worth a special trip. It's located within a fine bamboo grove that you traverse via a moss-lined path. Once inside there is a small stroll garden that leads to the centrepiece: a rectangle of moss and maple trees, backed by bamboo. Take some time on the verandah here to soak it all up.

Kyoto Imperial Palace
Historic Building

(京都御所, Kyoto Gosho; Map p100; ☎075-211-1215; www.kunaicho.go.jp; Kyoto Gyōen, Kamigyō-ku; ⊙9am-4.30pm Tue-Sun Mar-Sep, to 4pm Oct-Feb, last entry 40min before closing; ⑤Karasuma line to Marutamachi or Imadegawa) FREE The Kyoto Imperial Palace, known as the Gosho in Japanese, is a walled complex that sits in the middle of the **Kyoto Imperial Palace Park**. While no longer the official residence of the Japanese emperor, it's still a grand edifice, though it doesn't rate highly in comparison with other attractions in Kyoto. Visitors can wander around the marked route in the grounds where English signs explain the history of the buildings. Entrance is via the main Seishomon Gate, where you'll be given a map.

◉ Southern Higashiyama

Kiyomizu-dera   Buddhist Temple

(清水寺; Map p102; ☎075-551-1234;
www.kiyomizudera.or.jp; 1-294 Kiyomizu,
Higashiyama-ku; adult/child ¥400/200; ⊘6am-
6pm, closing times vary seasonally; ☒Kyoto
City bus 206 to Kiyomizu-michi or Gojō-zaka,
☒Keihan line to Kiyomizu-Gojō) A buzzing hive
of activity perched on a hill overlooking
the basin of Kyoto, Kiyomizu-dera is one of
Kyoto's most popular and most enjoyable
temples. It may not be a tranquil refuge,
but it represents the favoured expression
of faith in Japan. The excellent website is
a great first port of call for information on
the temple, plus a how-to guide to praying
here. Note that the Main Hall is undergoing
renovations and may be covered, but is still
accessible.

Shōren-in   Buddhist Temple

(青蓮院; Map p102; 69-1 Sanjōbō-chō, Awata-
guchi, Higashiyama-ku; adult/child ¥500/free;
⊘9am-5pm; Ⓢ Tōzai line to Higashiyama) This
temple is hard to miss, with its giant cam-
phor trees growing just outside the walls.

Fortunately, most tourists march right on
past, heading to the area's more famous
temples. That's their loss, because this
intimate little sanctuary contains a superb
landscape garden, which you can enjoy
while drinking a cup of green tea (¥500;
ask at the reception office, not available in
summer).

Chion-in   Buddhist Temple

(知恩院; Map p102; www.chion-in.or.jp; 400
Rinka-chō, Higashiyama-ku; adult/child
¥500/250, grounds free; ⊘9am-4.30pm, last
entry 3.50pm; Ⓢ Tōzai line to Higashiyama) A
collection of soaring buildings, spacious
courtyards and gardens, Chion-in serves
as the headquarters of the Jōdo sect,
the largest school of Buddhism in Japan.
It's the most popular pilgrimage temple
in Kyoto and it's always a hive of activity.
For visitors with a taste for the grand, this
temple is sure to satisfy.

Yasaka-jinja   Shintō Shrine

(八坂神社; Map p102; ☎075-561-6155; www.
yasaka-jinja.or.jp; 625 Gion-machi, Kita-
gawa, Higashiyama-ku; ⊘24hr; Ⓢ Tōzai line

Nijō-jō

Downtown Kyoto & Kyoto Station Area

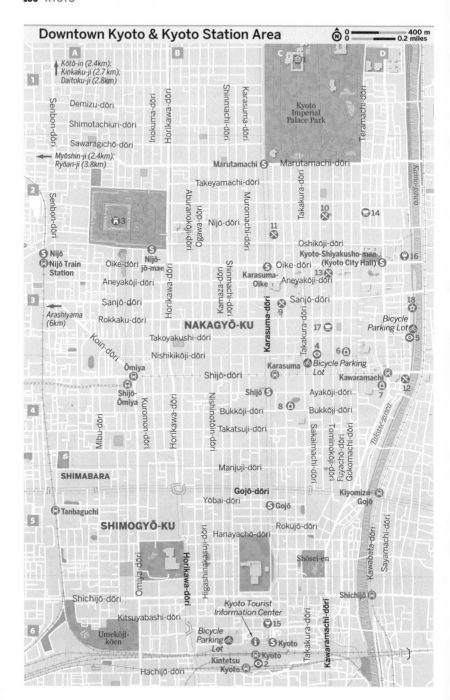

Downtown Kyoto & Kyoto Station Area

to Higashiyama) FREE This colourful and spacious shrine is considered the guardian shrine of the Gion entertainment district. It's a bustling place that is well worth a visit while exploring Southern Higashiyama; it can easily be paired with Maruyama-kōen, the park just up the hill.

Kyoto National Museum Museum
(京都国立博物館; Map p102; www.kyohaku. go.jp; 527 Chaya-machi, Higashiyama-ku; admission varies; ⊙9.30am-5pm, to 8pm Fri & Sat, closed Mon; 🚌Kyoto City bus 206 or 208 to Sanjūsangen-dō-mae, 🚃Keihan line to Shichijō) The Kyoto National Museum is the city's premier art museum and plays host to the highest-level exhibitions in the city. It was founded in 1895 as an imperial repository for art and treasures from local temples and shrines. The **Heisei Chishinkan**, designed by Taniguchi Yoshio and opened in 2014, is a brilliant modern counterpoint to the original red-brick **main hall** building, which was closed and undergoing structural work at the time of research. Check the *Kyoto Visitor's Guide* to see what's on while you're in town.

◎ Northern Higashiyama

Ginkaku-ji Buddhist Temple
(銀閣寺; Map p102; 2 Ginkaku-ji-chō, Sakyō-ku; adult/child ¥500/300; ⊙8.30am-5pm Mar-Nov, 9am-4.30pm Dec-Feb; 🚌Kyoto City bus 5 to Ginkakuji-michi stop) Home to a sumptuous garden and elegant structures, Ginkaku-ji

is one of Kyoto's premier sites. The temple started its life in 1482 as a retirement villa for shogun Ashikaga Yoshimasa, who desired a place to retreat from the turmoil of a civil war. While the name Ginkaku-ji literally translates as 'Silver Pavilion', the shogun's ambition to cover the building with silver was never realised. After Ashikaga's death, the villa was converted into a temple.

Nanzen-ji Buddhist Temple
(南禅寺; Map p102; www.nanzenji.com; 86 Fukuchi-chō, Nanzen-ji, Sakyō-ku; adult/child from ¥300/150, grounds free; ⊙8.40am-5pm Mar-Nov, to 4.30pm Dec-Feb; 🚌Kyoto City bus 5 to Eikandō-michi, Ⓢ Tōzai line to Keage) This is one of the most rewarding temples in Kyoto, with its expansive grounds and numerous subtemples. At its entrance stands the massive **San-mon**. Steps lead up to the 2nd storey, which has a great view over the city. Beyond the gate is the main hall of the temple, above which you will find the **Hōjō**, where the Leaping Tiger Garden is a classic Zen garden well worth a look.

Eikan-dō Buddhist Temple
(永観堂; Map p102; ✆075-761-0007; www. eikando.or.jp; 48 Eikandō-chō, Sakyō-ku; adult/ child ¥600/400; ⊙9am-5pm; 🚌Kyoto City bus 5 to Eikandō-michi, Ⓢ Tōzai line to Keage) Perhaps Kyoto's most famous (and most crowded) autumn-foliage destination, Eikan-dō is a superb temple just a short walk south of the famous Path of Philosophy. Eikan-dō

Higashiyama

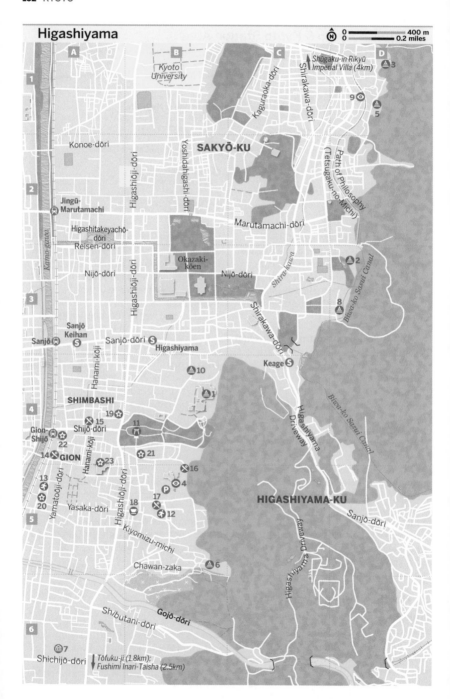

N ⬆
0 ▬▬▬▬ 400 m
0 ▬▬▬▬ 0.2 miles

Kyoto University

Kaguraoka-dōri

Shirakawa-dōri

↑ Shūgaku-in Rikyū
Imperial Villa (4km)

A **B** **C** **D**

9 ◎ ⚠ 3
⚠ 5

Konoe-dōri

Yoshidahigashi-dōri

SAKYŌ-KU

Higashiōji-dōri

Path of Philosophy
(Tetsugaku-no-Michi)

Jingū-
Marutamachi

Higashitakeyachō-
dōri
Reisen-dōri

Marutamachi-dōri

Kamo-gawa

Higashiōji-dōri

Nijō-dōri

Okazaki-
kōen

Nijō-dōri

Shira-kawa

⚠ 2

⚠ 8

Biwa-ko Sosui Canal

Sanjō
Keihan

Sanjō-dōri Ⓢ Higashiyama

Shirakawa-dōri

Sanjō Ⓡ

Higashiyama

⚠ 10

Keage Ⓢ

Biwa-ko Sosui Canal

Hanami-koji

⚠ 1

Higashiyama Driveway

SHIMBASHI

19 ✿

⊗ 15
Shijō-dōri

11 🏯

Gion-
Shijō

22 ✿

Hanami-koji

21 ✿

14 ⊗ **GION**

23 ✿

⊗ 16

HIGASHIYAMA-KU

Yamatoōji-dōri

13 ✿

Ⓟ 4

Sanjō-dōri

20 ✿

Yasaka-dōri

17 ✿ 12

Higashiōji-dōri

18 🍴

Kiyomizu-michi

Chawan-zaka

⚠ 6

Higashiyama Driveway

Shibutani-dōri

Gojō-dōri

⌂ 7

Shichijō-dōri

↓ Tōfuku-ji (1.8km);
Fushimi Inari-Taisha (2.5km)

1 **2** **3** **4** **5** **6**

Higashiyama

is made interesting by its varied architecture, its gardens and its works of art. It was founded as Zenrin-ji in 855 by the priest Shinshō, but the name was changed to Eikan-dō in the 11th century to honour the philanthropic priest Eikan.

Path of Philosophy (Tetsugaku-no-Michi) Area

(哲学の道; Map p102; Sakyō-ku; 🚌 Kyoto City bus 5 to Eikandō-michi or Ginkakuji-michi, Ⓢ Tōzai line to Keage) The Tetsugaku-no-Michi is one of the most pleasant walks in Kyoto. Lined with a great variety of flowering plants, bushes and trees, it is a corridor of colour throughout most of the year. Follow the traffic-free route along a canal lined with cherry trees that come into spectacular bloom in early April. It only takes 30 minutes to do the walk, which starts at Nyakuōji-bashi, above Eikan-dō, and leads to Ginkaku-ji.

Shūgaku-in Rikyū Imperial Villa Notable Building

(修学院離宮; ☎ 075-211-1215; www.kunaicho.go.jp; Shūgaku-in, Yabusoe, Sakyō-ku; ⊗ tours 9am, 10am, 11am, 1.30pm & 3pm Tue-Sun; 🚌 Kyoto City bus 5 from Kyoto Station to Shūgakuinrikyū-michi) FREE One of the highlights of northeast Kyoto, this superb imperial villa was designed as a lavish summer retreat for the imperial family. Its gardens, with their views

down over the city, are worth the trouble it takes to visit. The one-hour tours are held in Japanese, with English audio guides free of charge. You must be over 18 years to enter and bring your passport.

◎ Arashiyama

Arashiyama Bamboo Grove Park

(嵐山竹林; Ogurayama, Saga, Ukyō-ku; ⊗ dawn-dusk; 🚌 Kyoto City bus 28 from Kyoto Station to Arashiyama-Tenryuji-mae, 🚉 JR Sagano/San-in line to Saga-Arashiyama or Hankyū line to Arashiyama, change at Katsura) FREE The thick green bamboo stalks seem to continue endlessly in every direction and there's a strange quality to the light at this famous bamboo grove. It's most atmospheric on the approach to Ōkōchi Sansō villa and you'll be unable to resist trying to take a few photos, but you might be disappointed with the results: photos just can't capture the magic of the place. The grove runs from outside the north gate of Tenryū-ji to just below Ōkōchi Sansō.

Ōkōchi Sansō Historic Building

(大河内山荘; 8 Tabuchiyama-chō, Sagaogurayama, Ukyō-ku; adult/child ¥1000/500; ⊗ 9am-5pm; 🚌 Kyoto City bus 28 from Kyoto Station to Arashiyama-Tenryuji-mae, 🚉 JR Sagano (San-in) line to Saga-Arashiyama or Hankyū line to Arashiyama, change at Katsura) This is the lavish estate of Ōkōchi Denjirō, an actor famous for his samurai films. The sprawling gardens may well be the most lovely in all of Kyoto, particularly when you consider the brilliant views eastwards across the city. The house and teahouse are also sublime. Be sure to follow all the trails around the gardens. Hold onto the tea ticket you were given upon entry to claim the *matcha* and sweet that's included with admission.

Tenryū-ji   Buddhist Temple
(天龍寺; ☑075-881-1235; www.tenryuji.com; 68 Susukinobaba-chō, Saga-Tenryū-ji, Ukyō-ku; adult/child ¥800/600, garden only ¥500/300; ☺8.30am-5pm; 🚌Kyoto City bus 28 from Kyoto Station to Arashiyama-Tenryuji-mae, 🚉JR Sagano (San-in) line to Saga-Arashiyama or Hankyū line to Arashiyama, change at Katsura) A major temple of the Rinzai school, Tenryū-ji has one of the most attractive gardens in all of Kyoto, particularly during the spring cherry-blossom and autumn-foliage seasons. The main 14th-century Zen garden, with its backdrop of the Arashiyama mountains, is a good example of *shakkei* (borrowed scenery). Unfortunately, it's no secret that the garden here is world class, so it pays to visit early in the morning or on a weekday.

◎ Kyoto Station Area

Kyoto Station   Notable Building
(京都駅; Map p100; www.kyoto-station-building.co.jp; Karasuma-dōri, Higashishiokōji-chō, Shiokōji-sagaru, Shimogyō-ku; 🚉Kyoto Station) The Kyoto Station building is a striking steel-and-glass structure – a kind of futuristic cathedral for the transport age – with a tremendous space that arches above you as you enter the main concourse. Be sure to take the escalator from the 7th floor on the east side of the building up to the 11th-floor glass corridor, Skyway (open 10am to 10pm), that runs high above the main concourse of the station, and catch some views from the 15th-floor Sky Garden terrace.

✈ ACTIVITIES

Camellia Tea Experience   Tea Ceremony
(茶道体験カメリア; Map p102; ☑075-525-3238; www.tea-kyoto.com; 349 Masuya-chō,

Kyoto Station

Higashiyama-ku; per person ¥2000; Kyoto City bus 206 to Yasui) **Camellia** is a superb place to try a simple Japanese tea ceremony. It's located in a beautiful old Japanese house just off Ninen-zaka. The host speaks fluent English and explains the ceremony simply and clearly to the group, while managing to perform an elegant ceremony. The price includes a bowl of *matcha* and a sweet.

Funaoka Onsen   Onsen

(船岡温泉; 82-1 Minami-Funaoka-chō-Mura-sakino, Kita-ku; ¥430; ⊘3pm-1am Mon-Sat, from 8am Sun; Kyoto City bus 206 to Senbon Kuramaguchi) This old *sentō* (public bath) on Kuramaguchi-dōri is Kyoto's best. It boasts an outdoor bath, a sauna, a cypress-wood tub, an electric bath, a herbal bath and a few more for good measure. To get here, head west about 400m on Kuramaguchi-dōri from the Kuramaguchi and Horiikawa intersection. It's on the left, not far past Lawson convenience store. Look for the large rocks.

SHOPPING

Kyoto has a fantastic variety of both traditional and modern shops. Most are located in the Downtown Kyoto area, making the city a very convenient place to shop. Whether you're looking for fans, kimono and tea, or the latest electronics, hip fashion and ingenuous gadgets, Kyoto has plenty to offer.

Aritsugu   Homewares

(有次; Map p100; ☑075-221-1091; 219 Kaji-ya-chō, Nishikikōji-dōri, Gokomachi nishi-iru, Nakagyō-ku; ⊘9am-5.30pm; Hankyū line to Kawaramachi) While you're in Nishiki Market, have a look at this store – it has some of the best kitchen knives in the world. Choose your knife – all-rounder, sushi, vegetable – and the staff will show you how to care for it before sharpening and boxing it up. You can also have your name engraved in English or Japanese. Knives start at around ¥10,000.

 The Tea Ceremony

Chanoyu (literally 'water for tea') is usually translated as 'tea ceremony', but it's more like performance art, with each element – from the gestures of the host to the feel of the tea bowl in your hand – carefully designed to articulate an aesthetic experience. It's had a profound and lasting influence on the arts in Japan; whether you take part in a ceremony or simply pause to admire a teahouse, *sadō* (the way of tea) will colour your Kyoto experience.

GREG ELMS/LONELY PLANET ©

Ippōdō Tea   Tea

(一保堂茶舖; Map p100; ☑075-211-3421; www.ippodo-tea.co.jp; Teramachi-dōri, Nijō-agaru, Nakagyō-ku; ⊘9am-6pm; Tōzai line to Kyoto-Shiyakusho-mae) This old-style tea shop sells some of the best Japanese tea in Kyoto, and you'll be given an English leaflet with prices and descriptions of each one. Its *matcha* makes an excellent souvenir. Ippōdō is north of the city hall, on Teramachi-dōri. It has an adjoining teahouse, Kaboku Tearoom (p110); last orders at 5.30pm.

Wagami no Mise   Arts & Crafts

(倭紙の店; Map p100; ☑075-341-1419; 1st fl, Kajinoha Bldg, 298 Ōgisakaya-chō, Higash-inotōin-dōri, Bukkōji-agaru, Shimogyō-ku; ⊘9.30am-5.30pm Mon-Fri, to 4.30pm Sat; Karasuma line to Shijō) This place sells a fabulous variety of *washi* for reasonable prices and is a great spot to pick up a gift or souvenir. Look for the Morita Japanese Paper Company sign on the wall out the front.

Takashimaya

Takashimaya · Department Store

(高島屋; Map p100; ☑075-221-8811; Shijō-Kawaramachi Kado, Shimogyō-ku; ⊙10am-8pm; 🚊Hankyū line to Kawaramachi) The *grande dame* of Kyoto department stores, Takashimaya is almost a tourist attraction in its own right, from the mind-boggling riches of the basement food floor to the wonderful selection of lacquerware and ceramics on the 6th. Check out the kimono display on the 5th floor.

🍴 EATING

Kyoto is one of the world's great food cities. In fact, when you consider atmosphere, service and quality, it's hard to think of a city where you get more bang for your dining buck. You can pretty much find a great dining option in any neighbourhood, but the majority of the best spots are clustered downtown.

🍴 Downtown Kyoto

Café Bibliotec Hello! · Cafe ¥

(カフェビブリオティックハロー！; Map p100; ☑075-231-8625; 650 Seimei-chō, Nijō-dōri, Yanaginobanba higashi-iru, Nakagyō-ku; meals from ¥850; ⊙11.30am-midnight; 🛜; Ⓢ Tōzai line to Kyoto-Shiyakusho-mae) As the name suggests, books line the walls of this cool cafe located in a converted *machiya* attracting a mix of locals and tourists. It's a great place to relax with a book or to tap away at your laptop over a coffee (¥450) or light lunch. Look for the huge banana plants out the front.

Honke Owariya · Noodles ¥

(本家尾張屋; Map p100; ☑075-231-3446; www.honke-owariya.co.jp; 322 Kurumaya-chō, Nijō, Nakagyō-ku; dishes from ¥810; ⊙11am-7pm; Ⓢ Karasuma or Tōzai lines to Karasuma-Oike) Set in an old sweets shop in a traditional Japanese building on a quiet downtown street, this is where locals come for excellent soba (buckwheat-noodle) dishes. The highly recommended house speciality, *hourai soba* (¥2160), comes with a stack of five small plates of soba with a selection of toppings, including shiitake mushrooms, shrimp tempura, thin slices of omelette and sesame seeds.

Biotei
Vegetarian ¥

(びお亭; Map p100; ☑075-255-0086; 2nd fl, M&I Bldg, 28 Umetada-chō, Sanjō-dōri, Higash-inotōin nishi-iru, Nakagyō-ku; lunch/dinner sets from ¥890/1385; ⏰ 11.30am-2pm Tue-Fri, 5-8.30pm Tue, Wed, Fri & Sat; ☑; Ⓢ Tōzai or Karasuma lines to Karasuma-Oike) Located diagonally across from Nakagyō post office, this is a favourite of Kyoto vegetarians, serving à la carte and daily sets with dishes such as deep-fried crumbed tofu and black seaweed salad with rice, miso and pickles. The seating is rather cramped but the food is excellent, beautifully presented and carefully made from quality ingredients.

Roan Kikunoi
Kaiseki ¥¥¥

(露庵菊乃井; Map p100; ☑075-361-5580; www.kikunoi.jp; 118 Saito-chō, Kiyamachi-dōri, Shijō-sagaru, Shimogyō-ku; lunch/dinner from ¥7000/13,000; ⏰11.30am-1.30pm & 5-8.30pm Thu-Tue; ☒Hankyū line to Kawaramachi or Keihan line to Gion-Shijō) Roan Kikunoi is a fantastic place to experience the wonders of *kaiseki*. It's a lovely intimate space located right downtown. The chef takes an experimental and creative approach and the results are a wonder for the eyes and palate. Highly recommended. Reserve at least a few days in advance.

Yoshikawa
Tempura ¥¥¥

(吉川; Map p100; ☑075-221-5544; www.kyoto-yoshikawa.co.jp; 135 Matsushita-chō, Tominokōji, Oike-sagaru, Nakagyō-ku; lunch ¥3000-25,000, dinner ¥8000-25,000; ⏰11am-1.45pm & 5-8pm; Ⓢ Tōzai line to Karasuma-Oike or Kyoto-Shiyakusho-mae) This is the place to go for delectable tempura with a daily changing menu. Attached to the Yoshikawa ryokan, it offers table seating, but it's much more interesting to sit and eat around the small intimate counter and observe the chefs at work. Reservation is required for the private tatami room, and counter bar for dinner. Note: counter bar is closed Sunday.

 Kaiseki Cuisine

In a city blessed with excellent dining options, one not to be missed is the refined and elegant experience of *kaiseki* cuisine. *Kaiseki* consists of a number of small courses, largely vegetarian, served on exquisite dinnerware where the preparation and service is as outstanding as the food itself. Diners are usually served in private rooms at speciality restaurants, such as the highly regarded Kikunoi (p108) and Kitcho Arashiyama (p109). Prices are elevated for this fine-dining experience, but you don't need to spend a week's travel budget on dinner to get a taste of *kaiseki*.

Kaiseki dishes
KPG_PAYLESS/SHUTTERSTOCK ©

🌏 Southern Higashiyama

Kagizen Yoshifusa
Teahouse ¥

(鍵善良房; Map p102; ☑075-561-1818; www.kagizen.co.jp; 264 Gion machi, Kita-gawa, Higashiyama-ku; kuzukiri ¥1080, tea & sweet ¥880; ⏰9.30am-6pm, closed Mon; ☒Hankyū line to Kawaramachi, Keihan line to Gion-Shijō) This Gion institution is one of Kyoto's oldest and best-known *okashi-ya* (sweet shops). It sells a variety of traditional sweets and has a lovely tearoom out the back where you can sample cold *kuzukiri* (transparent arrowroot noodles) served with a *kuro-mitsu* (sweet black sugar) dipping sauce, or just a nice cup of *matcha* and a sweet.

Escape the Crowds

Gion Be sure to veer off the main drag in the Gion (p94) district, where you'll escape the crowds and see some of the area's impossibly atmospheric backstreets.

Path of Philosophy The crowds are usually gone by 5pm here, leaving this scenic pathway (p103) to locals and savvy travellers. A great option if your cruise schedule permits.

Hōnen-in Escape the crowds and find yourself at this lovely Buddhist **sanctuary** (法然院; Map p102; 30 Goshonodan-chō, Shishigatani, Sakyō-ku; ☉6am-4pm; 🚌Kyoto City bus 5 to Ginkakuji-michi) FREE.

Northwest Kyoto This area has some superb temples and shrines that are worth making the trek for. Aside from Kinkaku-ji (p99), the main attraction, you've got quiet temple complexes, Myōshin-ji and Ninna-ji, that are the perfect places to spend some time strolling around, minus the crowds.

Path of Philosophy
MYPIXELDIARIES/SHUTTERSTOCK ©

Omen Kodai-ji Noodles ¥
(おめん 高台寺店; Map p102; ☎075-541-5007; 362 Masuya-chō, Kōdaiji-dōri, Shimokawara higashi-iru, Higashiyama-ku; noodles from ¥1150; ☉11am-9pm; 🚌Kyoto City bus 206 to Higashiyama-Yasui) Housed in a remodelled Japanese building with a light, airy feeling, this branch of Kyoto's famed Omen noodle chain is the best place to stop while exploring the Southern Higashiyama district. Upstairs has fine views over the area.

The signature udon (thick, white wheat noodles) served in broth with a selection of fresh vegetables is delicious.

Chidoritei Sushi ¥
(千登利亭; Map p102; ☎075-561-1907; 203 Rokken-cho, Donguri-dori, Yamato-oji Nishi-iru, Higashiyama-ku; sushi sets ¥600-2200; ☉11am-8pm, closed Thu; 🚆Keihan line to Gion-Shijō) Family owned Chidoritei is a snug little sushi restaurant tucked away in the backstreets of Gion away from the bustle. It's a great place to try delicious traditional Kyoto *saba-zushi* – mackerel hand pressed into lightly vinegared rice and wrapped in *konbu* (a type of seaweed). In summer, the speciality here is conger-eel sushi.

Kikunoi Kaiseki ¥¥¥
(菊乃井; Map p102; ☎075-561-0015; www.kikunoi.jp; 459 Shimokawara-chō, Yasakatoriimae-sagaru, Shimokawara-dōri, Higashiyama-ku; lunch/dinner from ¥10,000/16,000; ☉noon-1pm & 5-8pm; 🚆Keihan line to Gion-Shijō) Michelin-starred chef Mutara serves some of the finest *kaiseki* in the city. Located in a hidden nook near Maruyama-kōen, this restaurant has everything necessary for the full over-the-top *kaiseki* experience, from setting to service to exquisitely executed cuisine, often with a creative twist. Reserve at least a month in advance.

❌ Arashiyama

Arashiyama Yoshimura Noodles ¥
(嵐山よしむら; ☎075-863-5700; Togetsu-kyō kita, Saga-Tenryū-ji, Ukyō-ku; soba from ¥1000, sets from ¥1278; ☉11am-5pm; 🚌Kyoto City bus 28 from Kyoto Station to Arashiyama-Tenryuji-mae, 🚆JR Sagano/San-in line to Saga-Arashiyama or Hankyū line to Arashiyama, change at Katsura) For a tasty bowl of soba noodles and a million-dollar view over the Arashiyama mountains and the Togetsu-kyō bridge, head to this extremely popular eatery (prepare to queue at peak times) just north of the famous bridge, overlooking the Katsura-gawa. There's an English menu but no English sign; look for the big glass windows and the stone wall.

Meal at Arashiyama Yoshimura

Shigetsu Vegetarian, Japanese ¥¥
(篩月; 075-882-9725; 68 Susukinobaba-chō, Saga-Tenryū-ji, Ukyō-ku; lunch sets ¥3500, ¥5500 & ¥7500; 11am-2pm; ; Kyoto City bus 28 from Kyoto Station to Arashiyama-Tenryuji-mae, JR Sagano/San-in line to Saga-Arashiyama or Hankyū line to Arashiyama, change at Katsura) To sample *shōjin-ryōri*, try Shigetsu in the precincts of Tenryū-ji (p104). This healthy fare has been sustaining monks for more than a thousand years in Japan, so it will probably get you through an afternoon of sightseeing, although carnivores may be left craving something more. Shigetsu has beautiful garden views. Prices include temple admission.

Kitcho Arashiyama Kaiseki ¥¥¥
(吉兆嵐山本店; 075-881-1101; www.kyoto-kitcho.com; 58 Susukinobaba-chō, Saga-Tenryūji, Ukyō-ku; lunch/dinner from ¥51,840/64,800; 11.30am-3pm & 5-9pm Thu-Tue; ; Kyoto City bus 28 from Kyoto Station to Arashiyama-Tenryuji-mae, JR Sagano/San-in line to Saga-Arashiyama or Hankyū line to Arashiyama, change at Katsura) Considered one of the best *kaiseki* restaurants in Kyoto (and Japan, for that matter), Kitcho Arashiyama is the place to sample the full *kaiseki* experience. Meals are served in private rooms overlooking gardens. The food, service, explanations and atmosphere are all first rate. Make bookings online via its website well in advance.

DRINKING

Kyoto is a city with endless options for drinking, whether it's an expertly crafted single-origin coffee in a hipster cafe, a rich *matcha* at a traditional tearoom, carefully crafted cocktails and single malts in a sophisticated six-seater bar, or Japanese craft beer in a brewery. Check ahead in *Kansai Scene* to see what's going on.

Downtown Kyoto

Weekenders Coffee Coffee
(ウィークエンダーズ コーヒー; Map p100; 075-746-2206; www.weekenderscoffee.com; 560 Honeyana-chō, Nakagyō-ku; coffee from ¥430; 7.30am-6pm Thu-Tue; Hankyū line to Kawaramachi) Weekenders is a tiny coffee

bar tucked away in a traditional-style building at the back of a parking lot in Downtown Kyoto. Sure, it's a strange location, but it's where you'll find some of the city's best coffee being brewed by roaster-owner Masahiro Kaneko. It's mostly takeaway with a small bench out front.

Taigu   Pub

(ダイグ ガストロ パブ; Map p100; ☎075-213-0214; 1st fl, 498 Kamikoriki-chō, Nakagyō-ku; ⊘11.30am-11pm; 🛜; ⑤Tōzai line to Kyoto-Shiyakusho-mae) Looking out on scenic Kiyamachi-dōri, Taigu (formerly Tadg's Gastro Pub) is a good spot for an evening drink. Choose from an extensive selection of craft beers (including several rotating Japanese beers on tap), a variety of wines, sake and spirits. It also does pub-style meals.

Kaboku Tearoom   Teahouse

(喫茶室嘉木; Map p100; Teramachi-dōri, Nijō-agaru, Nakagyō-ku; ⊘10am-6pm; ⑤Tōzai line to Kyoto-Shiyakusho-mae) A casual tearoom attached to the Ippōdō Tea (p105) store, Kaboku serves a range of teas and provides a great break while exploring the shops in the area. Try the *matcha* and grab a counter seat to watch it being prepared.

🍷 Southern Higashiyama

% Arabica   Coffee

(Map p102; ☎075-746-3669; 87 Hoshino-chō, Higashiyama-ku; coffee from ¥300; ⊘8am-6pm; 🚌Kyoto City bus 206 to Higashiyama-Yasui) This branch of % Arabica sits in the shadow of nearby Yasaka Pagoda on an atmospheric stone paved street. Grab a takeaway single-origin brew and continue strolling and sightseeing in the area. There's usually a queue out the front of Kyoto's pretty young things taking Instagrammable selfies as they wait.

🍶 Kyoto Station Area

Roots of all Evil   Bar

(Map p100; www.nokishita.net; Kyoto Tower, B1 Karasuma-dōri, Shichijō-sagaru, Shimogyō-ku; ⊘11am-11pm; 🚌Kyoto Station) 🍸 Stop by this standing bar in the Kyoto Tower Sando food basement for creative gin cocktails. It offers interesting herbal, spicy and floral gin infusions. Cocktails from ¥800.

Vermillion Espresso Bar   Cafe

(バーミリオン; www.vermillioncafe.com; 85 Onmae-chō, Fukakusa-inari, Fushimi-ku; ⊘9am-5pm; 🛜; 🚆JR Nara line to Inari or Keihan line to Fushimi-Inari) A Melbourne-inspired cafe, tiny Vermillion takes its name from the colour of the *torii* of the nearby Fushimi Inari-Taisha shrine. It does standout coffee, as well as a small selection of cakes, which can be taken away or enjoyed at the communal table. It's on the main street, just a short hop from Inari Station.

⭐ ENTERTAINMENT

Minamiza   Theatre

(南座; Map p102; www.kabukiweb.net; Shijō-Ōhashi, Higashiyama-ku; 🚆Keihan line to Gion-Shijō) This theatre in Gion is the oldest kabuki theatre in Japan. The major event of the year is the **Kaomise festival** in December, which features Japan's finest kabuki actors.

Miyako Odori   Dance

(都をどり; Map p102; ☎075-541-3391; www.miyako-odori.jp; Gion Kōbu Kaburen-jō Theatre, 570-2 Gion-machi, Minamigawa, Higashiyama-ku; tickets from ¥4000; ⊘shows 12.30pm, 2.20pm & 4.10pm; 🚌Kyoto City bus 206 to Gion, 🚆Keihan line to Gion-Shijō) This 45-minute dance is a wonderful geisha performance. It's a real stunner and the colourful images are mesmerising. It's held throughout April, usually at Gion Kōbu Kaburen-jō Theatre. The building is under ongoing renovations until around 2021 and performances will be held at Minamiza in the meantime.

ℹ️ INFORMATION

TOURIST INFORMATION

Kyoto Tourist Information Center (京都総合観光案内所, TIC; Map p100; ☎075-343-0548; 2F Kyoto Station Bldg, Shimogyō-ku; ⊘8.30am-7pm; 🚆Kyoto Station) Stocks bus and city maps, has plenty of transport info and English speakers are available to answer your questions. Note that it's called 'Kyo Navi' in Japanese (in case you have to ask someone). It also has a couple of computer terminals with internet (10 minutes ¥100).

ℹ️ GETTING AROUND

BUS

Kyoto has an intricate network of bus routes providing an efficient way of getting around at moderate cost. Most of the routes used by visitors have announcements and bus-stop information displays in English. Most buses run between 7am and 10pm, though a few run earlier or later.

Bus entry is usually through the back door and exit is via the front door. Inner-city buses charge a flat fare (¥230 for adults, ¥120 for children ages six to 12, free for those younger), which you drop into the clear plastic receptacle on top of the machine next to the driver on your way out. A separate machine gives change for ¥100 and ¥500 coins or ¥1000 notes.

TAXI

Taxis are a convenient, but expensive, way of getting from place to place about town. A taxi can usually be flagged down in most parts of the city at any time. There are also a large number of *takushī noriba* (taxi stands) in town, outside most train/subway stations, department stores etc.

There is no need to touch the back doors of the cars at all – the opening/closing mechanism is controlled by the driver.

TRAIN & SUBWAY

The main train station in Kyoto is Kyoto Station, which is in the south of the city, just below Shichijō-dōri and is actually two stations under one roof: JR Kyoto Station and Kintetsu Kyoto Station.

In addition to the private Kintetsu line that operates from Kyoto Station, there are two other private train lines in Kyoto: the Hankyū line that operates from Downtown Kyoto along Shijō-dōri and the Keihan line that operates from stops along the Kamo-gawa.

Kōfuku-ji

Nara

Japan's first permanent capital, Nara (奈良) is one of the country's most rewarding destinations. With eight Unesco World Heritage Sites, it's second only to Kyoto as a repository of Japan's cultural legacy.

Great For...

Don't Miss

The awe-inspiring Daibutsu (Great Buddha), a towering effigy first cast in the 8th century.

Nara's highlights all occupy a compact area in and around Nara-kōen, a large, grassy park home to many (somewhat) tame deer.

Tōdai-ji (東大寺; www.todaiji.or.jp; 406-1 Zōshi-chō; Daibutsu-den adult/child ¥600/300; ⊙Daibutsu-den 7.30am-5.30pm Apr-Oct, 8am-5pm Nov-Mar) is home to **Daibutsu (Great Buddha)**, Nara's star attraction and one of the largest bronze statues in the world. It was unveiled in 752, upon the completion of the **Daibutsu-den** (大仏殿, Great Buddha Hall), built to house it. Both have been damaged over the years; the present statue was recast in the Edo period. The Daibutsu-den is the largest wooden building in the world; incredibly, the present structure, rebuilt in 1709, is a mere two-thirds of the size of the original.

Southeast of Tōdai-ji is **Kasuga Taisha** (春日大社; www.kasugataisha.or.jp; 160 Kasugano-chō; ⊙6am-6pm Apr-Sep, 6.30am-5pm Oct-Mar) **FREE**. Founded in the 8th

Daibutsu (Great Buddha)

BENNY MARTY/SHUTTERSTOCK ©

Explore Ashore

The nearest ports to Nara are those in Kyoto (p89) and Osaka (p117). The Kintetsu Nara line is the fastest and most convenient connection between Kyoto (Kintetsu Kyoto Station, in Kyoto Station) and central Nara (Kintetsu Nara Station), via direct, all-reserved trains (¥1130, 35 minutes) or express trains (¥620, 50 minutes), which usually require a change at Yamato-Saidaiji. The Kintetsu Nara line connects Osaka (Namba Station) with Nara (Kintetsu Nara Station; ¥560, 45 minutes).

❶ Need to Know

Nara is popular as a day trip from Kyoto or Osaka – there's just enough time to see the highlights.

century, this sprawling shrine at the foot of Mikasa-yama was created to protect Nara. It was ritually rebuilt every 20 years, according to Shintō tradition, until the late 19th century and is still kept in pristine condition. Many of its buildings are painted vermilion, in bold contrast to the cedar roofs and surrounding greenery. The corridors are lined with hundreds of lanterns, which are illuminated during the twice-yearly **Mantōrō lantern festival** (⊘3 Feb, 14 & 15 Aug).

On the west side of Nara-kōen is the **Nara National Museum** (奈良国立博物館, Nara Kokuritsu Hakubutsukan; ☑050-5542-8600; www.narahaku.go.jp; 50 Noboriōji-chō; ¥520, special exhibitions ¥1100-1420; ⊘9.30am-5pm Tue-Sun), a world-class museum of Buddhist art. Built in 1894 and strikingly renovated in 2016, the Nara Buddhist Sculpture Hall & Ritual Bronzes Gallery

displays a rotating selection of about 100 *butsu-zō* (statues of Buddhas and bodhisattvas) at any one time, about half of which are National Treasures or Important Cultural Properties. Chinese bronzes in the Ritual Bronzes Gallery date as far back as the 15th century BC. Each image has detailed English explanations.

Further west is **Kōfuku-ji** (興福寺; www.kohfukuji.com; grounds free, Tōkondō ¥300, National Treasure Museum ¥600, combined ticket ¥800; ⊘grounds 24hr, Tōkondō 9am-5pm), which was founded in Kyoto in 669 and relocated here in 710. The original Nara temple complex had 175 buildings, though many have been lost over the years to fires and periods of medieval warfare. Of those that remain, the most impressive are the **Tōkondō** (東金堂; Eastern Golden Hall) and the temple's two pagodas: the **three-storey pagoda** (三重塔) dates to 1181 and is a rare example of Heian-era architecture, while the 50.1m **five-storey pagoda** (五重塔), last reconstructed in 1426, is Japan's second-tallest pagoda.

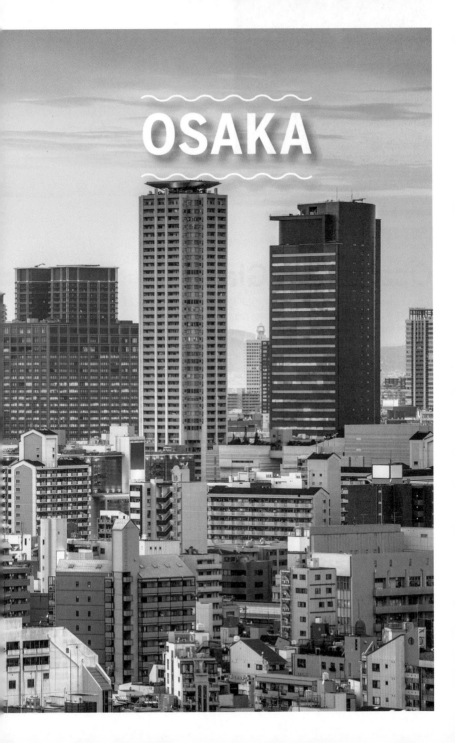

OSAKA

Osaka at a Glance

If Kyoto was the city of the courtly nobility and Tokyo the city of the samurai, then Osaka (大阪) was the city of the merchant class. Japan's third-largest city is a place where things have always moved a bit faster, where people are a bit brasher and interactions are peppered with playful jabs – and locals take pride in this. Osaka is not a pretty city in the conventional sense – though it does have a lovely river cutting through the centre – but it packs more colour than most. The acres of concrete are cloaked in dazzling neon; shopfronts are vivid, unabashed cries for attention.

With a Day in Port

Start with a visit to **Osaka-jō** (p122), then take the subway to Tennōji for a view over the city at **Abeno Harukas** (p124) and a dip at **Spa World** (p125), and enjoy a *kushikatsu* lunch at **Ganso Kushikatsu Daruma Honten** (p121). Hop back on the subway to Nipponbashi and wander through **Kuromon Ichiba** (p124) market before heading over to **Dōtombori** (p124). There are plenty of places to eat here – try Japanese haute cuisine at **Shoubentango-tei** (p121) or *okonomi-yaki* (savoury pancakes) at **Chibō** (p120). If you have time, stick around to see the area's neon lights at dusk.

Best Places for...

City views Abeno Harukas (p124)

Coffee Brooklyn Roasting Company (p128)

History Osaka-jō (p122)

Markets Kuromon Ichiba (p124)

Tempura Yotaro Honten (p127)

Youth culture Amerika-Mura (p124)

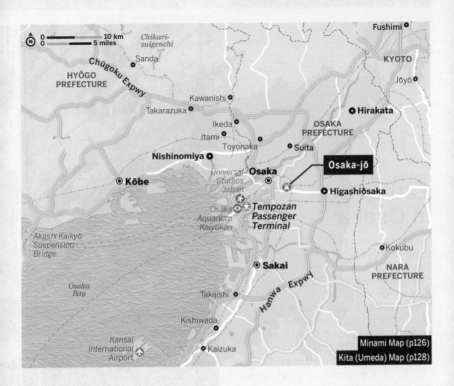

Chikari-suigenchi

Fushimi

KYOTO

Jōyō

HYŌGO PREFECTURE

Chūgoku Expwy

Sanda

Kawanishi

Takarazuka

Ikeda

Itami

Toyonaka

Hirakata

OSAKA PREFECTURE

Suita

Nishinomiya

Universal Studios Japan

Osaka

Osaka-jō

Kōbe

Higashiōsaka

Osaka Aquarium Kaiyūkan

Tempozan Passenger Terminal

Akashi Kaikyō Suspension Bridge

Kokubu

NARA PREFECTURE

Sakai

Osaka Bay

Takaishi

Hanwa Expwy

Kishiwada

Kansai International Airport

Kaizuka

Minami Map (p126)

Kita (Umeda) Map (p128)

0 — 10 km
0 — 5 miles

Getting from the Port

Ships dock at Tempozan Passenger Terminal. From the terminal it's an easy 500m walk to Osakako Station, from where you can get to either JR Osaka Station or Namba Station (near Dōtombori) by train in about 20 minutes. For Osaka-jō, head straight down the Chūō (green) line for 30 minutes to Morinomiya Station.

Fast Facts

Money ATMs in post offices and 7-Eleven convenience stores take international cards. Major banks and post offices have currency exchange services.

Wi-fi Increasingly available at cafes and public areas around town.

Tako-yaki (octopus dumpling) shops

Eating Out in Osaka

Osaka has a rich food culture that ranks as the number one reason to visit: its unofficial slogan is kuidaore *('eat until you drop'). You'll find great food at street counters, in train station basements and along shopping arcades, behind both graceful traditional facades and loud, over-the-top shopfronts. It's most famous for its comfort food – dishes that are deep-fried or grilled and stuffed with delicacies such as octopus and squid.*

Great For...

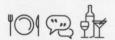

❶ Need to Know

The Minami district is the centre of Osaka's eating and drinking scene. Many street-food counters have tables and chairs out the back.

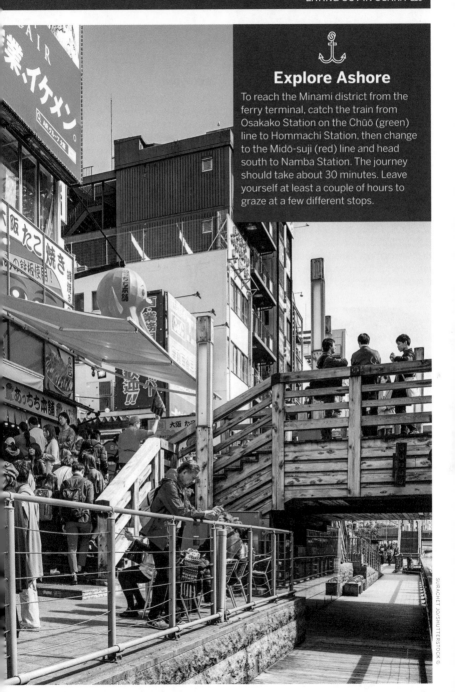

Explore Ashore

To reach the Minami district from the ferry terminal, catch the train from Osakako Station on the Chūō (green) line to Hommachi Station, then change to the Midō-suji (red) line and head south to Namba Station. The journey should take about 30 minutes. Leave yourself at least a couple of hours to graze at a few different stops.

Okonomiyaki

Thick, savoury pancakes filled with shredded cabbage and your choice of meat, seafood, vegetables and more (the name means 'cook as you like'). Often prepared on a *teppan* (steel plate) set into your table, the cooked pancake is brushed with a Worcestershire-style sauce, decoratively striped with mayonnaise and topped with dried bonito flakes, which seem to dance in the rising steam. Slice off a wedge using a tiny *kote* (trowel), and – warning – allow it to cool a bit before taking that first bite.

Chibō (千房; Map p126; ☏06-6212-2211; www.chibo.com; 1-5-5 Dōtombori, Chūō-ku; mains ¥885-1675; ⊙11am-1am Mon-Sat, to midnight Sun; Ⓢ Midō-suji line to Namba, exit 14) is one of Osaka's most famous *okonomiyaki* restaurants. It almost always has a line, but it moves fast because there is seating on multiple floors (though you might want to hold out for the coveted tables overlooking Dōtombori canal).

Tako-yaki

These doughy dumplings stuffed with octopus (*tako* in Japanese) are grilled in specially made moulds. They're often sold as street food, served with pickled ginger, topped with savoury sauce, powdered *aonori* (seaweed), mayonnaise and bonito flakes, and are eaten with toothpicks. Nibble carefully first as the centre can be molten hot!

Try them at **Wanaka Honten** (わなか本店; Map p126; ☏06-6631-0127; http://takoyaki-wanaka.com; 11-19 Sennichi-mae, Chūō-ku; tako-yaki per 8 from ¥450; ⊙10am-11pm Mon-Fri, from 8.30am Sat & Sun; Ⓢ Midō-suji line to Namba, exit 4), which uses custom copper

Kushikatsu

hotplates (instead of cast iron) to make dumplings that are crisper on the outside than usual (but still runny inside).

Kushikatsu

Yakitori refers to skewers of grilled meat, seafood and/or vegetables; *kushikatsu* is the same ingredients crumbed, deep fried and served with a savoury dipping sauce (double-dipping is a serious no-no). For many Japanese, a pilgrimage to **Ganso Kushikatsu Daruma Honten** (元祖串か つ だるま本店; Map p126; ☑06-6645-7056; www.kushikatu-daruma.com; 2-3-9 Ebisu-Higashi, Naniwa-ku; skewers ¥120-240; ⊗11am-10.30pm;

☑ Don't Miss

Dōtombori is Osaka's biggest street-food destination; it gets awfully crowded in the evening.

ⓢMidōsuji line to Dōbutsuen-mae, exit 5) is a necessary part of any visit to Osaka. Opened in 1929, it's said to be the birth-place of *kushikatsu*.

Kaiten-sushi

This Osaka invention (from the 1950s) goes by many names in English: conveyor-belt sushi, sushi-go-round or sushi train. It's all the same – plates of sushi that run past you along a belt built into the counter (you can also order off the menu). **Kaiten Sushi Ganko** (回転寿司がんこ; Map p128; ☑06-4799-6811; Eki Maré, Osaka Station City, Kita-ku; plates ¥130-735; ⊗11am-11pm; ☒JR Osaka, Sakurabashi exit), inside JR Osaka's Eki Marché food court, is a popular choice – meaning the two whirring tracks of plates are continuously restocked with fresh options.

Kappō-ryōri

Osaka's take on Japanese haute cuisine is casual: the dishes are similar to what you might find at a Kyoto *ryōtei* (a formal restaurant with tatami seating) – incorporating seasonal ingredients and elaborate presentation – but at *kappō* restaurants, diners sit at the counter, chatting with the chef, who hands over the dishes as they're finished. Despite the laid-back vibe these restaurants can be frightfully expensive. **Shoubentango-tei** (正弁丹吾亭; Map p126; ☑06-6211-3208; 1-7-12 Dōtombori, Chūō-ku; dinner course ¥3780-10,800; ⊗5-10pm; ⓢMidō-suji line to Namba, exit 14) isn't, despite its pedigree: established over 100 years ago, it was a literati hangout in the early 20th century. It's a wonderful option if your cruise schedule allows. Even the cheapest course, which includes five dishes decided that day by the chef, tastes – and looks – like a luxurious treat. Reservations are necessary for all but the cheapest course.

YOSHIO TOMII/GETTY IMAGES ©

Osaka-jō

After unifying Japan in the late 16th century, General Toyotomi Hideyoshi built this castle (1583) as a display of power using, it's said, the labour of 100,000 workers. Although the present structure is a 1931 concrete reconstruction (refurbished in 1997), it's nonetheless quite a sight, looming dramatically over the surrounding park and moat. Inside, a museum displays historical artefacts.

Great For...

☑ **Don't Miss**

Swing by bakery Gout (p127) to pick up gourmet picnic supplies.

The Castle Walls

Hideyoshi's original granite structure was said to be impregnable, yet it was destroyed in 1614 by the armies of Tokugawa Ieyasu (the founder of the Tokugawa shogunate). Ieyasu had the castle rebuilt – using the latest advancements to create terrifically imposing walls of enormous stones. The largest are estimated to weigh over 100 tonnes; others are engraved with the crests of feudal lords.

The Turrets & Gates

There are 13 structures on the castle grounds that date back to the 17th-century reconstruction of the castle. **Sengan-yagura** (千貫櫓, Sengan Turret), next to **Ote-mon** (大手門) – the main gate, on the western side of the castle – and **Inui-yagura** (乾櫓, Inui Turret), in the northwest-

Explore Ashore

Nearby Morinomiya Station is on the Chūō (green) line, as is Osakako Station (near the ferry terminal). Simply hop on an eastbound train and you'll be there in 30 minutes. You'll need about three hours if you want to properly explore the grounds, castle and museum.

❶ Need to Know

大阪城; Osaka Castle; Map p128; www.osaka castle.net; 1-1 Osaka-jō, Chūō-ku; grounds/ castle keep free/¥600, combined with Osaka Museum of History ¥900; ⏱9am-5pm, hours vary in spring & summer; ⑤Chūō line to Tanimachi 4-chōme, exit 9, ⑧JR Loop line to Osaka-jō-kōen

ern corner of the grounds, are the oldest: they date to 1620.

The Main Keep & Museum

By the 20th century, most of the castle was in ruins. Osaka citizens raised money themselves to rebuild the main keep; in 1931 the new tower was revealed, with bright white walls and glittering gold-leaf tigers stalking the eaves. Inside, a museum displays historical artefacts, paintings, scrolls and suits of armour from the feudal era.

The Grounds

From the 8th-floor observatory inside the main keep, there are excellent views of the castle's sprawling, grassy grounds. For local residents, these grounds are the ultimate draw of the historical structure. Where

soldiers once trained, families and couples now enjoy picnics and strolls.

Top Tips

∘ It's free to walk the castle grounds; admission is for the main keep only.

∘ You can take an elevator up to the 5th floor of the keep, but you have to hike the rest of the way to the 8th floor (visitors with disabilities can take the elevator to the 8th floor).

∘ The main keep, with its stairs and cramped, crowded passageways, can be challenging with small children.

∘ Visit the grounds on a warm weekend and you might catch local musicians staging casual shows on the lawns.

⊙ SIGHTS

Dōtombori
Area

(道頓堀; Map p126; www.dotonbori.or.jp; Ⓢ Midō-suji line to Namba, exit 14) Highly photogenic Dōtombori is the city's liveliest night spot and the centre of the southern part of town. Its name comes from the 400-year-old canal, Dōtombori-gawa, now lined with pedestrian walkways and with a riot of illuminated billboards glittering off its waters. Don't miss the famous **Glico running man** sign. South of the canal is a pedestrianised street that has dozens of restaurants vying for attention with the flashiest of signage.

Abeno Harukas
Notable Building

(あべのハルカス; Map p126; www.abenoharu kas-300.jp; 1-1-43 Abeno-suji, Abeno-ku; observation deck adult ¥1500, child from ¥500-700, under 4yr free; ⊗ observation deck 9am-10pm; Ⓢ Midō-suji to Tennōji, Ⓡ JR Loop line to Tennōji) This César Pelli–designed tower, which opened in March 2014, is Japan's tallest building (300m, 60 storeys). The observatory on the 16th floor is free, but admission is required for the highly recommended top-level **Harukas 300 observation deck**, which has incredible 360-degree views of the whole Kansai region through windows that run several storeys high. There's also an open-air atrium. It houses Japan's largest department store (Kintetsu, floors B2–14), the **Abeno Harukas Art Museum** (あべのハルカス美術館; Map p126; ☎ 06-4399-9050; www.aham.jp; 16th fl, Abeno Harukas; admission varies by exhibition; ⊗ 10am-8pm Tue-Fri, to 6pm Sat & Sun; Ⓢ Midō-suji line to Tennōji, Ⓡ JR Loop line to Tennōji), a hotel, offices and restaurants.

Amerika-Mura
Area

(アメリカ村, America Village, Ame-Mura; Map p126; www.americamura.jp; Nishi-Shinsaibashi, Chūō-ku; Ⓢ Midō-suji line to Shinsaibashi, exit 7) West of Midō-suji, Amerika-Mura is a compact enclave of hip, youth-focused and offbeat shops, plus cafes, bars, tattoo and piercing parlours, nightclubs, hair salons and a few discreet love hotels. In the middle is **Triangle Park** (三角公園, Sankaku-kōen; Map p126), an all-concrete 'park' with benches for sitting and watching the fashion parade. Come nighttime, it's a popular gathering spot.

Osaka Aquarium Kaiyūkan
Aquarium

(海遊館; ☎ 06-6576-5501; www.kaiyukan. com; 1-1-10 Kaigan-dōri, Minato-ku; adult ¥2300, child ¥600-1200; ⊗ 10am-8pm, last entry 7pm; Ⓢ Chuō line to Osaka-kō, exit 1) Kaiyūkan is among Japan's best aquariums. An 800m-plus walkway winds past displays of sea life from around the Pacific 'ring of fire': Antarctic penguins, coral-reef butterflyfish, unreasonably cute Arctic otters, Monterey Bay seals and unearthly jellyfish. Most impressive is the ginormous central tank, housing a whale shark, manta rays and thousands of other fish. Note there are also captive dolphins here, which some visitors may not appreciate; there is growing evidence that keeping cetaceans in captivity is harmful for the animals.

Kuromon Ichiba
Market

(黒門市場, Kuromon Market; Map p126; www. kuromon.com; Nipponbashi, Chūō-ku; ⊗ most shops 9am-6pm; Ⓢ Sakai-suji line to Nippon-bashi, exit 10) An Osaka landmark for over a century, this 600m-long market is in equal parts a functioning market and a tourist attraction. Vendors selling fresh fish, meat, produce and pickles attract chefs and local home cooks; shops offering takeaway sushi or with grills set up (to cook the steaks, oysters, giant prawns etc that they sell) cater to visitors – making the market excellent for grazing and photo ops.

☻ ACTIVITIES

Cycle Osaka
Cycling Tours

(Map p128; ☎ 080-5325-8975; www.cycle osaka.com; 2-12-1 Sagisu, Fukushima-ku; half-/full-day tours ¥5000/10,000; Ⓡ JR Loop line to Fukushima) The English-speaking guides here lead well-organised tours to sights both well known and less well known, along the riverbanks and through the markets.

The food route (¥8000) is particularly recommended. Fees include bicycle and helmet rental, water and food. It also rents out bikes (¥1500 per day).

Spa World Onsen

(スパワールド; Map p126; ☎06-6631-0001; www.spaworld.co.jp; 3-4-24 Ebisu-higashi, Naniwa-ku; day pass ¥1300; ⏲10am-8.45am the next day; Ⓢ Midō-suji line to Dōbutsu-en-mae, exit 5, Ⓡ JR Loop line to Shin-Imamiya) This huge, seven-storey onsen (hot-spring) complex contains dozens of options from saunas to salt baths, styled after a mini-UN's worth of nations. Gender-separated 'Asian' and 'European' bathing zones (bathe in the buff, towels provided) switch monthly. Swimsuits (rental ¥600, or BYO) are worn in swimming pools and *ganbanyoku* (stone baths; additional ¥800 Monday to Friday, ¥1000 Saturday and Sunday).

Universal Studios Japan Amusement Park

(ユニバーサルスタジオジャパン, Universal City; ☎0570-200-606; www.usj.co.jp; 2-1-33 Sakura-jima, Konohana-ku; 1-day pass adult/child ¥7400/5100; ⏲varies seasonally; Ⓡ JR Yumesaki line to Universal City) Modelled after sister parks in the US, 'USJ' bursts with Hollywood movie–related rides, shows, shops and restaurants. Top billing goes to the ¥45 billion (!) Wizarding World of Harry Potter, a painstakingly recreated Hogsmeade Village (shop for magic wands, Gryffindor capes and butterbeer) plus the 'Harry Potter and the Forbidden Journey' thrill ride through Hogwarts School.

SHOPPING

Osaka is the biggest shopping destination in western Japan, with an overwhelming number of malls, department stores, shopping arcades, electronics dealers, boutiques and second-hand shops. More and more places are offering to waive the sales tax on purchases over ¥10,000 (look for signs in the window; passport is required).

Bunraku puppet
COWARDLION/SHUTTERSTOCK ©

Bunraku

Bunraku is traditional Japanese puppet theatre. Almost-life-sized puppets are manipulated by black-clad, on-stage puppeteers, to evoke dramatic tales of love, duty and politics. The art form may not have originated in Osaka but it became popular here. Bunraku's most famous playwright, Chikamatsu Monzaemon (1653–1724), wrote plays about Osaka's merchants and the denizens of the pleasure quarters, social classes otherwise generally ignored in the Japanese arts at the time.

Bunraku has been recognised on the Unesco World Intangible Cultural Heritage list, and the **National Bunraku Theatre** (国立文楽劇場; Map p126; ☎06-6212-2531, ticket centre 0570-07-9900; www.ntj.jac.go.jp; 1-12-10 Nipponbashi, Chūō-ku; full performance ¥2400-6000, single act ¥500-1500; ⏲opening months vary, check the website; Ⓢ Sakai-suji line to Nipponbashi, exit 7) works to keep the tradition alive, with performances and an exhibition in the lobby about the history of bunraku and its puppeteers and main characters. Learn more at www2.ntj.jac.go.jp/unesco/bunraku/en.

Dōguya-suji Arcade Market

(道具屋筋; Map p126; www.doguyasuji.or.jp/map_eng.html; Sennichi-mae, Chūō-ku; ⏲10am-6pm; Ⓢ Midō-suji line to Namba, exit 4) This long arcade sells just about anything related to the preparation, consumption and

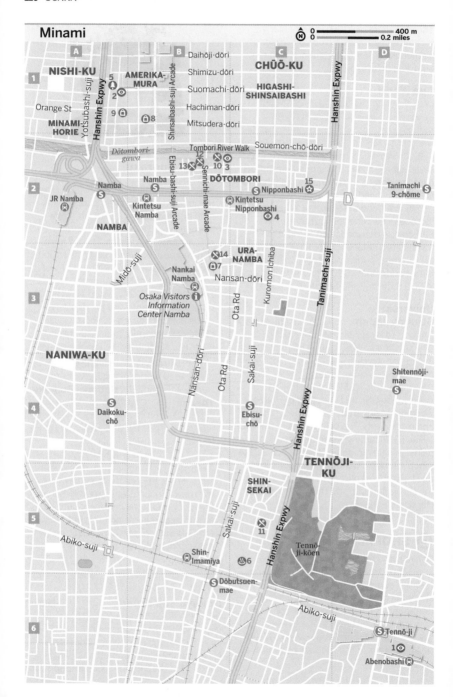

Minami

0 — 400 m
0 — 0.2 miles

NISHI-KU

Orange St

AMERIKA-MURA

Yotsubashi-suji

Hanshin Expwy

Shinsaibashi-suji Arcade

MINAMI-HORIE

Daihōji-dōri

Shimizu-dōri

Suomachi-dōri

Hachiman-dōri

Mitsudera-dōri

CHŪŌ-KU

HIGASHI-SHINSAIBASHI

Hanshin Expwy

Dōtombori-gawa

Tombori River Walk

Souemon-chō-dōri

Ebisu-bashi-suji Arcade

Namba

Namba

JR Namba

Kintetsu Namba

NAMBA

Sennichi-mae Arcade

DŌTOMBORI

Kintetsu Nipponbashi

Nipponbashi

15

Tanimachi 9-chōme

Midō-suji

Nankai Namba

Osaka Visitors Information Center Namba

URA-NAMBA

Nansan-dōri

Kuromon Ichiba

Tanimachi-suji

NANIWA-KU

Nansan-dōri

Ota Rd

Ota Rd

Sakai-suji

Shitennōji-mae

Daikoku-chō

Ebisu-chō

Hanshin Expwy

TENNŌJI-KU

SHIN-SEKAI

Sakai-suji

11

Tennō-ji-kōen

Abiko-suji

Shin-Imamiya

6

Dōbutsuen-mae

Abiko-suji

Tennō-ji

1

Abenobashi

Minami

selling of Osaka's principal passion: food. There's everything from bamboo steamers and lacquer miso soup bowls to shopfront lanterns, plastic food models and, of course, moulded hotplates for making *tako-yaki* (octopus dumplings). Hours vary by store.

Standard Books
Books

(スタンダードブックストア; Map p126; ☎06-6484-2239; www.standardbookstore.com; 2-2-12 Nishi-Shinsaibashi, Chūō-ku; ☉11am-10.30pm; Ⓢ Midō-suji line to Shinsaibashi, exit 7) This cult-fave Osaka bookstore prides itself on not stocking any bestsellers. Instead, it's stocked with small-press finds, art books, indie comics and the like, plus CDs, quirky fashion items and accessories.

Time Bomb Records
Music

(Map p126; ☎06-6213-5079; www.timebomb.co.jp; B1, 9-28 Nishi-Shinsaibashi, Chūō-ku; ☉noon-9pm; Ⓢ Midō-suji line to Shinsaibashi, exit 7) One of the best record stores in the city, Time Bomb stocks an excellent collection of vinyl and CDs from '60s pop and '70s punk to alternative, soul and psychedelic. Find out about gigs around town here, too.

🍴 EATING

For more on eating in Osaka, see p118.

Gout
Bakery ¥

(グウ; Map p128; ☎06-6585-0833; 1-1-10 Honmachi, Chūō-ku; bread from ¥200; ☉7.30am-8pm, closed Thu; Ⓢ Tanimachi line

to Tanimachi 4-chōme, exit 4) One of Osaka's best bakeries, Gout (pronounced 'goo', as in French) sells baguettes, pastries, croissants, sandwiches and coffee to take away or eat in. It's perfect for picking up picnic supplies before heading to nearby Osaka-jō.

Yoshino Sushi
Sushi ¥¥

(吉野鮓; Map p128; ☎06-6231-7181; www.yoshino-sushi.co.jp; 3-4-14 Awaji-machi, Chūō-ku; lunch from ¥2700; ☉11am-1.30pm Mon-Fri; Ⓢ Midō-suji line to Honmachi, exit 1) In business since 1841, Yoshino specialises in Osaka-style sushi, which is *hako-sushi* (pressed sushi). This older version of the dish (compared to the newer, hand-pressed Tokyo-style *nigiri-sushi)* is formed by a wooden mould, resulting in Mondrian-esque cubes of spongy omelette, soy-braised shiitake mushrooms, smokey eel and vinegar-marinated fish on rice. Reservations recommended.

Yotaro Honten
Tempura ¥¥

(与太呂本店; Map p128; ☎06-6231-5561; 2-3-14 Kōraibashi, Chūō-ku; tempura set ¥2500, sea bream rice ¥4300; ☉11am-1pm & 5-7pm, closed Thu; Ⓢ Sakaisuji line to Kitahama) This two-Michelin-starred restaurant specialises in exceptionally light and delectable tempura served at the counter, where you can watch the chefs, or in private rooms. The tasty sea bream dish serves two to three people and the filling tempura sets are fantastic value. Look for the black-and-white sign and black

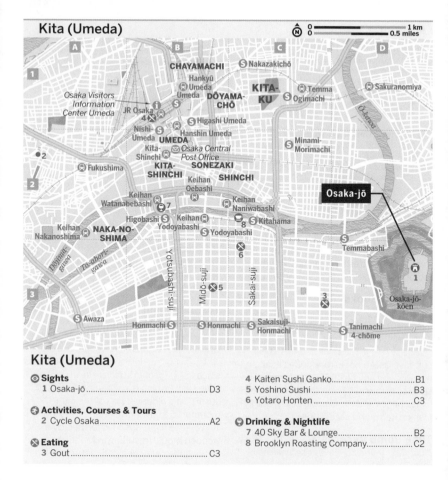

Kita (Umeda)

slatted bars across the windows. Reserve in advance through your hotel.

Imai Honten   Udon ¥¥

(今井本店; Map p126; ☎06-6211-0319; www.d-imai.com; 1-7-22 Dōtombori, Chūō-ku; dishes from ¥800; ⊙11am-10pm, closed Wed; ⑤Midō-suji line to Namba, exit 14) Step into an oasis of calm amid Dōtombori's chaos to be welcomed by staff at one of the area's oldest and most-revered udon specialists. Try *kitsune udon* – noodles topped with soup-soaked slices of fried tofu. Look for the traditional exterior and the willow tree outside.

🍷 DRINKING

Brooklyn Roasting Company   Coffee

(Map p128; ☎06-6125-5740; www.brooklynroasting.jp; 1-16 Kitahama, Chūō-ku; coffee from ¥350; ⊙8am-8pm Mon-Fri, 10am-7pm Sat & Sun; 🛜; ⑤Sakaisuji line to Kitahama, exit 2) With its worn leather couches, big communal table and industrial fittings, this is a little slice of Brooklyn in Osaka and the perfect pit stop while exploring Naka-no-shima. Sip well-crafted coffee (almond and soy milk available, too) on the wide riverside terrace and watch the boats go by. If hunger strikes, there's a small selection of donuts and pastries.

40 Sky Bar & Lounge Cocktail Bar

(Map p128; 📞06-6222-0111; www.conradhotels3.
hilton.com; 3-2-4 Nakanoshima, Kita-ku, Conrad
Osaka; cover after 8.30pm ¥1400; ⏱10am-mid-
night; Ⓢ Yotsubashi line to Higobashi, exit 2) If
heights aren't your thing, you'll need a stiff
drink once you've peered down over the
city from the 40th floor at this ultrasuave
hotel bar. Service is impeccable and there's
a good range of food and bar snacks to go
with well-made cocktails.

INFORMATION

DANGERS & ANNOYANCES

Osaka has a rough image in Japan, with the
highest number of reported crimes per capita of
any city in the country – though it remains sig-
nificantly safer than most cities of comparable
size. Still, it's wise to employ the same common
sense here that you would back home. Purse
snatchings are not uncommon, so be mindful.

INTERNET ACCESS

An increasing number of cafes have wi-fi or
internet access, and Osaka has been expanding
free wi-fi in public areas around town (details at
www.ofw-oer.com/en).

POST

Osaka Central Post Office (大阪中央郵便局;
Map p128; Basement fl, Eki-mae Dai-1 Bldg, 1-3-1
Umeda, Kita-ku; postal services 9am-9pm, ATM
7am-11.30pm Mon-Fri, 8am-11.30pm Sat, 8am-
9pm Sun; Ⓢ Yotsubashi line to Nishi-Umeda, Ⓡ JR
Osaka, Sakurabashi exit)

TOURIST INFORMATION

Osaka Visitors Information Center Umeda
(大阪市ビジターズインフォメーションセ
ンター・梅田; Map p128; 📞06-6345-2189;
www.osaka-info.jp; ⏱7am-11pm; Ⓡ JR Osaka,
north central exit) is the main tourist office, with
English information, pamphlets and maps. It's
on the 1st floor of the central north concourse
of JR Osaka Station. There is also a branch on
the 1st floor of **Nankai Namba Station** (大阪市
ビジターズインフォメーションセンター・
なんば; Map p126; 📞06-6631-9100; ⏱9am-
8pm; Ⓢ Midō-suji line to Namba, exit 4, Ⓡ Nankai

Discount Passes

Enjoy Eco Card (エンジョイエコカード;
weekday/weekend ¥800/600, child ¥300)
One-day unlimited travel on subways, city
buses and Nankō Port Town line, plus admission discounts. At subway ticket machines,
push 'English', insert cash, select 'one-day
pass' or 'one-day pass weekend'.

ICOCA Card Rechargeable, prepaid transport
pass with an IC-chip, which you wave over
the reader at ticket gates. Works on most
trains, subways and buses in the Kansai area.
Purchase it (¥2000, including ¥500 deposit)
at any ticket machine. Return the card to any
station window to get the deposit and any
credit back.

Osaka Amazing Pass (大阪周遊パス; www.
osp.osaka-info.jp/en/) Foreign visitors to
Japan can purchase one-day passes (¥2500)
for unlimited travel on city subways, buses
and trains, and admission to around 35 sights
(including Osaka-jō). Passes are sold at tourist
information centres and city subway stations.

Yokoso Osaka Ticket (www.howto-osaka.
com/en/ticket/ticket/yokoso.html; ¥1500)
Includes one-day travel on city subway
and Nankō Port Town lines, plus admission
discounts. Buy online in advance.

Namba). The tourist information website (www.
osaka-info.jp) is a good resource, too.

GETTING AROUND

Trains and subways should get you everywhere
you need to go. There are eight subway lines, but
the one that short-term visitors will find most useful is the Midō-suji (red) line, running north–south
and stopping at Shin-Osaka, Umeda (next to
Osaka Station), Shinsaibashi, Namba and Tennōji
stations. Single rides cost ¥180 to ¥370 (half-
price for children). Fair warning: Osaka's larger
stations can be disorienting, particularly Osaka
Station. Exits are often confusingly labelled, even
for Japanese. The Metro Osaka Subway app (available from the iTunes store) is very handy to have.

In This Chapter

Kōbe at a Glance

Perched on a hillside sloping down to the sea, Kōbe (神戸) is one of Japan's most attractive and cosmopolitan cities. It was a maritime gateway from the earliest days of trade with China and home to one of the first foreign settlements after Japan reopened to the world in the mid-19th century. Kōbe is compact and walkable, allowing you to immerse yourself in the city's distinct atmosphere and dining options.

With a Day in Port

Wander the streets of **Kitano-chō** (p134), admiring the historic streetscapes. Stop for lunch and sample Kōbe's famous beef. Learn about the sake-making process at **Hakutsuru Sake Brewery Museum** (p136), and sample the the end result at **Sake Yashiro** (p139).

Best Places for...

Kōbe beef Kōbe Plaisir (p138)

A quick snack Isuzu Bakery (p138)

A breath of fresh air Nunobiki Falls (p135)

Strolling the city streets Kitano-chō (p134)

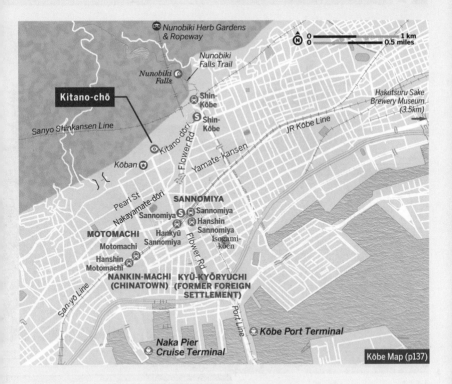

Nunobiki Herb Gardens & Ropeway

Nunobiki Falls Trail

Nunobiki Falls

Kitano-chō

0 — 1 km
0 — 0.5 miles

Hakutsuru Sake Brewery Museum (3.5km)

Sanyo Shinkansen Line

Shin-Kōbe

Shin-Kōbe

JR Kōbe Line

Kitano-dōri

Kōban

Yamate-kansen

Pearl St

Nakayamate-dōri

SANNOMIYA

Sannomiya

Sannomiya

Hanshin Sannomiya

MOTOMACHI

Hankyū Sannomiya

Isogami-kōen

Motomachi

Flower Rd

Hanshin Motomachi

NANKIN-MACHI (CHINATOWN)

KYŪ-KYORYŪCHI (FORMER FOREIGN SETTLEMENT)

San-yō Line

Port Line

Kōbe Port Terminal

Naka Pier Cruise Terminal

Kōbe Map (p137)

Getting from the Port

There are two main arrival points in Kōbe. Cruise ships generally dock at **Kōbe Port Terminal**, linked to centrally located Sannomiya Station by a frequent and fast monorail service, the **Port Liner** (ポートライナー; www.knt-liner. co.jp). **Naka Pier Cruise Terminal** is for smaller ships; there's usually a free shuttle running to central Kōbe, just five minutes away.

Fast Facts

Money There are money changers near Sannomiya Station and at both ports, and ATMs that accept foreign-issued cards at Sannomiya Station, Shin-Kōbe and Harbor Land.

Tourist information At Kōbe Port Terminal and Naka Pier.

Wi-fi Free wi-fi is available for tourists throughout Kōbe, including at both port terminals; stop by a tourist information centre for access.

Weathercock House

COWARDLION/SHUTTERSTOCK ©

Kitano-chō

Nestled between Mt Rokko and Kōbe city is lovely Kitano-chō. Kōbe's port was opened to foreign trade in the 1860s, and the incoming traders and immigrants settled in what is today Nankin-machi and here in Kitano-chō. The ijinkan (literally 'foreigners' houses') here are among the best-preserved in Japan.

Great For...

☑ Don't Miss

Exploring the area's house museums, cafes, shops and streets.

Historic Homes

For generations of Japanese tourists, the pleasant, hilly neighbourhood of Kitano-chō is Kōbe, thanks to the dozen or so well-preserved homes of (mostly) Western trading families and diplomats who settled here during the Meiji period. These *ijinkan* – strangely, though naturally, incongruent, as each is built in the architectural style of the owner's home country – are now mostly cafes, restaurants and souvenir shops.

Two of the best-preserved homes, the red-brick **Weathercock House**, built in 1909 for a German trader, and the wooden, jade-green **Moegi House**, built in 1903 for the former US consul, are open as museums (⊘9am to 6pm; combined ticket ¥650). Many of the original furnishings are intact – you'll see the lengths that expats a century ago went to in order to maintain their native lifestyles.

Nunobiki Herb Gardens & Ropeway

GAID KORNSILAPA/SHUTTERSTOCK ©

Explore Ashore

From Kōbe Port Terminal, take the Port Liner to Sannomiya Station; Kitano-chō is a short walk northwest of the station. From Naka Pier, take the shuttle to Motomachi Station, then take a train to Sannomiya Station and head northwest, or Shin-Kōbe Station and head southwest to Kitano-chō.

❶ Need to Know

北野町; ⑤Shin-Kōbe, ℝJR Shin-Kōbe

Coffee Break

A big chain wouldn't normally be worth listing, but **Starbucks Ijinkan** (スターバックス異人館; ☎078-230-6302; 3-1-31 Kitano-chō, Chūō-ku; ⏰8am-10pm; ℝJR Sannomiya) is different: it's housed in a beautifully preserved former *ijinkan*, c 1907. Buy a cuppa and ensconce yourself in period antiques and furniture (albeit amid some of the standard Starbucks decor). It can be crowded.

View from Above

At the northeastern edge of Kitano-chō, just before Shin-Kōbe Station, is **Nunobiki Herb Gardens & Ropeway** (布引ハーブ園&ロープウェイ; ropeway 1 way/return ¥950/1500, return after 5pm ¥900; ⏰10am-5pm Mon-Fri, to 8.30pm Sat & Sun 20 Mar-19 Jul & Sep-Nov, 10am-8.30pm daily 20 Jul-31 Aug, to 5pm Dec-19 Mar; ⑤Shin-Kōbe, ℝJR Shin-Kōbe), offering an

escape from the city on a 400m-high mountain ridge and sweeping views across town to the bay. During the day (to 5pm), after taking the ropeway up, you can descend on foot to the midway station through the landscaped herb gardens, which include some nicely placed benches and hammocks. From here you can return by ropeway or continue on for about 20 minutes to the **Nunobiki Falls** (布引の滝, Nunobikinotaki; ⑤Shin-Kōbe, ℝJR Shin-Kōbe) FREE; follow the road (it's signposted) and keep a lookout for the staircase on your right (not well signposted) that leads to the waterfall path.

You'd never guess that such a beautiful natural sanctuary could sit so close to the city. This revered waterfall in four sections (the longest is 43m tall) has been the subject of art, poetry and worship for centuries – some of the poems are reproduced on stone tablets at the site. It's accessible by a steep 400m path from Shin-Kōbe Station. Take the ground-floor exit, turn left and walk under the station building to the path.

⊙ SIGHTS

Hakutsuru Sake Brewery Museum
Brewery

(白鶴造酒資料館; ☎078-822-8907; www.hakutsuru-sake.com; 4-5-5 Sumiyoshi Minami-machi, Higashi-Nada-ku; ⊗9.30am-4pm; ⌂Hanshin main line to Sumiyoshi) FREE Hakutsuru is a major sake brewer in Kōbe's Nada-gogō district, a major sake-brewing centre. The self-guided tour through the old wooden brewery (the current, modern brewery is behind it) is a fascinating look at traditional sake-making methods: videos (with English) show real footage from inside the original brewery alongside old equipment. You can sample some sake at the end.

Take a local Hanshin-line train eight stops east from Sannomiya to Sumiyoshi Station (¥190, 15 minutes). Exit the station, walk south towards the elevated highway and cross under it, then take your first left and then a right; the entrance is on the right. Use the blue-and-white crane logo atop the factory as your guide.

Port of Kōbe Earthquake Memorial Park
Monument

(神戸港震災メモリアルパーク; Meriken Park; ⓢKaigan line to Minato Motomachi, ⌂Motomachi) FREE At 5.46am on 17 January 1995 the Great Hanshin Earthquake struck this region. It was Japan's strongest since the Great Kantō Quake of 1923 devastated Tokyo. Kōbe bore the brunt of the damage – 6000 killed, over 30,000 injured, toppled expressways and nearly 300,000 lost buildings. This simple, open-air, harbourside museum tells the story through artefacts and a video presentation in English. Most striking is a section of the dock that was left as it was after that devastating day.

Ikuta-jinja
Shinto Shrine

(生田神社; ☎078-321-3851; 1-2-1 Shimo-Yamate-dōri, Chūō-ku; ⊗7am-sunset; ⌂JR Sannomiya) FREE Kōbe's signature shrine is said to date from 201, though it's been rebuilt many a time – a symbol of resilience for the city. It's right in the middle of Sannomiya, providing a peaceful retreat from the urban bustle.

Ikuta-jinja

MTAIRA/SHUTTERSTOCK ©

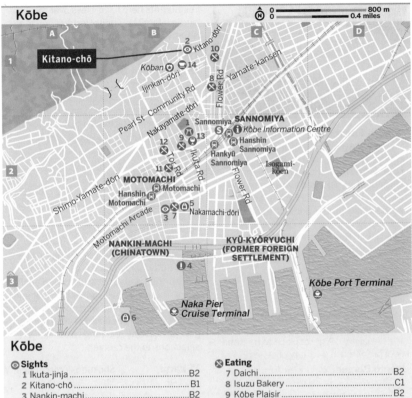

Kōbe

Nankin-machi   Area

(南京町; Chinatown; Sakaemachi-dōri, Chūō-ku; ⑤ Kaigan line to Kyūkyoryūchi-Daimaru-mae, Ⓡ JR or Hanshin lines to Motomachi) Kōbe's Chinatown – Nankin comes from Nanjing; *machi* just means town – dates to the early days of the city opening its port to foreign traders. It was rebuilt after the 1995 earthquake and has all the visual signifiers of Chinatowns the world over: tiered gates at the cardinal entrances (except for the north side, guarded by lions) and lots of restaurants.

It's definitely touristy, but it's fun: most restaurants have stalls out the front selling street food, like *nikuman* (steamed buns, usually filled with pork; *baozi*) and *chimaki* (sticky rice wrapped in bamboo leaves, also often filled with pork; they're also called *zongzi*) for a few hundred yen each.

🏠 SHOPPING

Kōbe Harbor Land   Mall

(神戸ハーバーランド; www.harborland.co.jp; Higashi Kawasaki-chō, Chūō-ku; ◷10am-9pm;

🍴 Famous Kōbe Beef

Kōbe is known worldwide for its top-class beef, considered by many to be the best in the world. Highly marbled, it's naturally tender and rich in flavour. It's also held to very strict regulations. Splurge on the cut rather than the size; the fat content makes Kōbe beef very filling.

Kōbe Plaisir (神戸プレジール; 📞078-571-0141; https://kobe-plaisir.jp; 2-11-5 Shimo-Yamate-dōri, Chūō-ku; lunch/dinner Kōbe-beef set menus from ¥7500/11,000; ⏱11.30am-3pm & 5-10.30pm; Ⓢ Sannomiya, 🚆JR Sannomiya) A great place to try Kōbe beef prepared in a variety of styles.

Wanto Burger (ワントバーガー; 📞078-392-5177; www.wantoburger.com; 3-10-6 Shimo-Yamate-dōri, Chūō-ku; burgers ¥1080-3800; ⏱noon-3pm & 5-10pm Tue-Fri, noon-10pm Sat, to 5pm Sun; 🚆JR Sannomiya) Serves towering, teetering burgers made with Kōbe beef.

Daichi (大地; 📞078-333-6688; www.koubegyuu.com/shop/daichi; 1-1-3 Motomachi-dōri, Chūō-ku; steak meals from ¥2500; ⏱11am-9pm; Ⓢ Kaigan line to Kyūkyorūchi-Daimaru-mae, 🚆Motomachi) Kōbe beef teppanyaki at entry-level prices.

🐾; Ⓢ Kaigan line to Harbor Land, 🚆JR Kōbe line to Kōbe) This bayside complex has several malls (Umie and Mosaic), with branches of many mainstream shops. Some restaurants here have views over the water and are family friendly. Harbor Land is a short walk from Naka Pier.

Daimaru Department Store   Department Store
(大丸; www.daimaru.co.jp/kobe; 40 Akashi-machi, Chūō-ku; ⏱10am-8pm; Ⓢ Kaigan line Kyūkyorūchi-Daimaru-mae) Large department store at the western edge of Kyū-Kyoryuchi (the former foreigners' settlement).

🍴 EATING

Isuzu Bakery   Bakery ¥
(イスズベーカリー; 📞078-222-4180; www.isuzu-bakery.jp; 2-1-4 Nunobiki-chō, Chūō-ku; bread & pastries ¥120-560; ⏱8am-8pm; 🚆JR Sannomiya) The most famous of Kōbe's bakeries, Isuzu is particularly famous for its crisp, fluffy 'curry pan' (カレーパン; ¥160), a deep-fried doughnut stuffed with beef curry. There's a huge variety of sweet and savoury options (and, with no English signs, you never quite know which you're going to get). Grab a tray and tongs and take your selections to the cashier.

Mikami   Shokudo, International ¥
(味加味; 📞078-242-5200; 2-5-9 Kanō-chō, Chūō-ku; mains ¥480-1800, set meals from around ¥850; ⏱11.30am-3pm & 5-11pm Wed-Mon; 🚆JR Sannomiya, 🚆JR Shin-Kōbe) Mikami is a beacon of good food in the otherwise forlorn zone between Shin-Kōbe Station and Sannomiya. It does excellent *teishoku* (set meals); the *katsu* (crumbed and fried) dishes are especially good.

It's located on the street one block west of the main road connecting Shin-Kōbe Station and Sannomiya, about halfway between the two; look for an ivy-covered building.

Modernark   Cafe ¥
(モダナーク; 📞078-391-3060; http://modern ark-cafe.chronicle.co.jp; 3-11-15 Kitanagasa-dōri, Chūō-ku; mains ¥950-1150; ⏱11.30am-10pm; 🚆Motomachi) This adorably funky cafe with a glassed-in verandah is Kōbe's go-to

spot for organic vegetarian and vegan meals and cakes, served with herbal tea or homemade sangria. Look for the thicket of potted trees out the front.

🍸 DRINKING

Sake Yashiro — Bar

(さけやしろ; ☎078-334-7339; 4-6-15 Ikuta-chō, Chūō-ku; ⊘4-11.30pm; 🚃JR Sannomiya) This standing bar has a daunting selection of 90 kinds of sake, including about 50 from local brewers, on its (Japanese-only) menu. Anticipating your needs, staff have made a cheat sheet in English of their top five local picks, all priced ¥880 by the glass. Look for the denim door curtains. A great option if your cruise schedule allows it.

ℹ️ INFORMATION

Kōbe Information Centre (神戸市総合インフォメーションセンター; ☎078-322-0220; www.feel-kobe.jp; JR Sannomiya; ⊘9am-7pm; 🚃Sannomiya) On the ground floor outside of JR Sannomiya Station's east gate. There's a smaller information counter on the 2nd floor of Shin-Kōbe Station, outside the main *shinkansen* gate. Both have good English city maps.

ℹ️ GETTING AROUND

Kōbe is small enough to get around on foot.

 Connections to Surrounding Cities

Kōbe is well connected to surrounding cities. The JR Kōbe line runs fast *shinkaisoku* (special rapid trains) from Sannomiya Station to **Himeji** (¥970, 40 minutes), **Kyoto** (¥1080, 50 minutes) and **Osaka** (¥410, 20 minutes). Shin-Kōbe Station, north of Sannomiya, is on the Tōkaidō/San-yō and Kyūshū *shinkansen* lines. Destinations include **Himeji** (¥2700, 25 minutes), **Hiroshima** (¥9490, 70 minutes), **Kyoto** (¥2810, 30 minutes) and **Shin-Osaka** (¥1500, 15 minutes).

BUS

City-loop buses (per ride/day pass ¥260/660, children half-price) stop at most of the city's sightseeing spots and its main stations several times an hour (10am to 6pm); look for the retro-style green buses. Purchase tickets on board or at the information centre.

TRAIN

The Seishin-Yamate subway line connects Shin-Kōbe and Sannomiya Stations (¥210, two minutes).

The Kaigan subway line runs from just south of Sannomiya Station to Minato Motomachi and Harbor Land Stations.

KŌCHI

Kōchi at a Glance

Kōchi (高知) is a smart, compact city with a deserved reputation for enjoying a good time. The castle here is largely undamaged and remains a fine example of Japanese architecture. Also claimed by Kōchi is a samurai of great national significance – during the Meiji Restoration, Sakamoto Ryōma was instrumental in bringing down the feudal government. The central part of the city is 12km north and inland from the sea and the liveliest part of town is where the tramlines cross near Harimaya-bashi, a tiny red replica of a bridge made famous by song and film in Japan. The main Obiyamachi shopping arcade runs perpendicular to Harimayabashi-dōri.

With a Day in Port

Eat your way along Obiyamachi Arcade to **Kōchi-jō** (p145). Visit **Chikurin-ji** (p146), one of the famed 88 Sacred Temples of Shikoku, then learn about the art of making *washi* (Japanese paper) at **Ino Japanese Paper Museum** (p148).

Best Places for...

History Kōchi-jo (p144)

Cheap eats Hirome Ichiba (p145)

A quiet drink Kinako Cafe (p149)

Spectacular scenery Iya Valley (p150)

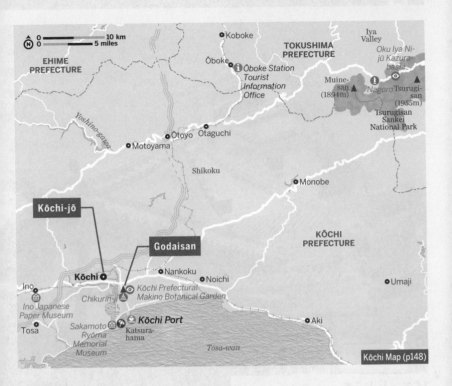

Kōchi Map (p148)

Getting from the Port

Cruise operators generally put on a free shuttle bus from Kōchi port into town, stopping at Kōchi bus terminal (p151). Otherwise a taxi is a good option. There's no public transport between the port and downtown.

Fast Facts

Money International ATMs are available at the post office next to JR Kōchi Station. Currency exchange available at port.

Tourist information Temporary quayside information booths greet most arrivals. See p150 for other tourist information offices.

Wi-fi Log on to Kōchi Free Wi-fi (www.visitkochijapan.com/travelers_kit/wifi).

MARLON TROTTMANN/SHUTTERSTOCK ©

Kōchi-jō

A visit to Kōchi-jo offers plenty of variety: gardens, views, a museum, a walk through Kōchi's eating and entertainment district and, of course, a well-preserved historic castle.

Great For...

☑ Don't Miss

The views: the main castle keep offers sweeping views across the city, and this is the only castle in Japan where both the main keep and gate can be viewed at once, making for a great photo op.

History

Kōchi-jō is one of just a dozen castles in Japan to have survived with its original *tenshu-kaku* (keep) intact. The castle was originally built during the first decade of the 17th century by Yamanouchi Katsu-toyo, who was appointed *daimyō* (domain lord) by Tokugawa Ieyasu after he fought on the victorious Tokugawa side in the Battle of Sekigahara in 1600. A major fire destroyed much of the original structure in 1727; the castle was largely rebuilt between 1748 and 1753.

Kōchi-jō was the product of an age of peace – it never came under attack and for the remainder of the Tokugawa period it was more like a stately home than a military fortress. The fee is for entry to the castle itself; it's free to walk in the surrounding grounds. The approach to

Obiyamachi Arcade

WINHORSE/GETTY IMAGES ©

⚓

Explore Ashore

Take a shuttle or taxi from the port to the Kōchi bus terminal (p151), adjacent to JR Kōchi train station. From here, it's a half-hour walk to the castle. Alternatively, take a tram (about 10 minutes), changing lines at Harimaya-bashi (はりまや橋) junction.

❶ Need to Know

高知城; 1-2-1 Marunouchi; ¥420; ⊗9am-5pm

the castle is a steep climb, with plenty of stairs, and can be hot in summer.

Kōchi Castle Museum of History

This **museum** (高知城歴史博物館; ☎088-871-1600; www.kochi-johaku.jp; 2-7-5 Ōtesuji; ¥500; ⊗9am-6pm Mon-Sat, from 8am Sun) celebrating the history of Kōchi castle is an architectural achievement in its own right. Entry is free to the museum shop (1st floor) and to the 2nd floor cafe and terrace – both with marvellous views of the castle and its grounds. The entry fee gives you access to the 3rd floor, where you'll find interesting exhibitions on the history of the castle and the city of Kōchi.

Obiyamachi Arcade

Kōchi's main eating and entertainment district is in the area around the Obiyamachi Arcade and the Harimaya-bashi junction where the tramlines meet. Walking through the arcade up to the castle (about 2km) gives you a good taste of what Kōchi has to offer, and there's plenty to see along the way. **Hirome Ichiba** (ひろめ市場; ☎088-822-5287; www.hirome.co.jp; 2-3-1 Obiyamachi; dishes from ¥300; ⊗8am-11pm, from 7am Sun), a full block of mayhem at the end of the main arcade, just before the castle, is the hub of Kōchi's cheap-eats scene. On weekends, it positively heaves with young people. Dozens of mini-restaurants and bars specialising in everything from *gomoku rāmen* (seafood noodles) to *tako-yaki* (octopus balls) surround communal tables.

Chikurin-ji

Godaisan

Several kilometres east of the town centre, and north of the port, is the mountain of Godaisan (五台山), where you can enjoy excellent views of the city from a lookout point (展望台). Near the top of the hill is Chikurin-ji, one of the famous 88 temples of Shikoku. By the entrance gates is the Kōchi Prefectural Makino Botanical Garden, a network of gardens and parkland.

Great For...

☑ Don't Miss

Tropical plants are on display year-round in the botanic gardens' greenhouse.

Chikurin-ji

The extensive grounds of **Chikurin-ji** (竹林寺; ☎088-882-3085; www.chikurinji.com; 3577 Godaisan) **FREE** feature a five-storey pagoda and thousands of statues of the Bodhisattva Jizō, guardian deity of children and travellers. The temple's Treasure House (¥400; ⊙8am to 5pm) hosts an impressive collection of Buddhist sculpture from the Heian and Kamakura periods; the same ticket gets you in to see the temple's lovely Kamakura-period garden opposite.

The 88 Sacred Temples of Shikoku

Shikoku (四国), the island upon which Kōchi sits, is home to the 88 Sacred Temples of Shikoku, Japan's most famous pilgrimage.

Five-storey pagoda, Chikurin-ji

THANYARAT07/GETTY IMAGES ©

Kōchi

Kōchi Prefectural
Makino Botanical
Garden

Godaisan

Chikurin-ji

Kōchi Port

Explore Ashore

Take a shuttle into town to Kōchi bus station (p151). From here, take a My-Yū tourist bus (p151) to Godaisan. The gardens lie between the port and the city centre, so a taxi is a more direct option.

❶ Need to Know

There's a restaurant and cafe in the gardens; otherwise grab a bento box on the way in and enjoy a picnic in the beautiful gardens.

The *henro* (pilgrim on the 88 Temple Circuit) is one of the most distinctive sights of any trip to Shikoku – solitary figures in white, trudging purposefully through heat haze and downpour alike on their way from temple to temple.

Although the backgrounds and motives of the *henro* may differ widely, they all follow in the legendary footsteps of Kōbō Daishi, the monk who attained enlightenment on Shikoku, established Shingon Buddhism in Japan and made significant contributions to Japanese culture. The idea behind making the 1400km, 88 Temple Circuit is to do so accompanied by the spirit of Kōbō Daishi himself – hence the inscription on pilgrims' backpacks and other paraphernalia: 同行二人 (*dōgyō ninin*), meaning 'two people on the same journey'.

A pilgrim's routine at each temple is mostly the same: a bang on the bell and a chant of the Heart Sutra at the Daishi-dō (one of the two main buildings in each temple compound), before filing off to the *nōkyō-jo* (desk), where the pilgrims' book is inscribed with beautiful characters detailing the name of the temple and the date of the pilgrimage.

Kōchi Prefectural Makino Botanical Garden

Next to the Chikurin-ji entrance gates on the south side of Godaisan is the impressive **Kōchi Prefectural Makino Botanical Garden** (高知県立牧野植物園; ☑088-882-2601; www.makino.or.jp; 4200-6 Godaisan; ¥720; ◷9am-5pm), which features more than 3000 different plant species.

◉ SIGHTS

Ino Japanese
Paper Museum   Museum

(いの町紙の博物館; ☎088-893-0886; www.
kamihaku.com/en; 110-1 Saiwai-chō, Ino-chō;
¥500; ⊙9am-5pm Tue-Sun) Discover the history and development of *washi* (Japanese
paper) at Ino, about 10km west of downtown Kōchi. There are demonstrations
of *nagashizuki* papermaking techniques
and on the first Sunday of every month,
there's a papermaking class (¥400; in
Japanese only). Check out the excellent
English website for details. The museum is
a 10-minute walk from both the Ino JR and
tram stations.

Harimaya-bashi   Landmark

(播磨屋橋) This tiny reconstructed bridge
from the Edo period is renowned throughout Japan thanks to a romantic song
in which it features. For older Japanese
people, this is *the* major Kōchi landmark
and obligatory photos are taken, though
many are surprised by how small it is. The
tram station and the city's busiest intersection are named after it.

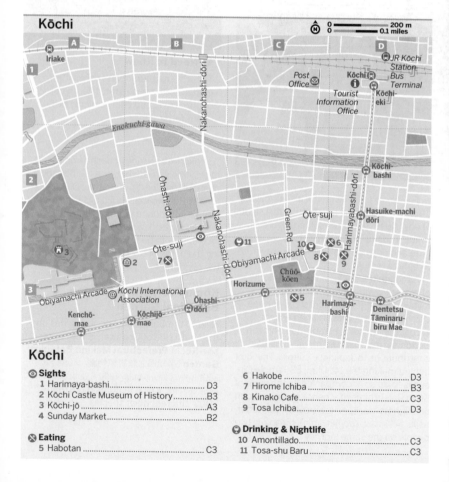

Kōchi

Katsura-hama · Beach

(桂浜) Katsura-hama is a popular beach 12km south of central Kōchi at the point where Kōchi's harbour empties out into the bay. Strong currents prohibit swimming, but it's a lovely spot to stroll, with a small **shrine** perched on an oceanside promontory. Just before the beach itself is **Sakamoto Ryōma Memorial Museum** (坂本龍馬記念館; ☑088-841-0001; www. ryoma-kinenkan.jp; 830 Urado-shiroyama; ¥700; ⏰9am-5pm), with exhibits dedicated to the life of a local hero who was instrumental in bringing about the Meiji Restoration in the 1860s.

Public buses run to Katsura-hama from Kōchi Station (¥690, 35 minutes, six daily) and Harimaya-bashi (¥620, 25 minutes, frequent). The My-Yū bus runs as far as Katsura-hama before heading back to Kōchi.

EATING

With its long Pacific coastline, Kōchi Prefecture is known for its seafood, particularly *katsuo-tataki,* seared bonito fish that is thinly sliced and eaten with grated ginger. *Sawachi-ryōri* is a huge plate (a *sawachi*) of seafood, with various varieties of both sashimi and sushi.

Central Obiyamachi Arcade offers a plethora of tasty dining options.

Kinako Cafe · Cafe ¥

(きなこCafe; ☑088-875-2255; www.hitosara. com/0006109127; 1-1-7 Obiyamachi; meals from ¥800; ⏰11am-3pm & 5-11pm Tue-Sat, lunch only Sun) This tiny, lovingly run place serves tasty set meals at lunchtime, then morphs into a jazz and wine bar serving top-quality *otsumami* (snacks) in the evenings. A great little place to relax after time on your feet in the Obiyamachi shopping arcade.

Hakobe · Okonomiyaki ¥

(はこべ; ☑088-823-0084; 1-2-5 Obiyamachi; dishes ¥650-1200; ⏰11am-midnight) This is one of the few remaining cook-it-yourself

Sunday Street Market

Our favourite **street market** (日曜市; Ōte-suji; ⏰5am-6pm Sun Apr-Sep, 5.30am-5pm Sun Oct-Mar) in Shikoku is 300 years old and takes place every Sunday along 1.3km of Ōte-suji, the main road leading to the castle. Around 430 colourful stalls sell fresh produce, tonics and tinctures, knives, flowers, garden stones, wooden antiques and everything else imaginable.

Antiques for sale
AKIYOKO/SHUTTERSTOCK ©

okonomiyaki (pancake) joints in Kōchi serving cheap and cheerful Japanese pancakes. The 'mix' of *ika* (squid), *ebi* (shrimp) and *tori* (chicken) is heavenly. Other alternatives include *buta* (pork) and *yasai* (vegetables). They bring it out and you cook it on the hotplate. It's slap bang in the heart of the arcade.

Habotan · Izakaya ¥

(葉牡丹; ☑088-872-1330; www.habotan.jp; 2-21 Sakai-machi; dishes ¥150-1100; ⏰11am-11pm) Red lanterns mark out this locals' *izakaya* opposite Chūō-kōen that opens at the shockingly early hour of 11am. The food is under glass on the counter, so you can point at what you'd like to order. *Sashimi moriawase* (a selection of sashimi) is ¥1050. Local booze includes Tosa-tsuru sake and Dabada Hiburi, a *shōchū* (distilled grain liquor) made from chestnuts.

Tosa Ichiba · Japanese ¥¥

(土佐市場; ☑088-872-0039; 1-3-11 Harima-yachō; set meals from ¥1100; ⏰11am-10.30pm)

 Iya Valley

The spectacular Iya Valley (祖谷渓) is a special place: winding your way around narrow cliff-hanging roads as the icy water of the Iya-gawa shoots along the ancient valley floor is a blissful travel experience. Beyond the remarkable scenery, highlights of the valley include the vine-covered bridges of **Oku Iya Ni-jū Kazura-bashi** (奥祖谷二重かずら橋; ¥550; ⏰7am-5pm), and the surreal **Nagoro** (名頃かかしの里; Nagoro Scarecrow Village), populated by life-size scarecrow-type dolls.

You will need to be organised in order to set off and return to Kōchi port in a single day. To get here, take a train from Kōchi to JR Ōboke Station (¥3180, 50 minutes). From here infrequent buses head off around the valley, and it is also possible to hire a car (be aware that in this mountainous area, roads can be narrow).

With limited time, however, you'll make the most of a day trip with a tour. The extremely efficient **Ōboke Station Tourist Information Office** (大歩危駅観光内所; ☎0883-76-0877; www.miyoshi-tourism.jp/en; ⏰8.30am-3.30pm Mon, Tue, Thu & Fri, to 5.30pm Sat & Sun) can help with organising your trip over the hill and into the Iya Valley. The English-speaking staff have tons of brochures and maps on hand.

Oku Iya Ni-jū Kazura-bashi
WORLDROADTRIP/SHUTTERSTOCK ©

Near the start of Obiyamachi Arcade, this is a good place to try local set meals, especially if you're struggling with Japanese menus. Most of the menu is displayed either outside or in the windows in plastic-model form. Pick what looks good and point it out to the friendly staff. There are lots of seafood options.

🍷 DRINKING

Kōchi is a lively town. Head into the streets just north of Obiyamachi Arcade to find more than a few options for a drink. If your cruise schedule allows, check out the following places.

Tosa-shu Baru
Bar

(土佐酒バル; ☎088-823-2216; 1-9-5 Ōte-suji; ⏰6pm-midnight Tue-Sun) Without doubt, this nonsmoking bar with an extremely convivial atmosphere is the place to go to try Kōchi-made sake. Owner Kōji is passionate about sake and has offerings from all 18 breweries in Kōchi, three daily-changing *nomi-kurabe* (tasting sets) and serves superb small dishes featuring local produce. He is a fountain of sake knowledge and plays great jazz.

Amontillado
Pub

(アモンティラード; ☎088-875-0599; www.irishpub-amontillado.owst.jp; 1-5-2 Obiyamachi; ⏰5pm-1am) If you feel like a pint of Guinness (¥880), pop into this Irish pub right on Obiyamachi Arcade. There's always plenty going on as it's popular with locals.

ℹ️ INFORMATION

Kōchi International Association (高知県国際交流協会; ☎088-875-0022; www.kochi-kia.or.jp; 2nd fl, 4-1-37 Honmachi; ⏰8.30am-5.15pm Mon-Sat) Friendly English-speaking staff, free internet access, a library and English newspapers and magazines.

Tourist Information Office (高知観光案内所; ☎088-826-3337; www.visitkochijapan.com; ⏰8.30am-5pm, accommodation info to 7.30pm)

Tram at Harimayabashi Station

The helpful tourist-information pavilion out the front of JR Kōchi Station provides English-language maps, Kōchi mini-guidebooks and more. There's always an enthusiastic English speaker on hand.

ⓘ GETTING AROUND

BICYCLE

Free rental bicycles can be picked up from the Tourist Information Office at the front of JR Kōchi Station. They're available from 8.30am to 5pm (bring ID).

BUS

The **My-Yū bus** (MY遊バス; www.visitkochijapan.com/about/Kochi_MYyou_EN.pdf; 1-/2-day pass ¥1000/1600) runs from **Kōchi bus terminal** (高知駅バスターミナル) to Godaisan to Katsura-hama and back. Purchase the pass at the Tourist Information Office in front of Kōchi Station; show your foreign passport and you'll get the pass for half price.

Public buses to Katsura-hama (¥270, 35 minutes, hourly) leave from the bus terminal.

TRAM

Kōchi's colourful tram service (¥200 per trip) has been running since 1904. There are two lines: the north–south line from the station intersects with the east–west tram route at the Harimaya-bashi junction. Pay when you get off and ask for a *norikae-ken* (transfer ticket) if you have to change lines.

Explore Ashore

Some cruise companies offer a shuttle to the park, and taxis are readily available. Tram 3 (30 minutes, ¥180) runs here from the Ujina Wharf area. From Itsukaichi Wharf, take a taxi, shuttle bus or walk the couple of kilometres to Hiroden-Itsukaichi tram stop. From here, tram line 2 runs to the park (about 40 minutes, ¥180).

The Bombing of Hiroshima

At 8.15am on 6 August 1945, the US B-29 bomber *Enola Gay* released the 'Little Boy' atomic bomb over Hiroshima. The 2000°C (3630°F) blast obliterated 90% of the city and instantly killed 80,000 people. The bomb exploded over the town centre, filled with wooden homes and shops. This created intense firestorms that raced through the city for three days and destroyed 92% of buildings, fuelled by broken gas pipes and electrical lines. Toxic black rain fell 30 minutes after the blast, carrying 200 different types of radioactive isotopes, contaminating the thirsty wounded who drank it.

Around 350,000 people were present that day. In the following months, 130,000 died of radiation exposure and other secondary effects, including intensive burns. Most casualties were civilians, including firefighters and 90% of the city's doctors who came to help; 20,000 forced Korean labourers; and 6000 junior-high-school students who had been clearing fire breaks in anticipation of a regular attack.

The Japanese government says around 187,000 atomic-bomb survivors were still alive in 2015, many living through the mental trauma, cancers and other effects of radiation. No residual radiation remains today.

Atomic Bomb Dome

The starkest reminder of the destruction visited upon Hiroshima in WWII is the **Atomic Bomb Dome** (原爆ドーム, Genbaku Dome; 1-10 Otemachi; ⊙24hr; 🚃Genbaku-dōmu-mae) **FREE**. Built by a Czech architect in 1915, it was the Industrial Promotion Hall until the bomb exploded almost directly above it. Everyone

Children's Peace Monument

inside was killed, but the building was one of very few left standing near the epicentre. A decision was taken after the war to preserve the shell as a memorial.

Hiroshima Peace Memorial Museum

The main building, **Hiroshima Peace Memorial Museum** (広島平和記念資料館; www.pcf.city.hiroshima.jp; 1-2 Nakajima-chō, Naka-ku; adult/child ¥200/free; ⏲8.30am-7pm Aug, to 6pm Mar-Jul & Sep-Nov, to 5pm Dec-Feb; 🚋Genbaku-dōmu-mae or Chūden-mae), houses a collection of items salvaged from the bomb's aftermath. The displays are con-

---

☑ Don't Miss

The pond's **Flame of Peace** (平和の灯) will only be extinguished when every nuclear weapon has been destroyed.

DFLC PRINTS/SHUTTERSTOCK © DESIGNERS: KAZUO KIKUCHI & KIYOSHI IKEBE

fronting and personal – ragged clothes, a child's melted lunch box, a watch stopped at 8.15am – and there are some grim photographs. The east building presents a history of Hiroshima and of the development and destructive power of nuclear weapons.

Memorial Hall for the Atomic Bomb Victims

A softly lit internal walkway leads down into this deeply moving, memorial **space** (国立広島原爆死没者追悼平和祈念館; www.hiro-tsuitokinenkan.go.jp; 1-6 Nakajima-chō, Naka-ku; ⏲8.30am-7pm Aug, to 6pm Mar-Jul & Sep-Nov, to 5pm Dec-Feb; 🚋Genbaku-dōmu-mae or Hon-dōri) FREE whose walls show a panorama of Hiroshima at the time of the bomb. A fountain at the centre represents the moment the bomb was dropped, while the water offers relief to the victims. An adjoining room shows the names and photographs of those who perished.

Children's Peace Monument

The **Children's Peace Monument** (原爆の子の像) was inspired by Sasaki Sadako, just two years old at the time the bomb was dropped in 1945. At age 11 she developed leukaemia, and decided to fold 1000 paper cranes. In Japan, the crane is a symbol of longevity and happiness, and Sadako believed if she folded 1000 she would recover. Sadly she died before reaching her goal, but her classmates folded the rest. Surrounding the monument are strings of thousands of colourful paper cranes sent by school children from around the country and the world.

Cenotaph

The curved concrete **cenotaph** (原爆死没者慰霊碑) houses a list of the names of all the known victims of the atomic bomb. It stands at one end of the pond at the centre of the park, framing the Flame of Peace.

✕ Take a Break

Choose a park bench along the riverside opposite the Atomic Bomb Dome.

⊙ SIGHTS & ACTIVITIES

Hiroshima City
Manga Library   Library
(広島市まんが図書館; ☑082-261-0330; www.
library.city.hiroshima.jp/manga; 1-4 Hijiyama-
kōen; ⊙10am-5pm Tue-Sun; ☐Hijiyama-shita)
An obvious pit stop for manga (Japanese
comics) enthusiasts, this library has a small
section of foreign-language manga and a
collection of vintage and rare manga. Grab

the English-language pamphlet and head
up to the 2nd floor.

Hiroshima-jō   Castle
(広島城, Hiroshima Castle; www.rijo-castle.
jp; 21-1 Moto-machi; tower ¥370; ⊙9am-6pm
Mar-Nov, to 5pm Dec-Feb; ☐Kamiya-chō)
Also known as Carp Castle (鯉城; Rijō),
Hiroshima-jō was originally constructed in
1589, but much of it was dismantled following the Meiji Restoration. What remained

Hiroshima

was totally destroyed by the bomb and rebuilt in 1958. In the north end there's a small five-level museum with historical items, but most visitors go for the tower with views over the impressive moat. The surrounding park is a pleasant (and free) place for a stroll. Enter from the east or south.

Mazda Museum
Museum

(マツダミュージアム; ☑082-252-5050; www.mazda.com/about/museum; ☉by reservation Mon-Fri; ☒Mukainada) **FREE** Mazda is popular for the chance to see the impressive 7km assembly line. English-language tours (90 minutes) are available at 10am weekdays, but it's best to check the website or with the tourist office for the current times. Reservations are required and can be made online or by phone.

The museum is a short walk from JR Mukainada (向洋) Station, two stops from Hiroshima on the San-yō line.

Hiroshima Sightseeing Loop Bus
Bus

(www.chugoku-jrbus.co.jp; single/day pass ¥200/400) The *meipurū-pu* (loop bus) has two overlapping routes – orange and green – taking in the main sights and museums of the city, including the Peace Memorial Park and Atomic Bomb Dome. Both routes begin and end on the *shinkansen* entrance (north) side of Hiroshima Station, running from about 9am to 6pm (the green route runs later during summer).

SHOPPING

Browse the busy shop-filled Hon-dōri covered arcade for clothes and beauty products. Namiki-dōri is another shopping street, with a range of fashionable boutiques. Hiroshima also has branches of the big-name department stores, such as **Tokyu Hands** (東急ハンズ広島店; http://hiroshima.tokyu-hands.co.jp; 16-10 Hatchō-bori; ☉10am-8pm; ☒Tate-machi), packed with homewares, must-have gadgets, and

Hiroshima Reading

'Hiroshima' (1946) by John Hersey – the article by the Pulitzer Prize–winning writer (available at www.newyorker.com).

Hiroshima: Three Witnesses (1990); ed Richard H Minear – translation of first-hand accounts of three authors.

Black Rain (1965) by Ibuse Masuji – a novel depicting the lives of those who survived.

Sadako and the Thousand Paper Cranes (1977) by Eleanor Coerr – aimed at younger readers, based on the true story of Sasaki Sadako.

---

gifts; and classy **Mitsukoshi** (広島三越; http://mitsukoshi.mistore.jp/store/hiroshima; 5-1 Ebisu-chō; ☉10.30am-7.30pm; ☒Ebisu-chō), with its designer labels and small basement-floor gourmet food hall and supermarket.

Global Lounge
Books

(グローバル・ラウンジ; ☑082-244-8145; www.hiroshima-no1.com/lounge.html; 2nd fl, Kensei Bldg, 1-5-17 Kamiya-chō; ☉11.30am-9pm Mon-Thu, to 11pm Fri & Sat; ☒Kamiya-chō-higashi) Global Lounge (aka Outsider) has a big selection of second-hand English-language books (mostly paperbacks). You can grab a coffee and use the internet (¥200 per 15 minutes) while you're here.

⊗ EATING

Hiroshima has an excellent range of Japanese and international eating options for all budgets, especially west of Peace Memorial Park and south of the Hon-dōri covered arcade. Many restaurants offer good-value set-lunch menus, and mall basements are budget-friendly. Hiroshima is famous for oysters (often available right

 **Day Trip
to Miyajima**

The small island of Miyajima (宮島) is home to some good hikes, temples and a much-photographed *torii* (shrine gate) that seems to float on the water at high tide. Unfortunately, the *torii* is closed for repairs for two to three years from June 2019, but **Itsukushima-jinja** (厳島神社; 1-1 Miyajima-chō; ¥300; ⊙6.30am-5.30pm Jan-Nov, to 5pm Dec), which traces its origins back as far as the late 6th century, is open throughout. The shrine's unique pier-like construction is a result of the island's sacred status: commoners were not allowed to set foot on the island and had to approach by boat through the *torii*.

Beyond the shrine, sacred **Misen** is Miyajima's highest mountain (530m), and the island's finest walk. You can avoid most of the uphill climb by taking the two-stage **ropeway** (弥山; www.miyajima -ropeway.info; ropeway one way/return adult ¥1000/1800, child ¥500/900; ⊙9am-5pm) with its giddying sea views, which leaves you with a 30-minute walk to the top, where there is an excellent observatory. The cheeky deer will eat your map right out of your pocket if you're not careful.

There are a few ferry options to Miyajima. The mainland ferry terminal is a short walk from Hiroden-miyajima-guchi tram stop, about 20 minutes from Itsukaichi station on tram line 2. **Setonaikai Kisen** operates high-speed ferries direct to Miyajima from Ujina Wharf. The walk from your cruise berth to the ferry pier can be up to a couple of kilometres – you may prefer a taxi. A handy **Aqua Net** ferry runs directly from the Peace Memorial Park.

Itsukushima-jinja
ITZAVU/SHUTTERSTOCK ©

on the dock) and *Hiroshima-yaki* (noodle- and meat-layered *okonomiyaki*; savoury pancakes).

Okonomi-mura
Okonomiyaki ¥

(お好み村; www.okonomimura.jp; 2nd-4th fl, 5-13 Shintenchi; dishes ¥800-1300; ⊙11am-2am; 🚊Ebisu-chō) This Hiroshima institution is a touristy but fun place to get acquainted with *okonomiyaki* and chat with the cooks over a hot griddle. There are 25 stalls spread over three floors, each serving up hearty variations of the local speciality. Pick a floor and find an empty stool at whichever counter takes your fancy. Look for the entrance stairs off Chūō-dōri, on the opposite side of the square to the white Parco shopping centre.

Tōshō
Tofu ¥¥

(豆匠; ☎082-506-1028; www.toufu-tosho. jp; 6-24 Hijiyama-chō; set meals ¥2000-5000; ⊙11am-3pm & 5-10pm Mon-Sat, to 9pm Sun; 🖋; 🚊Danbara-1-chōme) In a traditional wooden building overlooking a large garden with a pond and waterfall, Tōshō specialises in homemade tofu, served in a variety of tasty and beautifully presented forms by kimono-clad staff. Even the sweets are tofu based. There is a range of set courses, with some pictures and basic English on the menu.

INFORMATION

In addition to the tourist offices, check out Hiroshima Navigator (www.hiroshimacvb.jp) for tourism and practical information, as well as downloadable audio guides to the sights.

Hiroshima Rest House (広島市平和記念 公園レストハウス; ☎082-247-6738; www. mk-kousan.co.jp/rest-house; 1-1 Nakajima-machi; ⊙8.30am-7pm Aug, to 6pm Mar-Jul & Sep-Nov, to 5pm Dec-Feb; 🚊Genbaku-dōmu-mae) In Peace Memorial Park next to Motoyasu-bashi bridge; has comprehensive information, English-speaking staff and a small shop selling souvenirs.

Chefs at Okonomi-mura

Tourist Information Office (観光案内所; 📞082-261-1877; ⊙9am-5.30pm; 🛜) Inside Hiroshima Station near the south exit, with English-speaking staff. There is another branch at the **north (shinkansen) exit** (📞082-263-6822; ⊙9am-5.30pm).

 GETTING AROUND

Most sights in Hiroshima are accessible either on foot or with a short tram (streetcar) ride.

Hiroshima's trams (www.hiroden.co.jp) will get you almost anywhere you want to go for a flat fare of ¥180. You pay by dropping the fare into the machine by the driver as you get off the tram. If you have to change trams to get to your destination, you should ask for a *norikae-ken* (transfer ticket).

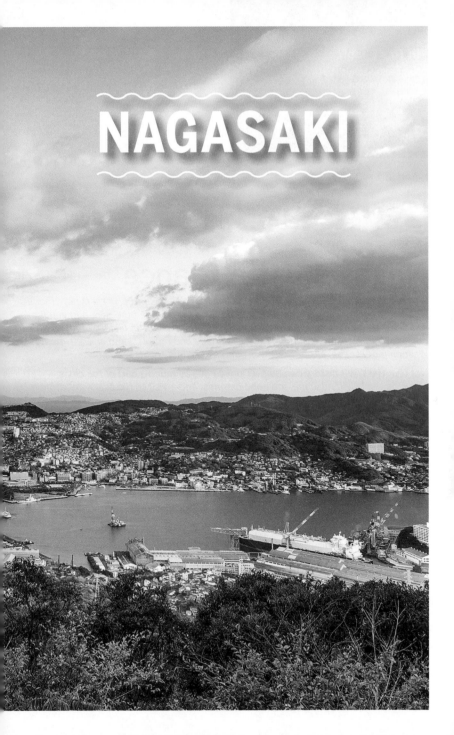

NAGASAKI

Nagasaki at a Glance

It's both unfortunate and important that the name Nagasaki (長崎) is synonymous with the dropping of the second atomic bomb. Spend some time here and you'll find that this welcoming, peaceful city also boasts a colourful history of trade with Europe and China, interesting churches, shrines and temples, and an East-meets-West culinary scene, all set prettily around a gracious harbour.

Not that the WWII history can be overlooked: it's as much a part of the city's fabric as the hilly landscape and cobblestones, and a visit to the scenes of atomic devastation is a must.

With a Day in Port

Visit the **Nagasaki Atomic Bomb Museum** (p168) and surrounding sites, then explore the beautiful gardens and historic homes of **Glover Garden** (p171). You can also take a cable car up **Inasa-yama** (p171) and soak in the hot baths of **Onsen Fukunoyu** (p171).

Best Places for...

Historic sites Dejima (p170)

Shopping Hamanmachi (p172)

Nagasaki-style kaiseki Shippoku Hamakatsu (p172)

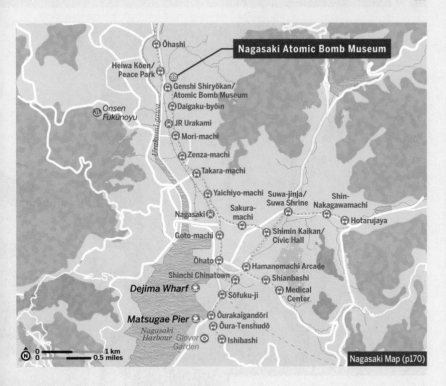

Nagasaki Map (p170)

Getting from the Port

Cruise ships dock at Matsugae Pier. It's a short walk from here to Ourakaigandori tram stop. A tram to downtown takes about five minutes.

Fast Facts

Money Currency exchange is available at the wharf.

Tourist information Information services greet arrivals. Also see p173 for tourist information offices.

Wi-fi There is free wi-fi at the port, JR Nagasaki Station, Dejima Wharf and many other locations.

Nagasaki National Peace Memorial Hall for the Atomic Bomb Victims

FIJPHOTO/SHUTTERSTOCK ©

Nagasaki Atomic Bomb Museum

Urakami, the hypocentre of the atomic explosion, is today a prosperous, peaceful suburb. While nuclear ruin seems comfortably far away seven decades later, many sights here keep the memory alive.

Great For...

☑ Don't Miss

Recording a message for peace, and hearing those left by others, at the Memorial Hall.

The Museum

On 9 August 1945, the world's second nuclear weapon detonated over Nagasaki. This sombre place recounts the city's destruction and loss of life through photos and artefacts, including mangled rocks, trees, furniture, pottery and clothing, a clock stopped at 11.02 (the time of the bombing), first-hand accounts from survivors, and stories of heroic relief efforts. Exhibits also include the post-bombing struggle for nuclear disarmament, and conclude with a chilling illustration of which nations bear nuclear arms.

Nagasaki National Peace Memorial Hall for the Atomic Bomb Victims

Adjacent to the museum and completed in 2003, this minimalist **memorial** (国立長崎原爆死没者追悼平和祈念館; www.peace-nagasaki.

Peace Park

RYUSHI/SHUTTERSTOCK ©

Peace Park
Atomic Bomb
Hypocentre Park
Heiwa Kōen/
Peace Park
Nagasaki National Peace
Memorial Hall for the
Atomic Bomb Victims
Genshi Shiryokan/
Atomic Bomb Museum
**Nagasaki
Atomic Bomb
Museum**

Explore Ashore

It's a short walk from Matsugae Pier to Ourakaigan-dori tram stop. The tram ride from here to the Atomic Bomb Museum takes about half an hour.

ℹ Need to Know

長崎原爆資料館; ☎095-844-1231; www. nagasakipeace.jp; 7-8 Hirano-machi; ¥200, audioguide ¥154; ⊗8.30am-6.30pm May-Aug, to 5.30pm Sep-Apr; ☒Genshi Shiryokan/ Atomic Bomb Museum

go.jp; 7-8 Hirano-machi; admission free; ⊗8.30am-6.30pm May-Aug, to 5.30pm Sep-Apr; ☒Heiwa Kōen/Peace Park) by Kuryū Akira is a profoundly moving place. It's best approached by quietly walking around the sculpted water basin, commemorating those who cried for water in their dying days. In the hall below, 12 'pillars of light', containing shelves of books of the names of the deceased, reach skyward. Listen to survivors' messages and leave your own digital message for peace at 'peace information counters'.

Atomic Bomb Hypocentre Park

A must-see for anyone coming to Nagasaki for its historic significance, this **park** (長崎爆心地公園; ☒Heiwa Kōen/Peace Park) houses a smooth, black-stone column that marks the point above which the atomic bomb exploded. Nearby are bomb-blasted

relics, including a section of the wall of the **Urakami Cathedral** (浦上天主堂; 1-79 Motō-machi; ⊗9am-5pm; ☒Atomic Bomb Museum).

Peace Park

North of the hypocentre, **Peace Park** (平和公園, Heiwa-kōen; ☒Ōhashi) is presided over by the 10-tonne bronze **Nagasaki Peace Statue** (平和祈念像), designed in 1955 by Kitamura Seibō. It also includes the dove-shaped Fountain of Peace (1969) and the Peace Symbol Zone, a sculpture garden with contributions on the theme of peace from around the world. On 9 August a rowdy antinuclear protest is held within earshot of the more formal official memorial ceremony for those lost to the bomb.

Take a Break

Stop by **Hibakusha no Mise** (被爆者の店; ☎095-844-8809; 8-20 Okamachi; ⊗8.45am-5pm) for snacks, candy, castella, toys or trinkets – profits go to hibakusha (atomic-bomb survivor) organisations.

◎ SIGHTS

Dejima Historic Site

(出島; ☎095-829-1194; www.nagasakidejima.
jp; 6-1 Dejima-machi; ¥510; ◎8am-7pm mid-Jul–
mid-Oct, to 6pm mid-Oct–mid-Jul; ☐Dejima) In
1641 the Tokugawa shogunate banished all
foreigners from Japan, with the exception
of one place: Dejima, an artificial island
in Nagasaki harbour. From then until the

1850s, this tiny Dutch trading post was the
sole sanctioned foreign presence in Japan.
Today, 17 buildings, walls and structures
(plus a miniature Dejima) have been painstakingly reconstructed here. The buildings
are as instructive inside as they are appealing outside, filled with exhibits covering
the spread of trade, Western learning and
culture, archaeological digs, and rooms

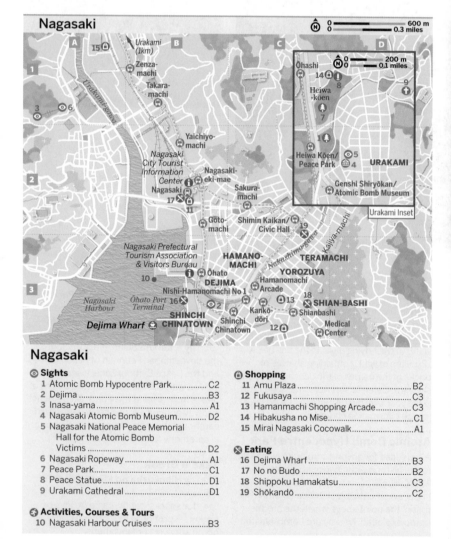

Nagasaki

combining Japanese tatami (tightly woven floor matting) with Western wallpaper. There's excellent English signage. Allow at least two hours.

Free walking-tour maps of the entire site are available, and there's even a kimono-rental shop (¥2000/6000 per hour/day) for those who want to feel even more historically connected.

Glover Garden   Gardens

(グラバー園; ☎095-822-8223; www.glover -garden.jp; 8-1 Minamiyamate-machi; adult/ student ¥610/300; ⏰8am-9.30pm May–mid-Jul, to 6pm mid-Jul–Apr; 🚋Ōura Tenshudō) Some two-dozen former homes of the city's Meiji-period European residents and other important buildings have been reassembled in this beautifully landscaped hillside garden, with breathtaking views across the harbour. Glover Garden is named after Scottish merchant and industrialist Thomas Glover (1838–1911), who built Japan's first railway and helped establish the shipbuilding industry, and whose arms-importing operations influenced the course of the Meiji Restoration.

Start by taking the moving walkways to the top of the hill, then work your way back down. The 'audio pen' guide, available near the ticket office, gives lots of detailed commentary and costs ¥700, although the map that comes with it can be confusing. The garden is about a 10-minute walk from the port.

Inasa-yama   Mountain

(稲佐山, Mt Inasa) West of the harbour, the **Nagasaki Ropeway cable car** (長崎ロープウエイ; ☎095-861-3640; www.nagasaki -ropeway.jp; 8-1 Fuchi-machi; return ¥1230; ⏰9am-10pm; 🚋Mori-machi) ascends every 15 to 20 minutes to the top of 333m-high Inasa-yama, offering superb views over Nagasaki. A tower at the top offers even more panoramic views. Elsewhere on the mountain is **Onsen Fukunoyu** (温泉ふくの湯; ☎095-833-1126; 451-23 Iwami-machi; ¥800; ⏰9.30am-1am Sun-Thu, to 2am Fri & Sat), which has wet baths, as well as *ganbanyoku* stone baths (an additional ¥700), with tempera-

🍴 Castella Cake

No visit to Nagasaki is complete without a taste of *castella*, a Portuguese-inspired dense sponge cake. This yellow, brick-shaped treat has become a must-have Nagasaki treat and souvenir. There seems to be a *castella* shop by every tourist attraction.

Two of the finer shops are **Fukusaya** (福砂屋; ☎095-821-2938; www.fukusaya. co.jp; 3-1 Funadaiku-machi; ⏰8.30am-8pm; 🚋Shianbashi), making the cakes since 1624, and **Shōkandō** (匠寛堂; ☎095-826-1123; www.shokando.jp; 7-24 Uo-no-machi; ⏰9am-7pm; 🚋Megane-bashi), across from Megane-bashi, supplier to the Japanese imperial family.

MELON SODA/SHUTTERSTOCK ©

tures from a balmy 38°C to an are-you-nuts 70°C. Family-style (private) baths are also available.

⏩ TOURS

One-hour **Nagasaki Harbour Cruises** (長崎港めぐりクルーズ; ☎095-822-5002; Nagasaki Harbour Terminal Bldg; adult/child ¥2000/1000; ⏰noon & 4pm Thu-Mon) are a great way to see the picturesque city. Check at the ferry terminal for up-to-date schedules.

🔒 SHOPPING

Local crafts and products are sold around and opposite JR Nagasaki Station, as well as in shops along busy Hamano-machi

SANGA PARK/ALAMY STOCK PHOTO ©

Dejima Wharf

shopping arcade near Shianbashi tram stop. Ignore **tortoiseshell crafts** (べっ甲) sold around town: these may land you in jail if the shell is from an endangered species.

For mall shopping, **Amu Plaza** (アミュプラザ長崎; 1-1 Onouemachi; ⓡ JR Nagasaki) at the station is nice and easy, and you can't miss **Mirai Nagasaki Cocowalk** (みらい長崎ココウォーク; ☎ 095-848-5509; www.cocowalk.jp; 1-55 Morimachi; ⏰ 10am-9pm; ⓡ Morimachi, ⓡ JR Urakami), a massive shopping, dining and cinema complex with a Ferris wheel (¥500) on the roof.

Youme Town, with ubiquitous mall shops, is by the harbour, and in the city centre **Hamanmachi** (www.hamanmachi.com/hamabura_map/en.htm) is a covered arcade housing an astonishing 700 shops.

✖ EATING

The Mirai Nagasaki Cocowalk shopping mall features some 20 restaurants on its 4th and 5th floors. Other good places for restaurant browsing and great views include the restaurant floors of the shopping mall Amu Plaza, especially the restaurants with a view on its 5th floor, and the harbourside **Dejima Wharf** (出島ワーフ; ☎ 095-828-3939; www.dejimawharf.com; 1-1-109 Dejimamachi; ⓡ Dejima).

Shippoku Hamakatsu   Kaiseki ¥¥
(卓袱浜勝; ☎ 095-826-8321; www.sippoku.jp; 6-50 Kajiya-machi; lunch/dinner from ¥1500/3500, shippoku courses ¥3900-7900; ⏰ 11am-10pm; ⓡ Shianbashi) Come here if you'd like to experience *shippoku-ryōri* (Nagasaki-style *kaiseki*) and still have something left to spend at the shops. Menus are filling and varied, and there's a choice of Japanese- or Western-style seating.

No no Budo   Buffet ¥¥
(野の葡萄; ☎ 095-895-8515; 5th fl, Amu Plaza, 1-1 Onouemachi; buffet lunch/dinner ¥1600/2100; ⏰ 11am-11pm; ⓡ Nagasaki-eki-mae, ⓡ JR Nagasaki) Come for the buffet, stay for the view at the new Nagasaki branch of this much-loved casual buffet chain. Dozens of savoury and dessert offerings concentrate on organic and local produce, including an

entire counter of Nagasaki specialities. The views from the far windows overlooking the harbour offer a great perspective on the city.

INFORMATION

A new multilingual **call centre** (☏095-825-5175) caters to English-speaking visitors.

Nagasaki City Tourist Information Center (長崎市総合観光案内所; ☏095-823-3631; www. at-nagasaki.jp/foreign/english; 1st fl, JR Nagasaki Station; ⊙8am-8pm) Has brochures and maps in English. The English spoken is minimal, though.

Nagasaki Prefectural Tourism Association & Visitors Bureau (☏095-828-9407; www. visit-nagasaki.com; 8th fl, 14-10 Motofuna-machi; ⊙9am-5.30pm; 🚇Ōhato)

❶ GETTING AROUND

Nagasaki is easy to navigate, with most sights easily accessible on foot or by tram.

There are four colour-coded tram routes numbered 1, 3, 4 and 5 (route 2 is for special events), and stops are signposted in English. It costs ¥120 to travel anywhere in town, but you can transfer for free at the Shinchi Chinatown (新地中華街) stop only: ask for a *noritsugi* (transfer pass). Alternatively, all day, unlimited tram passes are available for ¥500 from tourist information centres.

KANAZAWA

Kanazawa at a Glance

The array of cultural attractions in Kanazawa (金沢) makes the city the drawcard of the Hokuriku region and a rival to Kyoto as the historical jewel of mainland Japan. Best known for Kenroku-en, a castle garden dating from the 17th century, it also boasts beautifully preserved samurai and geisha districts, attractive temples, a wealth of museums and a wonderful market (and far fewer tourists than Kyoto – for now).

With a Day in Port

Stroll the serene pathways of **Kenroku-en** (p178), one of Japan's best gardens, and pause for reflection at nearby **DT Suzuki Museum** (p179). You can explore **Kanazawa Castle Park's** (p180) original and masterfully recreated buildings, surrounded by paths and gardens, and then step back in time at former geisha house **Kaikarō** (p182).

Best Places for...

Thatched cottages Shirakawa-gō (p184)

Tea ceremonies Gyokusen-an Rest House (p181)

Market shopping Ōmi-chō Market (p182)

Golden souvenirs Sakuda Gold Leaf Company (p184)

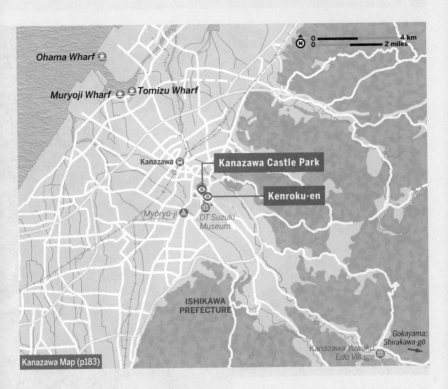

Kanazawa Map (p183)

Ohama Wharf

Muryoji Wharf · Tomizu Wharf

Kanazawa

Kanazawa Castle Park

Kenroku-en

Myōryū-ji · DT Suzuki Museum

ISHIKAWA PREFECTURE

Kanazawa Yuwaku Edo Village

Gokayama; Shirakawa-gō

Getting from the Port

Some cruise operators offer a shuttle service for the short trip to downtown – it usually takes about 20 minutes. Otherwise, a taxi (around ¥2500) is your best bet.

Fast Facts

Money Head into town for ATMs and currency exchange.

Tourist information Temporary information booths greet arrivals. See also p187 for tourist information centres.

Wi-fi Free wi-fi is available at the port, JR Kanazawa Station, Ishikawa Foundation for International Exchange (p187), and key sights around town.

Kenroku-en

Those in the know rate Kenroku-en as among the finest gardens in Japan, and a visit doesn't disappoint. Strolling the gentle paths reveals delightful details and vistas at every turn, and each season brings its own charm and palette.

Great For...

☑ Don't Miss

Look for poles, ropes and wires supporting and guiding trees and expert gardeners at work.

The Gardens

This Edo-period garden draws its name (*kenroku* means 'combined six') from a renowned Sung-dynasty garden in China that dictated six attributes for perfection: seclusion, spaciousness, artificiality, antiquity, abundant water and broad views. Kenroku-en has them all. Arrive before the crowds.

It's believed that the garden, originally belonging to an outer villa of Kanazawa-jō, was developed from the 1620s to the 1840s and was so named in 1822. It was first opened to the public in 1871.

Sigure-tei Teahouse

Kenroku-en's Sigure-tei teahouse offers green (¥310) and *matcha* tea (¥720), accompanied by seasonal, traditional

DT Suzuki Museum

LEE YIU TUNG/SHUTTERSTOCK © ARCHITECT: TANIGUCHI, YOSHIO

Kenroku-en

21st Century Museum of
Contemporary Art

Ishikawa Prefectural
Museum of Traditional
Products & Crafts

DT Suzuki Museum

Explore Ashore

Buses regularly make the 20-minute trip (¥200) from JR Kanazawa Station to the gardens. A taxi from the station costs around ¥1200 and takes about 10 minutes.

❶ Need to Know

兼六園; ☑076-234-3800; www.pref.ishika wa.jp/siro-niwa/kenrokuen/e; 1-1 Marunouchi; adult/child/senior ¥310/100/free; ⊘7am-6pm Mar–mid-Oct, 8am-4.30pm mid-Oct–Feb

Japanese sweets and gorgeous views, in a beautiful traditional building.

What's Nearby?

The spiritual **DT Suzuki Museum**
(鈴木大拙館; ☑076-221-8011; www.kanazawa -museum.jp/daisetz; 3-4-20 Honda-machi; adult/child/senior ¥300/free/200; ⊘9.30am-4.30pm Tue-Sun) is a tribute to Daisetsu Teitaro Suzuki, one of the foremost Buddhist philosophers of the modern age. Published in Japanese and English, Suzuki is largely credited with introducing Zen to the West. This stunning concrete complex embodies the heart of Zen.

A low-slung glass cylinder, 113m in diameter, forms the perimeter of the **21st Century Museum of Contemporary Art** (金沢21世紀美術館; ☑076-220-2800; www. kanazawa21.jp; 1-2-1 Hirosaka; ⊘10am-6pm Tue-Thu & Sun, to 8pm Fri & Sat). Museum entry is free, but admission fees are charged for special exhibitions. Inside, galleries are arranged like boxes on a tray. Check the website for event info and fees.

The small **Ishikawa Prefectural Museum of Traditional Products & Crafts** (石川県立伝統産業工芸館; ☑076-262-2020; www.ishikawa-densankan.jp; 2-1 Kenroku-machi; adult/child/senior ¥260/100/200; ⊘9am-5pm, closed 3rd Thu of month Apr-Nov, closed Thu Dec-Mar) offers fine displays of over 20 regional crafts; many pieces are for sale if you fall in love with something. Pick up the free English-language audioguide.

ANDREAS H/SHUTTERSTOCK ©

Kanazawa Castle Park

The original castle on this site burned down long ago, with only one original gate still standing, supplemented by a couple of skilful reconstructions. Nevertheless, it's an imposing sight; spend an hour or two wandering through the gardens, admiring the buildings and conjuring the castle's dramatic past.

Great For...

☑ Don't Miss

A tea ceremony at Gyokusen-an Rest House in the adjacent Gyokusen Inmaru Garden.

History

Originally built in 1580, this massive structure was called the 'castle of 1000 tatami' and housed the Maeda clan for 14 generations until it was destroyed by fire in 1881. The elegant surviving gate, **Ishikawa-mon** (built in 1788), provides a dramatic entry from Kenroku-en; holes in its turret were designed for hurling rocks at invaders. Two additional buildings, the **Hishi-yagura** (diamond-shaped turret) and **Gojikken-nagaya** (armoury), were reconstructed using traditional means in 2001.

What's Nearby?

Adjacent to the Kanazawa Castle Park, **Gyokusen Inmaru Garden** (玉泉院丸庭園, Gyokusen Inmaru Teien; ☑076-234-3800; www.pref.ishikawa.jp/siro-niwa/kanazawajou/e/gyokusen-in; 1-1 Marunouchi; admission free;

Gyokusen Inmaru Garden

MANUEL ASCANIO/SHUTTERSTOCK ©

Explore Ashore

The castle is directly across from Kenroku-en, so it's easy to move from one to the other. From JR Kanazawa Station, take a bus (20 minutes, ¥200) or taxi (¥1200, 10 minutes).

❶ Need to Know

金沢城公園, Kanazawa-jō Kōen; ☑076-234-3800; www.kanazawa-tourism.com/eng/guide/guide1_1.php?no=2; 1-1 Marunouchi; buildings/grounds ¥310/free; ⊘grounds 7am-6pm Mar-15 Oct, 8am-5pm 16 Oct-Feb, castle 9am-4.30pm

⊘7am-6pm) was first constructed in 1634 but abandoned in the Meiji era. Its five-year reconstruction was completed in 2015. Features include a small waterfall, bridges and many traditional elements. While the garden's focal point is the Gyokusen-an Rest House, it's the overall picture of beauty and refinement that impresses most. The garden and teahouse are illuminated spectacularly on Friday and Saturday evenings between sunset and 9pm.

The handsome **Gyokusen-an Rest House** (玉泉庵; ☑076-234-3800; 1-1 Marunouchi; tea ceremony ¥720; ⊘7am-6pm Mar-15 Oct, 8am-5pm 16 Oct-Feb) is the perfect setting in which to experience *cha-dō* (a tea ceremony), one of Japan's oldest,

most intricate and unique customs. Enjoy serene views accompanied by *matcha* green tea with *wagashi* (Japanese sweets; ¥720).

Audio buffs will dig the **Kanazawa Phonograph Museum** (金沢蓄音器館; ☑076-232-3066; www.kanazawastation.com/kanazawa-phonograph-museum; 2-11-21 Owari-chō; adult/student/senior ¥300/free/200; ⊘10am-5pm) of old-time phonographs and SP records, with daily demonstrations at 11am, 2pm and 4pm.

Ishikawa Local Products Center (石川県観光物産館, Ishikawa-ken Kankō-bussankan; ☑076-222-7788; www.kanazawa-kankou.jp; 2-20 Kenroku-machi; ⊘10am-6pm) offers an overview of Kanazawa crafts, on the kitschy side, under one roof.

◎ SIGHTS

Just north of the Asano-gawa, Higashi-chaya-gai (Higashi Geisha District) is an enclave of narrow streets established early in the 19th century for geisha to entertain wealthy patrons. The slatted wooden facades of the geisha houses are romantically preserved. It's very picturesque around sunset.

Ōmi-chō Market   Market

(近江町市場; 35 Ōmi-chō; ⏱9am-5pm) Between Kanazawa Station and Katamachi you'll find this market, reminiscent of Tokyo's old Tsukiji market. A bustling warren of fishmongers, buyers and restaurants, it's a great place to watch everyday people in action or indulge in the freshest sashimi and local produce. The nearest bus stop is Musashi-ga-tsuji.

Kaikarō   Museum

(懐華樓; ☎076-253-0591; www.kaikaro.jp/eng/index.html; 1-14-8 Higashiyama; adult/child ¥750/500; ⏱9am-5pm) In Higashi-chaya-gai, Kaikarō is an early-19th-century geisha house refinished with contemporary fittings and art, including a red-lacquered staircase. If your cruise schedule allows, evening geisha performances include a short lecture in English by the proprietor, followed by a demonstration of traditional party games by geisha themselves. Performances last 1½ hours; tickets start at ¥6500.

Myōryū-ji   Buddhist Temple

(妙立寺; Ninja-dera; ☎076-241-0888; www.myouryuji.or.jp/en.html; 1-2-12 Nomachi; adult/child ¥1000/700; ⏱by reservation only 9am-4pm Mon-Fri, to 4.30pm Sat & Sun) Completed in 1643 in Teramachi, the temple was designed to protect its lord from attack. It contains hidden stairways, escape routes, secret chambers, concealed tunnels and trick doors. Contrary to popular belief, it has nothing to do with ninja. Admission is by tour only (in Japanese with an English guidebook). Phone for reservations with English-speaking staff.

Nagamachi Yūzen-kan   Museum

(長町友禅館; ☎076-264-2811; www.kagayuzen-club.co.jp; 2-6-16 Nagamachi; ¥350; ⏱9.30am-5pm Thu-Mon Mar-Nov) In

Ōmi-chō Market

TKURIKAWA/GETTY IMAGES ©

Kanazawa

Kanazawa

a non-traditional building at the edge of
the Nagamachi district, the Nagamachi
Yūzen-kan displays some splendid
examples of *Kaga Yūzen* kimono dyeing
and demonstrates the process. Enquire
ahead about trying the silk-dyeing process
yourself (¥4000).

Shima
Museum

(志摩; ☎076-252-5675; www.ochaya-shima.
com; 1-13-21 Higashiyama; adult/child ¥500/300;
⊙9am-6pm) This traditional-style former
geisha house dates from 1820 and has an
impressive collection of elaborate combs,
and picks for *shamisen* (three-stringed
instruments resembling a lute or banjo).

 Exploring
Shirakawa-gō

The remote, mountainous districts of
Shirakawa-gō (白川郷) and Gokayama
are best known for farmhouses in the
thatched *gasshō-zukuri* style. They're
rustic and lovely whether set against the
vibrant colours of spring, draped with
the gentle mists of autumn, or peeking
through a carpet of snow, and they hold
a special place in the Japanese heart.

Most of Shirakawa-gō's sights (and
crowds) are in **Ogimachi** (often referred
to simply as Shirakawa-gō). The less
crowded, more isolated villages of
Suganuma and **Ainokura**, in the Gokayama district of Toyama Prefecture,
have the most ambience; other sights
are spread over many kilometres along
Rte 156. All three villages are Unesco
World Heritage Sites.

Passionate debate continues around
the impact that tour buses have upon
these unique communities, and how
best to mitigate disruption to local
life. To avoid the crowds, steer clear of
weekends, holidays and cherry-blossom
and autumn-foliage seasons.

A plethora of day tours are available
from Kanazawa; ask at the Kanazawa
Tourist Information Center (p187).
Nōhi Bus (濃飛バス; ☑0577-32-1688;
www.nouhibus.co.jp/english) services
Shirakawa-gō (1½ hours, ¥3600 round-
trip) approximately once an hour, and
Suganuma slightly less frequently (one
hour, ¥3600 round-trip); reserve your
ticket in advance.

Suganuma
BEIBAOKE/SHUTTERSTOCK ©

**Kanazawa
Yuwaku Edo Village**   Historic Building
(金沢湯涌江戸村, Kanazawa Yuwaku Edo-mura;
☑076-235-1267; www.kanazawa-museum.jp/edo
mura/english/index.html; 35-1 Yurakuwara-machi;
adult/student/senior ¥300/free/200; ☺9am-5pm
Wed-Mon; 🚌12) In Yuwaku Onsen, about 14km
southeast of Kanazawa along Rte 10, you'll
find this attractive collection of reconstructed Edo-period buildings arranged as an
open-air museum showcasing artefacts from
the era (1603–1868). Take the bus from JR
Kanazawa Station (¥600, 45 minutes) – get
off at Yuwaku Onsen stop and walk for about
300m, following the signs.

TOURS

Kanazawa Walking Tours   Walking
(☑803 044 3191; www.kanazawa-tours.com;
half-day tours from ¥3700) KWT's English-
speaking guides get rave reviews from
happy customers. Public tours go ahead
when a minimum of six people have
booked; private tours start at ¥22,000 per
half-day and are fully customisable.

🔒 SHOPPING

The Hirosaka shopping street, between
Kōrinbō 109 department store and
Kenroku-en, has some upmarket craft
shops on its south side. Other major
department stores are found towards JR
Kanazawa Station (Forus, Meitetsu M'za)
and on Hyakumangoku-dōri between Kōrin-
bō and Katamachi (Daiwa, Atrio Shopping
Plaza). The funky Tatemachi Shopping
Promenade is also here.

**Sakuda Gold Leaf
Company**   Arts & Crafts
(金銀箔工芸さくだ; ☑076-251-6777; www.
goldleaf-sakuda.jp; 1-3-27 Higashiyama; ☺9am-
6pm) Here you can observe the *kinpaku*
(gold-leaf) process and pick up all sorts
of gilded souvenirs, including pottery, lacquerware and, er...golf balls. It also serves
tea containing flecks of gold leaf, which is
reputedly good for rheumatism. Even the
toilet walls are lined with gold and platinum.

Murakami   Food

(村上; ☑076-264-4223; 2-3-32 Nagamachi;
⊙8.30am-5pm) If a flowering tree made of
candy excites you, head to Murakami. At this
handsome *wagashi* (Japanese sweets) shop
you'll also find *fukusamochi* (red-bean paste
and pounded rice in a crêpe) and *kakiho*
(soybean flour rolled in black sesame seeds).

EATING & DRINKING

The shiny, architecturally stunning JR
Kanazawa Station building is brimming
with eateries. Its neighbour, Forus department store (p186), has excellent dining
floors, as does the basement of Meitetsu
M'Za department store, opposite Ōmi-chō
Market (p182) with its fresh-from-the-boat
restaurants.

Daiba Kanazawa Ekimae   Izakaya ¥

(台場金沢駅前店; ☑076-263-9191; Kanazawa
Miyako Hotel 1F, 6-10 Konohana-machi; items
from ¥460; ⊙11am-3pm & 5pm-midnight) This
trendy spot in the Kanazawa Miyako Hotel
building has a comprehensive Japanese
menu and a limited English one with all the

Western favourites and some local specialities. It's a great place for your first *izakaya*
(pub-restaurant) experience.

Full of Beans   Cafe ¥

(フルオブビーンズ; ☑076-222-3315; www.
fullofbeans.jp; 41-1 Satomi-chō; meals from ¥850;
⊙11.30am-3.30pm & 5-10pm Thu-Tue) A variety of
Japanese dishes and *yōshoku* (Western-style
meals) are served at this stylish cafe in the
quieter backstreets of Katamachi – the
website will give you a sense of the vibe. It's
a good place to try inimitable Kanazawa
speciality *hanton raisu:* a bowl of rice topped
with an omelette, fried seafood, ketchup and
tartare sauce (available at lunch).

Curio Espresso
& Vintage Design   Cafe ¥

(☑076-231-5543; 1-13 Yasue-cho; sandwiches
from ¥600; ⊙9am-6pm Sat-Mon, from 8am Wed-
Fri) Brewing Seattle-style coffee that would
satisfy even the most hardened coffee
snob, this sweet little cafe is a quaint spot
to grab a break near the station. The menu
features Western favourites (including barbecue pulled pork) you'll be hard-pressed
to find elsewhere in this part of Japan.

Forus (p186)

TK KURIKAWA/SHUTTERSTOCK ©

Traditional Crafts

During the Edo period Kanazawa's ruling Maeda family fuelled the growth of important crafts. Many are still practised today.

Kanazawa and Wajima lacquerware
Decoration is applied to luminous black lacquerware through *maki-e* (decorating with gold or silver power) or gilding. Artists must take great care that dust does not settle on the final product.

Ōhi pottery The deliberately simple, almost primitive designs, rough surfaces, irregular shapes and monochromatic glazes of Ōhi pottery have been favoured by tea practitioners since the early Edo period.

Kutani porcelain Known for its elegant shapes, graceful designs and bright, bold colours. Typical motifs include birds, flowers, trees and landscapes.

Kaga Yūzen silk dyeing This laborious, specialised method is characterised by strong colours and realistic depictions of nature, such as flower petals that have begun to brown around the edges. White lines between elements where ink has washed away are typical.

Gold leaf A lump of pure gold the size of a ¥10 coin is rolled to the size of a tatami mat, becoming as thin as 0.0001mm. The gold leaf is then cut into squares of 10.9cm – the size used for mounting on walls, murals or paintings – or cut again for gilding on lacquerware or pottery. Over 98% of Japan's gold leaf is produced in Kanazawa.

Ōhi pottery
QUANG MINH/SHUTTERSTOCK ©

Forus Food Hall ¥
(☎076-265-8111; www.forus.co.jp/kanazawa; 3-1 Horikawa Shin-machi; ⊙11am-10pm) Forus department store has a wide variety of great Japanese restaurants and bakeries on its 6th floor.

Sentō Chinese ¥¥
(仙桃; ☎076-234-0669; 2F Ōmichō Ichiba, 88 Aokusa-machi; dishes from ¥650, set menus from ¥980; ⊙11am-3pm & 5-10.30pm Wed-Mon) Upstairs in Ōmi-chō Market (p182), chefs from Hong Kong prepare authentic Szechuan- and Hong Kong–style dishes (including dim sum) from scratch. Delicious set menus are excellent value.

Janome-sushi Honten Sushi ¥¥
(蛇之目寿司本店; ☎076-231-0093; 1-1-12 Kōrinbō; set menu ¥3000, Kaga ryōri sets from ¥4400; ⊙noon-2pm & 5.30-10.30pm Thu-Tue) Kanazawa institution Janome-sushi Honten has been known for sashimi and Kaga cuisine since 1931.

Kanazawa Todoroki-tei Bistro ¥¥
(金沢とどろき亭; ☎076-252-5755; 1-2-1 Higashi-yama; plates from ¥1500; ⊙11.30am-3.30pm & 6-11.30pm) The art-deco, woody, candelit atmosphere of this Western-style bistro near Higashi-chaya-gai is a big selling point. The Taisho-era (1912–26) building with vaulted ceilings is a little rough around the edges, but that's part of its charm.

Restaurant Jiyūken Shokudo ¥¥
(レストラン自由軒; ☎076-252-1996; www.jiyuken.com; 1-6-6 Higashiyama; meals ¥700-1890; ⊙11.30am-3pm & 5-9pm) This *shokudō* (all-round, inexpensive restaurant) in the heart of Higashi-chaya-gai has been serving *yōshoku* (Western food) – or at least Japanese takes on Western food – such as omelettes, hamburgers and curry rice, since 1909. Daily set lunches (¥995) are good value.

Chōhachi Kanazawa Ekimae-ten Japanese ¥¥
(長八 金沢駅前店; ☎076-256-1843; www.cho-hachi.jp; 5-5 Konohana-machi; items from ¥420; ⊙11am-11pm) This upmarket regional *izakaya* has an emphasis on seafood – as

you'd expect – with plenty of sushi and sashimi to sample in a classy though booze-friendly setting.

Kaiseki Tsuruko
Japanese ¥¥¥

(懐石 つる幸; ☎076-264-2375; www.turukou. com; 6-5 Takaoka-machi; lunch/dinner from ¥10,000/15,000; ⊙noon-3pm & 6-10pm) *Kaiseki* (Japanese haute cuisine) dining is a holistic experience of hospitality, art and originality. This outstanding restaurant is a true gourmand's delight, offering an experience beyond what you might enjoy in a ryokan. Dress to impress.

Oriental Brewing
Brewery

(☎076-255-6378; www.orientalbrewing.com; 3-2-22 Higashiyama; ⊙11am-10pm) You can't miss this trendy brewhouse at the entrance to Higashi-chaya-gai: it's always humming with Japanese and international guests, who love the mellow, friendly vibe and the original yeasty ales brewed on-site.

❶ INFORMATION

Check out https://visitkanazawa.jp for general city information.

Kanazawa Tourist Information Center (石川 県金沢観光情報センター; ☎076-232-6200, KGGN 076-232-3933; http://kggn.sakura.ne.jp; 1 Hirooka-machi; ⊙9am-7pm) This brilliant office inside JR Kanazawa Station, one of Japan's best, has helpful staff, maps and pamphlets in a variety of languages, and the excellent, free English-language magazine *Eye on Kanazawa*. The Goodwill Guide Network (KGGN) is also here to assist with free guiding in English – two weeks' notice is requested.

Ishikawa Foundation for International Exchange (☎076-262-5931; www.ifie.or.jp; 1-5-3 Honmachi; ⊙9am-8pm Mon-Fri, to 5pm Sat & Sun) Offers information, a library, satellite-TV news and free internet access. It's on the 3rd floor of the Rifare building, a few minutes' walk southeast of JR Kanazawa Station.

❶ GETTING AROUND
BICYCLE

Bikes can be rented from **JR Kanazawa Station Rent-a-Cycle** (駅レンタサイクル; ☎076-261-

🍴 Kanazawa Specialities

Seafood is the staple of Kanazawa's *Kaga ryōri* (Kaga cuisine); even the most humble train-station *bentō* (boxed meal) usually features some type of fish. *Oshizushi*, a thin layer of fish pressed atop vinegar rice, is said to be the precursor to modern sushi. Another favourite is *jibuni*, flour-coated duck or chicken stewed with shiitake and green vegetables.

Jibuni
BONCHAN/SHUTTERSTOCK ©

1721; per hour/day ¥200/1200; ⊙8am-8.30pm) and **Hokutetsu Rent-a-Cycle** (北鉄レンタサイ クル; ☎076-263-0919; per 4hr/day ¥630/1050; ⊙8am-5.30pm), both by the station's west exit.

There's also a pay-as-you-go bicycle-rental system called 'Machi-nori'. For the low-down in English, a downloadable map is available at www. machi-nori.jp.

BUS

Buses depart from the circular terminus in front of JR Kanazawa Station's east exit. Any bus from station stop 7, 8 or 9 will take you to the city centre (¥200). The round-trip journey is free if you have a JR pass. The Kanazawa Loop Bus (single ride/day pass ¥200/500, every 15 minutes from 8.30am to 6pm) circles the major tourist attractions in 45 minutes. On Saturday, Sunday and holidays, the Machi-bus goes to Kōrinbō for ¥100. Purchase day passes from the Hokutetsu Kankō service centre inside JR Kanazawa Station; there's another centre opposite the Ōmi-chō Market bus stop.

For more information, see www.hokutetsu. co.jp/en/en_round.

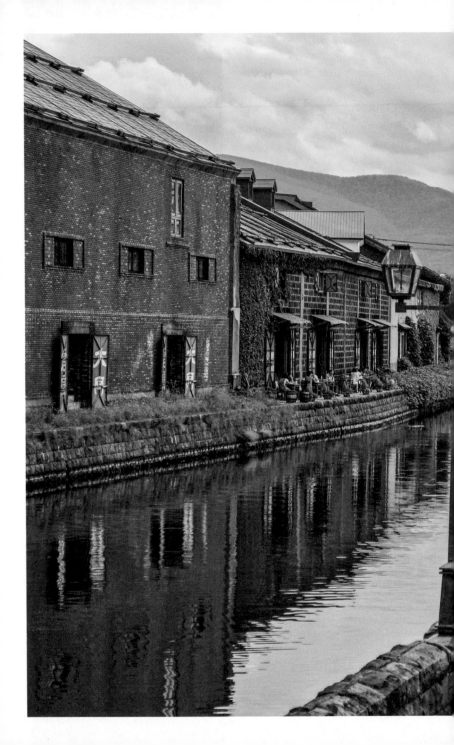

HOKKAIDŌ

Hokkaidō at a Glance

Hokkaidō (北海道) is a land of wide-open spaces, with large swathes of wilderness, primeval forests, tropical-blue caldera lakes and bubbling hot springs. In the summer, all this (plus the cooler, drier weather) draws hikers, cyclists and strollers, while winter is a different beast entirely, with cold fronts from Siberia bringing huge dumps of light, powdery snow. The island's stunning natural scenery tends to overshadow everything else that Japan's northernmost island has to offer, which is a lot: there is excellent food, a vibrant capital city and a compelling history.

With a Day in Port

In Otaru, explore the museums and restaurants along historic **Otaru Canal** (p198). In Sapporo, visit Japan's oldest **brewery** (p194) or the Hōheikyō **hot spring** (p201). Take in the views from **Hakodate-yama** (p202) in Hakodate, and in Kushiro make tracks for **Kushiro-shitsugen National Park** (p197).

Best Places for...

Seafood Kikuyo Shokudo (p203)
Souvenir shopping Kitaichi Sangōkan (p198)
Ramen Menya Saimi (p200)
Snow sports Sapporo Teine (p200)

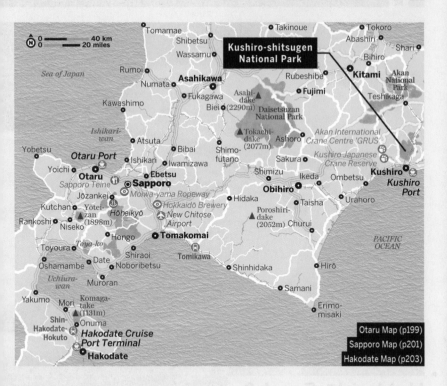

Otaru Map (p199)

Sapporo Map (p201)

Hakodate Map (p203)

Getting from the Port

Hokkaidō has three port areas: Otaru (near Sapporo), Hakodate and Kushiro.

Otaru Otaru Port is a 1.5km walk from Otaru Canal and 2km from Otaru Station. From here regular trains make the 30-minute journey to Sapporo.

Hakodate A regular shuttle (¥320, 30 minutes) runs between the Cruise Port Terminal and the main train station; a taxi costs about ¥2000. Buses 1 and 19 also head to the city centre.

Kushiro The port is a five-minute walk to Kushiro Fisherman's Wharf MOO, 15 minutes to downtown. From Nishi-koku Pier 4 it's a 15-minute drive to downtown.

Fast Facts

Otaru ATMs accepting foreign cards are at Canal Plaza. There is tourist information at Canal Plaza (p199) and Otaru Station. Wi-fi is free at Otaru Station.

Hakodate There are plenty of ATMs in the city centre. Tourist information can be found at the cruise port and at JR Hakodate Station. Wi-fi is available at the pier, main train station and on trams.

Kushiro Look for Japan Post Bank and 7-Eleven ATMs at Kushiro Station. Tourist-information booths greet arrivals and there's also a tourist office (p205). There is wi-fi is free at the port and Kushiro Fisherman's Wharf MOO (p205).

Ramen

MACKNIMAL/SHUTTERSTOCK ©

Hokkaidō Food & Beer Culture

Hokkaidō is a fantastic place to eat, serving up specialities different from what you might find elsewhere in Japan – thanks to its bountiful land, ample coast and a climate that favours belly-warming dishes. Sapporo has the liveliest dining scene, while in coastal areas, fresh, seasonal seafood is tops.

Great For...

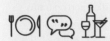

☑ Don't Miss

The Tsugaru Strait is famous for its squid, which can be sampled in Hakodate's morning seafood market.

Food

Want to make the most of your meals in Hokkaidō? Keep an eye out for the following regional delicacies.

Seafood

For many Japanese travellers, Hokkaidō is synonymous with crab. Winter is the season for *tarabagani* (タラバガニ; king crab), *zuwaigani* (ズワイガニ; snow crab) and *kegani* (毛蟹; horse hair crab) from the frigid waters of the Sea of Okhotsk. Restaurants in Sapporo do lavish crab feasts but you don't have to spend heaps: *kani-jiru* (かに汁) – miso soup made with crab – is a decadent treat that many *shokudō* (inexpensive restaurants) will serve.

Summer, meanwhile, is *uni* (うに; sea urchin) season. Fish markets, sushi restaurants and *shokudō* serve *uni-don* (うに

King crab

Eating Out

If you're generally an adventurous (or curious) eater, don't let the absence of an English menu put you off. Instead, tell the staff (or ideally the chef), 'omakase de onegaishimasu' (I'll leave it up to you).

Almost every city in Hokkaidō, large or small, has its own ji-biru (地ビール; microbrew). Microbrewed beer makes a great companion for local dishes.

丼), a bowl of rice topped with a mountain of fresh roe; you can also get it with other toppings, for example kaisen-don (海鮮丼; mixed seafood on rice).

Spring is the start of squid season, which moves slowly north through autumn. Hakodate is particularly known for squid (it even has a squid festival!). Try ika-sōmen (イカそうめん), which is raw squid sliced thin like noodles.

Ramen

In Sapporo the signature style is hearty miso-ramen (味噌ラーメン) and in Hakodate, it's shio-ramen (塩ラーメン), a light, salt-seasoned broth. In a nod to two of the prefecture's staple products, butter and corn, you'll often have the option to top off your ramen with either (or both).

Jingisukan

This dish of charcoal-grilled mutton is the unofficial symbol of Hokkaidō, a legacy of the island's short-lived, 19th-century sheep-rearing program. Its name – a Japanese rendering of Genghis Khan – comes from the unique shape of the cast-iron hotplate used to grill the meat, thought to resemble the warlord's helmet. The meat is grilled on the peak of the hotplate, allowing the juices to run down the sides to the onions and leeks sizzling on the brim. Jingisukan (ジンギスカン) is served all over the island and is best accompanied by copious amounts of beer.

Beer

Sapporo Brewery, founded in 1876, was Japan's first brewery. Its first brewmaster, Nakagawa Seibei, trained in Germany, bringing home knowledge of the beverage, considered exotic in Japan. Today, Sapporo is the most popular Japanese beer outside of Japan – though much of what is sold overseas is also produced overseas. For die-hard beer fans, a trip to Hokkaidō means not only getting to sample Sapporo from the source, but also tasting Sapporo Classic, a beer in the Sapporo lineup sold only in Hokkaidō. You can try both at the original factory, now the Sapporo Beer Museum, or the newer factory, Hokkaidō Brewery.

Sapporo may be synonymous with beer, but beer in Hokkaidō is not synonymous with Sapporo. Almost every city has its own microbrew.

Note that breweries have become very strict about drinking and driving. If you'll be driving, you won't be allowed to taste at the end of a tour.

The legendary **Sapporo Beer Museum** (サッポロビール博物館; ☎011-748-1876; www.sapporoholdings.jp/english/guide/sapporo; N7E9 Higashi-ku; admission free; ☯10.30am-6.30pm; 🅿; 🚌88 to Sapporo Biiru-en, ⒮Tōhō line to Higashi-Kuyakusho-mae, exit 4) is in the original Sapporo Beer brewery – a pretty, ivy-covered brick building. There's no need to sign up for the tour; there are plenty of English explanations throughout about Japan's oldest beer. At the end there's a tasting salon (beers ¥200 to ¥300).

Afterwards, head next door to the Sapporo Biergarten for more beer and *jingisukan*.

From the subway it's a 10-minute walk; the bus stops right out front.

Pubs & Breweries

The **Sapporo Biergarten** (サッポロビール園; ☎reservation hotline 0120-150-550; www.sapporo-bier-garten.jp; N7E9 Higashi-ku; ☯11.30am-10pm; 🚌88 to Sapporo Biiru-en, ⒮Tōhō line to Higashi-Kuyakusho-mae, exit 4), next to the Sapporo Beer Museum, has no fewer than five beer halls, the best of which is Kessel Hall. Here you can tuck into *jingisukan* washed down with all-you-can-drink draught beer direct from the factory (¥3900 per person). Reservations are highly recommended. From the subway it's a 10-minute walk; the bus stops right out front.

Sapporo Beer Museum

Hokkaidō Brewery (サッポロビール 北海道工場; ☎011-748-1876; www.sapporo holdings.jp/english/guide/hokkaido; 542-1 Toiso, Eniwa; admission free; ⊙tours 10am-4pm Tue-Sun) is one of the current brewing and bottling facilities for Sapporo beer. Guided tours are led (in Japanese only) by very enthusiastic brand ambassadors past windows that allow visitors to peer into the high-tech factory. You need to make reservations by 5pm the day before (best get a Japanese-speaker to do this).

★ **Local Knowledge**

As Hokkaidō's capital city and transport hub, Sapporo gets all the seafood (such as crab), produce (eg potatoes and corn) and dairy products (such as butter and cream) for which Hokkaidō is famous.

Note that the facility is not in operation every day; when you reserve be sure to ask. Non-drivers get two free beers at the end!

Hokkaidō Brewery is a 40-minute train ride from Sapporo; take the JR Chitose line towards the airport and get off at JR Sapporo Beer Teien Station.

Hakodate Beer (はこだてビール; ☎0138-23-8000; www.hakodate-factory. com/beer; 5-22 Ōtemachi; pints ¥875, dishes ¥400-1700; ⊙11am-3pm & 5-10pm Thu-Tue; 🚃Uōichiba-dōri) makes its beer right here on the bay with groundwater from Hakodate-yama. You can buy bottles or sample the brews on tap, served here along with typical Japanese-inflected pub food (like chips and fried squid). The Hakodate Weizen is its most popular brew.

Visit **Otaru Sōko No 1** (小樽倉庫 No 1; ☎0134-21-2323; www.otarubeer.com/jp; 5-4 Minato-machi; beer ¥500-1300; ⊙11am-11pm), a converted warehouse on the canal, to taste the local microbrew, Otaru Beer, on tap. Its pilsner and dunkel beers are the best, though even Germans give the thumbs up to the *Hefeweizen*.

T.IMAI/SHUTTERSTOCK ©

Akan International Crane Centre 'GRUS'

Kushiro-shitsugen National Park

Kushiro-shitsugen National Park (釧路湿原 国立公園), at 269 sq km, is Japan's largest undeveloped wetland. It was designated a national park in 1987 to combat urban sprawl and protect the habitat of numerous species, chiefly the tanchō-zuru (red-crowned white crane), the traditional symbol of both longevity and Japan.

Great For...

☑ Don't Miss

From JR Kushiro-shitsugen Station, walk uphill for 15 minutes to the Hosooka Marsh Viewpoint (細岡展望台) for great views.

Cranes

In the early 20th century, cranes were thought to be extinct due to overhunting and habitat destruction. In 1926, however, some 20 birds were discovered in the marshes here; with concentrated conservation efforts, they now number over 1000.

You can see a few cranes in breeding pens at the **Akan International Crane Centre 'GRUS'** (阿寒国際ツルセンター【グ ルス】; ☏0154-66-4011; www.aiccgrus.wixsite. com/aiccgrus; 23-40 Kami-Akan, Akan-chō; adult/child ¥470/240; ◷9am-5pm Apr-Oct, to 4.30pm Nov-Mar) but the real attraction is the Crane Observation Centre (8.30am to 4.30pm November to March), a winter feeding ground that is your best chance to see cranes outside of a bird park. Inside there are lots of interesting photos and some fun exhibits.

Shibecha

Akan International
Crane Centre 'GRUS'

**Kushiro-shitsugen
National Park**

Kushiro-shitsugen
Norokko Train

Kushiro Japanese
Crane Reserve

Kushiro

Shiranuka

Explore Ashore

A rental car or organised tour is the easiest way to get around the park. The JR Senmō main line train runs from Kushiro to Kushiro-shitsugen (¥360, 20 minutes), on the east side of the park. The bus from Kushiro Station to Akanko Onsen stops at the Japanese Crane Reserve (¥910, one hour) and Akan International Crane Centre (¥1450, 1¼ hours).

❶ Need to Know

Cranes can be seen year-round, but the best time to spot them is during winter when they gather at feeding spots.

The bus from Kushiro Station to Akanko Onsen stops here (¥1450, 1¼ hours), or follow Rte 240 between Kushiro and Akanko.

Run by Kushiro Zoo, the **Kushiro Japanese Crane Reserve** (釧路市丹頂鶴自然公園, Tanchō-zuru Shizen-kōen; ☏0154-56-2219; www.kushiro-tancho.jp; 112 Tsuruoka; adult/child ¥470/110; ⊗9am-6pm Apr-early Oct, 9am-4pm early Oct-Mar) has been instrumental in increasing the crane population. There are currently 14 tanchō-zuru living here, though they are free to leave anytime they like (the fences are for people, not the birds).

The bus from Kushiro Station to Akanko Onsen stops here (¥910, one hour), or follow Rte 240 between Kushiro and Akanko.

Kushiro-shitsugen Norokko Train

The **Kushiro-shitsugen Norokko Train** (釧路湿原ノロッコ号; ⊗Jun-Oct) is the best way to see the wetlands without a car: once or twice daily, a vintage train with large picture windows makes a slow journey from Kushiro via Kushiro-shitsugen (¥360) as far as Tōro Station (¥540). It's very popular so be sure to reserve a seat (plus ¥520). The tourist info booth at Kushiro Station can help.

In February, an old steam locomotive, the **Fuyu-shitsugen Norokko Train**, plies the same route; it doesn't run every day though and you'll need to book ahead.

Otaru

⊙ SIGHTS & ACTIVITIES

Otaru's sights are clustered around its canal. The area is easily walkable. A few of the museums and historical buildings require a bus trip or a short taxi ride.

Mt Tengu looms above the town. Take a bus (http://tenguyama.ckk.chuo-bus.co.jp; 20 minutes, two to three an hour) to the foot of the mountain; from here a scenic ropeway continues up the mountain. Views spread out across the city and the Sea of Japan. There's plenty to explore up here, including ski fields, a restaurant, chipmunk park and a scenic bobsleigh.

Otaru Canal   Canal

(小樽運河) Historic Otaru canal is lined with warehouses from the late 19th and early 20th centuries. This was a time when traditional Japanese architecture was infused with Western-style building techniques, so some of the buildings are quite interesting. Most have been restored and now house museums and cafes. Unfortunately the canal itself is half-buried by a major thoroughfare, despite the best lobbying efforts of local preservationists.

Otaru Music Box Museum   Museum

(小樽オルゴール堂; ☑0134-22-1108; www. otaru-orgel.co.jp; 4-1 Sumiyoshi-chō; ⊙9am-6pm, to 7pm mid-Jul–mid-Sep) **FREE** This museum has clearly, uh, struck a chord: there are now five of them in town, with over 25,000 music boxes on display. Actually everything is for sale. While it's mostly new stuff for the tourist market, on the 2nd floor of this main museum (a charming red-brick structure from 1912) there are some truly impressive antiques.

Otaru Canal Cruise   Cruise

(☑0134-31-1733; www.otaru.cc; 5-4 Minato-machi; adult/child day cruise ¥1500/500, night cruise ¥1800/500; ⊙9am-9pm) The view of the canal is prettiest from this vantage point on the water. Cruises depart from Chūō-bashi and last 40 minutes; though recommended, no advance booking is necessary.

🛍 SHOPPING

Shichifuku   Antiques

(七福; ☑0134-22-2257; 1-16 Sakaimachi; ⊙11am-5pm Wed-Mon) This tiny cluttered shop has all sorts of fascinating stuff, from expensive ornamental hairpins to kitschy lamps to 100-year-old sake cups.

Kitaichi Sangōkan   Glass

(北一硝子三号館; ☑0134-33-1993; www. kitaichiglass.co.jp; 7-26 Sakaimachi; ⊙8.45am-6pm) Local glassmaker Kitaichi is a hit with tourists, with numerous shops clustered east of the canal, including this, the biggest one. Pretty souvenirs include etched crystal tumblers and delicate pendant lamps.

🍴 EATING

Kita-no Aisukurīmu-ya-san   Ice Cream ¥

(北のアイスクリーム屋さん; ☑0134-23-8983; 1-2-18 Ironai; ice cream from ¥300; ⊙9.30am-6pm) Housed in a converted warehouse that was built in 1892, just back from the canal, this legendary Otaru ice-cream parlour scoops up some seriously 'special' ice cream flavours, such as wasabi, beer, and natto. The ika-sumi (squid ink) is actually just mildly sweet. Melon, a more ice-cream friendly flavour, is divine.

Otaru Sushi-kō   Sushi ¥¥

(小樽 すし耕; ☑0134-21-5678; www.denshi-parts.co.jp/sushikou; 2-2-6 Ironai; sushi sets ¥2000-3800; ⊙noon-9pm Thu-Tue) Come here for excellent sushi sets and kaisen-don (bowls of rice topped with sashimi) featuring Hokkaidō specialities such as sake (salmon), ikura (salmon roe), uni (sea urchin) and kani (crab). Note that it often closes for a few hours in the afternoon and fills up fast at dinner, so reservations are recommended.

Otaru

◎ **Sights**

🎯 **Activities, Courses & Tours**

🛍 **Shopping**

✖ **Eating**

🍸 **Drinking & Nightlife**

ℹ INFORMATION

Canal Plaza Tourist Information Centre
(運河プラザ観光案内所; ☎0134-33-1661;
2-1-20 Ironai; ⏰9am-6pm) Housed in Otaru's
oldest warehouse, with lots of pamphlets and
brochures in English for Otaru and surrounding
areas.

Otaru Station Tourist Information Centre
(小樽駅観光案内所; ☎0134-29-1333; ⏰9am-
6pm) Pick up an English map at this kiosk in the
station.

ℹ GETTING AROUND

Kitarin (きたりん; ☎070-5605-2926; www.
kitarin.info; 2-22 Inaho; 2hr ¥900; ⏰9am-6.30pm
Mon, Tue & Thu-Sat, from 6.30am Sun Apr-Nov,
9am-6.30pm Mon-Sat, from 6.30am Sun Jul-Sep)
is a friendly bike rental spot near JR Otaru
Station that has everything you'll need for a fun
day touring around town.

Sapporo

Japan's fifth-largest city, and the prefectural capital of Hokkaidō, Sapporo (札
幌) is a dynamic urban centre that offers

From Sapporo: Jōzankei

Jōzankei (定山渓) sits along the Toyohira-gawa, deep in a gorge. It's the closest major onsen town to Sapporo and an easy escape for those after some R&R. The resort is especially pretty (and popular) in autumn, when the leaves change colour – a sight that can be viewed from many an outdoor bath. Five buses run between Sapporo Eki-mae Bus Terminal and Jōzankei daily (¥770, one hour).

Most hotels and ryokan allow nonguests to use their onsen baths for a fee (¥500 to ¥1500). There's also **Hōheikyō** (豊平峡; ☎011-598-2410; www.hoheikyo.co.jp; 608 Jōzankei; adult/child ¥1000/500; ⊙10am-10.30pm) further up the road, often voted as one of Hokkaidō's best onsen. It's home to Hokkaidō's largest outdoor bath, and is a stunner, set above town on the gorge's forested slope. The whole rambling structure is shack-like, which adds to the appeal of having stumbled upon something great. The door curtains indicating which baths are for men and which are for women are swapped daily. These waters are purportedly ideal for improving women's skin.

Oddly enough, there's an Indian restaurant on the ground floor.

beer and food festivals. In February, despite the bitter cold, Sapporo's population literally doubles during the famous Snow Festival.

⊙ SIGHTS & ACTIVITIES

Hokkaidō Chūō Bus Tours (http://teikan.chuo-bus.co.jp/en) runs half-day city tours (adult/child ¥2600/1300) that take in sights that are awkward to reach by public transport.

Moiwa-yama Ropeway   Cable Car
(もいわ山ロープウェイ; ☎011-561-8177; http://moiwa.sapporo-dc.co.jp; 5-3-7 Fushimi; adult/child return ¥1700/850; ⊙10.30am-10pm; ☐Rōpuwei-iriguchi) At 531m, Moiwa-yama has fantastic, panoramic views over the city. Part of the fun is getting there. First you take a gondola for five minutes, then switch to a cute little cable car for two more minutes. Free shuttle buses run to the ropeway from the Rōpuwei-iriguchi tram stop; otherwise it's a 10-minute walk.

Sapporo Teine   Snow Sports
(サッポロテイネ; ☎011-223-5830, bus pack reservations 011-223-5901; www.sapporo-teine.com; day pass adult/child ¥5200/2600; ⊙9am-5pm Nov-May, to 9pm Dec-Mar; ☝) You can't beat Teine for convenience, as the slopes, which hosted skiing events for the 1972 Winter Olympics, lie quite literally on the edge of Sapporo. Teine has two zones: the lower, more beginner- and family-oriented **Olympia Zone**; and the higher, more challenging **Highland Zone**. There are 15 runs and nine lifts. A variety of packages bring the price down.

Frequent trains on the JR Hakodate line run between Sapporo and Teine (¥260, 10 minutes). From JR Teine Station, shuttle buses run to both zones.

everything you'd want from a Japanese city: a thriving food scene, stylish cafes, neon-lit nightlife, shopping galore – and then some. Summer is the season for

✖ EATING

Menya Saimi   Ramen ¥
(麺屋彩未; ☎011-820-6511; Misono 10-jō Toyohira-ku; ramen from ¥750; ⊙11am-3.15pm

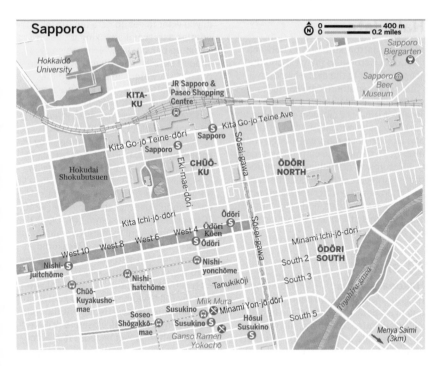

Sapporo

& 5-7.30pm Tue-Sun; [P]; [S]Tōhō line to Misono, exit 1) Sapporo takes its ramen very seriously and Saimi is oft-voted the best ramen shop in the city (and sometimes the country) – and it's not overrated. You will have to queue, which is annoying, but you will be rewarded with a mind-blowing meal for the same price as a convenience store *bentō*. Get the *miso ramen*.

Ganso Ramen Yokochō   Ramen ¥

(元祖さっぽろラーメン横丁; www.
ganso-yokocho.com; S5W3 Chūō-ku; ramen from ¥800; ⏱11am-3am; [S]Namboku line to Susukino, exit 3) This famous alleyway in the Susukino entertainment district is crammed with ramen shops, including branches of several venerable Hokkaidō shops. It's been around since 1952, and is keen to distinguish itself from all the 'imposter' ramen alleys.

It can be a little tricky to find (old as it is, it doesn't glow as bright as everything else

in Susukino), but all locals know where it is. Look for 'Ganso' as there are other ramen alleys nearby. Hours for individual shops vary.

Milk Mura   Ice Cream ¥

(ミルク村; ☎011-219-6455; S4W3-7-1; per serving ¥1300; ⏱noon-11pm Tue-Sun; [S]Namboku line to Susukino, exit 1) A grown-up twist on the classic ice-cream parlour, Milk Mura serves mugs of soft-serve ice cream accompanied by three tiny chalices of your choice of liquors – and there are dozens to choose from. Bottles, some ancient-looking, cover the counters, fairy lights twinkle and chansons play in the background. Bonus: one free refill of ice cream.

ⓘ GETTING THERE & AWAY

Twice-hourly *kaisoku* (rapid) trains on the JR Hakodate line connect Otaru and Sapporo (¥1160, 30 minutes).

Hakodate

Built on a narrow strip of land between Hakodate Harbour to the west and the Tsugaru Strait to the east, Hakodate (函館) is the southern gateway to the island of Hokkaidō. Under the Kanagawa Treaty of 1854, the city was one of the first ports to open up to international trade, and as such hosted a small foreign community. That influence can still be seen in the Motomachi district, a steep hillside that's sprinkled with European buildings and churches; the waterfront lined with red-brick warehouses; and in the nostalgic streetcar that still makes the rounds of the city.

◎ SIGHTS

Hakodate-yama   Mountain

(函館山) Mention you've been to Hakodate and every Japanese person you know will ask if you took in the night view from atop Hakodate-yama (334m) – it's that famous! If your cruise schedule allows

it, you want to get up here for sunset or after dark: what's striking is seeing the lit-up peninsula (which locals say is shaped like Hokkaidō itself) against the pitch-black waters. In addition to the viewing platform and parking area, those who hunt will find the remains of an old fort behind the buildings, with interesting foundations intact.

There are a few ways to get here: by **ropeway** (函館山ロープウェイ; ☏0138-23-3105; www.334.co.jp; 19-7 Motomachi; adult/child return ¥1280/780; ◷10am-10pm 25 Apr-15 Oct, 10am-9pm 16 Oct-24 Apr), bus, car or foot. Buses for the ropeway (¥240, 10 minutes) and the summit (¥400, 30 minutes, mid-April to mid-November) depart from bus stop 4 at JR Hakodate Station. You can also walk to the ropeway in 10 minutes from the Jūjigai tram stop; alternatively you can hike up one of several trails (all take about an hour) between May and late October. Note that the road to the summit is often closed to private vehicles after sunset because it gets too crowded.

Hakodate

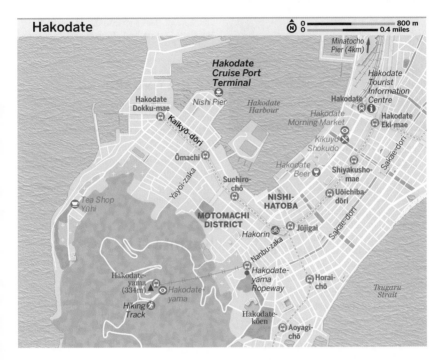

Hakodate
Hakodate Morning Market
Market

(函館朝市, Hakodate Asa-ichi; www.hakodate
-asaichi.com; 9-19 Wakamatsu-chō; ⏰5am-noon;
🚆JR Hakodate) **FREE** With crabs grilling over
hot coals, freshly caught squid packed
tightly in ice-stuffed styrofoam and the
sing-song call of vendors, Hakodate Morning Market does a fantastic impression of
an old-time seafood market – though the
visitors today are tourists not wholesale
buyers. (The commercial market that was
here originally has since moved to a bigger
space.)

🍴 EATING & DRINKING

For many visitors, eating is the whole
reason to come to Hakodate. Squid, caught
in the Tsugaru Strait, is the city's speciality.
Hakodate is also known for its *shio-ramen*
(塩ラーメン; ramen in a light, salt-flavoured
broth).

Kikuyo Shokudo
Seafood ¥

(きくよ食堂; www.hakodate-kikuyo.com/
asaichi; Hakodate Morning Market; mains from
¥1080; ⏰5am-2pm; 🚆JR Hakodate) Inside
Hakodate Morning Market, Kikuyo Shokudo got its start in the 1950s as a counter
joint to feed market workers and is now
one of the top reasons to come to Hakodate. The speciality here is the *Hakodate
tomoe-don* (函館巴丼; ¥1780), rice topped
with raw *uni* (sea urchin), *ikura* (salmon
roe) and *hotate* (scallops). There's a
picture menu.

You can also custom-make *kaisen-don*
(raw seafood over rice) from the list of
toppings or sample another Hakodate
speciality: *ika-sōmen* (raw squid sliced very
thinly like noodles; ¥1150).

Tea Shop Yūhi
Teahouse

(ティーショップ夕日; ☎0138-85-8824; 25-18
Funami-chō; tea sets from ¥600; ⏰10am-dusk
Fri-Tue mid-Mar–Nov; 🚌Funami-chō Kōryū-ji
mae, 🚋Hakodate Dokku-mae) Filling the halls

 Ōnuma Kōen

Sitting inside Ōnuma Quasi-National Park (大沼国定公園), Ōnuma Kōen (大沼公園), 25km north of Hakodate, is a popular getaway, especially for families. Sitting beneath the impressive volcano, Komaga-take (駒ケ岳; 1131m), is the lake Ōnuma (大沼), punctuated by tiny islands. It's a pretty diversion if you're craving some fresh air.

A series of linked walking paths around Ōnuma's small islands starts not far from the train station; pick up a map at the **tourist information centre** (大沼観光案内所; ☑0138-67-2170; www. onuma-guide.com; ☺8.30am-5.30pm; 🛜). Rental bicycles (¥500/1000 per hour/ day), which you can use to ride the 14km perimeter road around the lake, are available outside JR Ōnuma Kōen Station.

CHONGBUM THOMAS PARK/SHUTTERSTOCK ©

of a wooden building from 1885 (actually the old Hakodate Quarantine Office) is this magical teahouse overlooking the water. It's lit only by natural light so closes after the sun sets. In the meantime, you can while away the afternoon refilling your tiny pot of single-origin green tea, and nibbling on the *wagashi* (Japanese sweets) and pickles that accompany it.

 INFORMATION

Hakodate Tourist Information Centre (函館市観光案内所; ☑0138-23-5440; ☺9am-

7pm Apr-Oct, 9am-5pm Nov-Mar) is inside JR Hakodate Station, and offers English brochures and maps.

 GETTING AROUND

Single-trip fares on trams and buses generally cost around ¥250. One-day transport passes can be purchased at the tourist information centre (p204) or on-board.

You can rent bikes from **Hakorin** (はこりん; ☑0138-22-9700; 4-19 Suehiro-chō; per day ¥1600; ☺9am-6.30pm), which can be found at the community center outside JR Hakodate Station.

Kushiro

 SIGHTS

Just 600m south of the main train station, **Kushiro Children's Museum Kodomo Yugakukan** (http://kodomoyugakukan.jp/; ☺closed Mon) has science displays, a planetarium, a big indoor sandpit and plenty more besides.

Washō Market   Market
(和商市場, Washō Ichiba; ☑0154-22-3226; www. washoichiba.com; 13-25 Kurogane-chō; mains ¥1000-2000; ☺8am-5pm Mon-Sat, to 4pm Sun Apr-Dec, closed Sun Jan-Mar) This fish market is as much a sightseeing spot as a place to eat. The speciality here is called *katte-don* (勝手丼) – literally 'rice bowl as you like it'. First buy a bowl of rice from one of the vendors on the perimeter then head to a fish monger and have them top it off with your choice of raw fish. If you want to get even more in the mood, rent a kimono (¥1000) and walk around in style.

It's a couple of minutes' walk south of JR Kushiro Station.

 EATING & DRINKING

As you'd expect from a port city, seafood is Kushiro's speciality. Look for *robatayaki* (seafood and vegetables grilled over a charcoal fire) and *katte-don*.

Kushiro

There are cafes and bakeries in the train station, but few options in the streets nearby.

Kushiro Fisherman's Wharf MOO

Mall

(http://www.moo946.com) A short walk or shuttle ride from the town's ports is this large mall packed with shops, restaurants and bars. In the warmer months, *robata* seafood grills are set up along the riverside here. During the colder months, the gardens in EGG, next door, offer indoor greenery.

INFORMATION

The **Kushiro City Tourist Information Center** (⊙9am-5.30pm) at JR Kushiro Station provides info on Kushiro and the surrounding area, and can help with sightseeing tours.

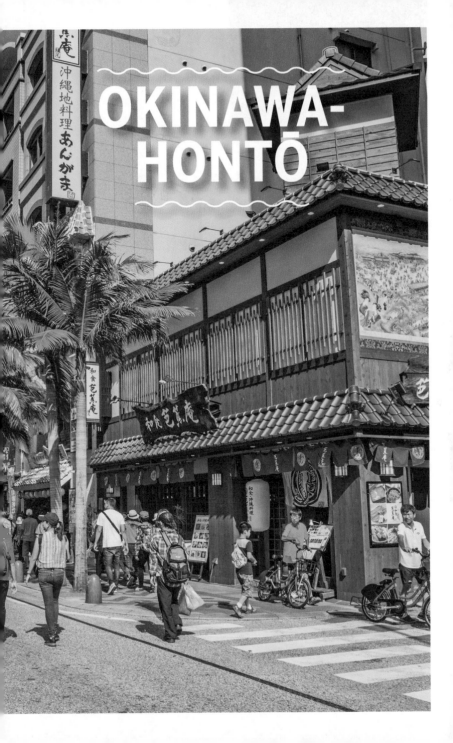

OKINAWA-HONTŌ

Okinawa-hontō at a Glance

Okinawa-hontō is the largest island in the Nansei-shotō (Southwest Islands) and its capital, Naha (那覇), is the busiest city. If Tokyo were a pie, and you cut a tiny slice, dropped it on an island in the Pacific, and served it with a dollop of Florida, Naha might be what you'd get. The city plays host to an interesting mix of young Japanese holidaymakers, American GIs looking for off-base fun and a growing number of foreign tourists. The action centres on Kokusai-dōri (International Blvd), and overlooking it all from a safe distance to the east is Shuri-jō, a wonderfully restored castle that was once the home of royalty.

With a Day in Port

Wander along **Tsuboya Pottery Street** (p210), admiring the handcrafted pottery and local houses, then gain insight into Okinawa's wartime past at **Okinawa Prefectural Peace Memorial Museum** (p213). Don't miss sampling distinctive Okinawan specialities at **Daichi Makishi Kōsetsu Ichiba** (p214).

Best Places for...

DIY crafting Naha City Traditional Arts & Crafts Center (p211)

People-watching Kokusai-dōri (p217) and surrounding arcades

Shopping American Village (p216)

Castle reconstructions Shuri-jō (p214)

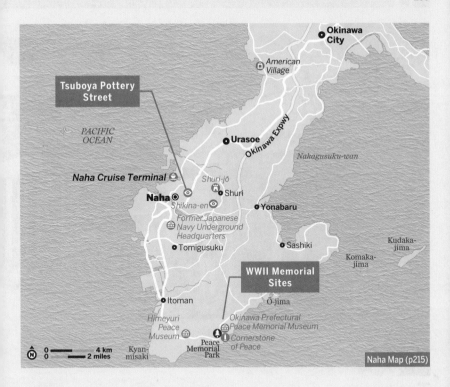

Tsuboya Pottery Street

Okinawa City

American Village

PACIFIC OCEAN

Urasoe

Okinawa Expwy

Nakagusuku-wan

Naha Cruise Terminal

Shuri-jō

Naha

Shuri

Shikina-en

Yonabaru

Former Japanese Navy Underground Headquarters

Tomigusuku

Sashiki

Kudaka-jima

Komaka-jima

WWII Memorial Sites

Ō-jima

Itoman

Himeyuri Peace Museum

Okinawa Prefectural Peace Memorial Museum

Cornerstone of Peace

Peace Memorial Park

Kyan-misaki

0 — 4 km
0 — 2 miles

Naha Map (p215)

Getting from the Port

Most cruise arrivals have a shuttle service to town. Otherwise it's a 1.5km walk or taxi ride to Naha town.

Fast Facts

Money There's currency exchange at the dock and ATMs in town.

Tourist information English-language information services are set up to greet cruise ships, and there's a tourist office in Naha (p217).

Wi-fi There is free wi-fi at the port and at a number of hotspots in town.

Tsuboya Pottery Street

One of the best parts of Naha is this neighbourhood, a centre of ceramic production from 1682, when Ryūkyū kilns were consolidated here by royal decree. Even if you're not looking for pottery souvenirs, the area is well worth a wander.

Great For...

☑ Don't Miss

The lanes off the main street contain some classic crumbling, old Okinawan houses.

Slender, cobblestone Tsuboya Pottery Street is lined with pottery workshops, and with shops that sell the resulting products. You can watch the craftspeople at work, see the kilns used, and take a short class in pottery making.

Most shops along this old-timey street sell all the popular Okinawan ceramics, including *shiisā* (lion-dog roof guardians) and containers for serving *awamori* (Okinawan liquor distilled from rice), the local firewater.

As you wander around town, here and elsewhere, keep an eye out for *shiisā* on the rooftops, as well as traditional red earthenware roof tiles. There's plenty of variety available here, from antique wares to freshly made pottery in traditional styles, to some modern new designs. A handcrafted teapot, pendant necklace or hanging *shiisā* makes for a wonderful souvenir, unique to Okinawa.

Shīsā (lion-dog guardian)

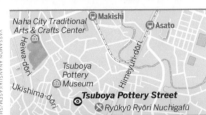

Explore Ashore

Take the shuttle from the port to town, then take the monorail to Makishi Station. From here it's a 600m walk southwest to Tsuboya Pottery Street. To get here from Kokusai-dōri, walk south through the entirety of Heiwa-dōri arcade (about 350m).

❶ Need to Know

When the wandering and shopping get too much, there's no shortage of cafes in the area, many of them serving up your order on locally made pottery.

Tsuboya Pottery Museum

This excellent **museum** (壺屋焼物博物館; ☎098-862-3761; www.edu.city.naha.okinawa. jp/tsuboya; 1-9-32 Tsuboya; adult/concession ¥350/280; ☉10am-6pm Tue-Sun) houses some fine examples of traditional Okinawan pottery. Here you can also inspect potters' wheels and *arayachi* (unglazed) and *jōyachi* (glazed) pieces. There's even a cross-section of a *nobori-gama* (kiln built on a slope) set in its original location, where crushed pieces of pottery that date back to the 17th century lie embedded in earth.

Ryūkyū Ryōri Nuchigafū

For a memorable, elegant meal in Naha, don't pass up a meal at the hilltop **Nuchigafū** (琉球料理ぬちがふう; ☎098-861-2952; www.facebook.com/RyukyuCuisine. Nuchigafu; 1-28-3 Tsuboya; set meals from

¥3000; ☉11.30am-5pm & 5.30-10pm Wed-Mon), off the southern end of Tsuboya Pottery Street. The building was formerly a lovely Okinawan teahouse, and before that a historic Ryūkyūan residence. Children aged 11 and older are welcome.

What's Nearby?

Right on Kokusai-dōri, **Naha City Traditional Arts & Crafts Center** (那覇市伝統工芸館; ☎098-868-7866; www. kogeikan.jp; 2nd fl, 3-2-10 Makishi; ¥350; ☉9am-6pm) houses a notable collection of traditional Okinawan crafts by masters of the media. You can also try your hand at Ryūkyūan glassblowing, weaving, *bingata* (painting on fabric) and pottery-making in workshops (¥1500 to ¥3000), and make your own souvenir from Okinawa.

VASSAMON ANANSUKKASEM/SHUTTERSTOCK ©

Peace Memorial Park

HELLORF ZCOOL/SHUTTERSTOCK ©

WWII Memorial Sites

Okinawa's most important war memorials are clustered in the Peace Memorial Park, located in the city of Itoman on the southern coast of the island. A visit to the area is highly recommended for those with an interest in wartime history or seeking a deeper understanding of the modern Okinawan identity.

Great For...

☑ Don't Miss

Take a break from the museums to admire the coastal scenery and ocean views.

During the closing days of the Battle of Okinawa, the southern part of Okinawa-hontō served as one of the last holdouts of the Japanese military and an evacuation point for wounded Japanese soldiers. A number of sites memorialise this history.

Peace Memorial Park

Housing Okinawa's most important war memorials, the **Peace Memorial Park** (平和祈念公園; 550 Mabuni; ⊙dawn-dusk) occupies an appropriately peaceful coastal location in the southern city of Itoman.

To reach the park, take bus 89 from Naha Bus Terminal to the Itoman Bus Terminal (¥580, one hour, every 20 minutes), then transfer to bus 82, and get off at Heiwa Kinen-dō Iriguchi (¥470, 30 minutes, hourly).

Cornerstone of Peace

HARISMOYO/SHUTTERSTOCK ©

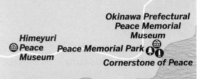

Himeyuri 🏛 **Peace Museum**   **Peace Memorial Park** 🅘🅘   **Okinawa Prefectural Peace Memorial Museum** 🏛

Cornerstone of Peace

PACIFIC OCEAN

⚓

Explore Ashore

Southern Okinawa-hontō is conveniently served by regular buses from Naha. Renting a car or hiring a taxi, while expensive, will give you more freedom to explore the area's diverse attractions. A one-way taxi to the Peace Memorial Park is approximately ¥3000 to ¥3500.

ⓘ Need to Know

Most points of interest in this area either have restaurants on site, or have eateries nearby that are geared towards tourist traffic.

Okinawa Prefectural Peace Memorial Museum

This **museum** (沖縄県平和祈念資料館; ☎098-997-3844; www.peace-museum.pref. okinawa.jp; 614-1 Aza Mabuni, Itoman; ¥300; ☺9am-5pm), the centrepiece of the Peace Memorial Park, focuses on the suffering of the Okinawan people during the island's invasion and under the subsequent American Occupation. While some material may stir debate, the museum's mission is to serve as a reminder of the horrors of war, so that such suffering is not repeated. There is a free English-language audio guide available, providing great detail on the 2nd-floor exhibit.

Outside is the **Cornerstone of Peace** (平和の礎; ☺dawn-dusk) FREE, inscribed with the names of everyone who died in the Battle of Okinawa.

What's Nearby?

Located above a cave that served as an emergency field hospital during the closing days of the Battle of Okinawa, the **Himeyuri Peace Museum** (ひめゆり平和 祈念資料館; ☎098-997-2100; www.himeyuri. or.jp; 671-1 Ihara; ¥310; ☺9am-5.30pm) is a haunting monument whose mission is to promote peace, driven by survivors and alumnae of the school. Here 240 female high-school students were pressed into service as nurses for Japanese military wounded.

As American forces closed in, the students were summarily dismissed and, thus abandoned, most perished. Excellent, comprehensive interpretive signage is provided in English. Bus 82 stops outside.

Naha

◉ SIGHTS

Okinawa Prefectural
Museum & Art Museum   Museum
(沖縄県立博物館・美術館; ☎098-941-8200;
www.museums.pref.okinawa.jp; Omoromachi
3-1-1; prefectural/art museum ¥410/310; ⊗9am-
6pm Tue-Thu & Sun, to 8pm Fri & Sat) Opened
in 2007, this museum of Okinawa's history,
culture and natural history is easily one of
the best museums in Japan. Displays are
well laid out, attractively presented and
easy to understand, with excellent bilingual
interpretive signage. The art-museum
section holds interesting special exhibits
(admission prices vary) with an emphasis
on local artists. It's about 15 minutes' walk
northwest of the Omoromachi monorail
station.

Shuri-jō   Castle
(首里城; ☎098-886-2020; www.oki-park.jp; 1-2
Kinjō-chō, Shuri; ¥820, with 1- or 2-day monorail
pass discounted to ¥660; ⊗8.30am-7pm Apr-Jun
& Oct-Nov, to 8pm Jul-Sep, to 6pm Dec-Mar,
closed 1st Wed & Thu Jul) This reconstructed castle was originally built in the 14th
century and served as the administrative
centre and royal residence of the Ryūkyū
kingdom until the 19th century. Enter
through the **Kankai-mon** (歓会門) and
go up to the **Hōshin-mon** (奉神門), which
forms the entryway to the inner sanctum of
the castle. Visitors can enter the impressive
Seiden (正殿), which has exhibits on the
castle and the Okinawan royals.

Daichi Makishi
Kōsetsu Ichiba   Market
(第一牧志公設市場; 2-10-1 Matsuo; ⊗8am-
8pm, restaurants 10am-7pm) A great place to
sample everyday Okinawan eats is at one
of the 2nd-floor eateries in this covered
food market just off Ichibahon-dōri, about
200m south of Kokusai-dōri. The colourful
variety of fish and produce on offer here is
amazing.

Shikina-en   Gardens
(識名園; ☎098-855-5936; 421-7 Aza Māji;
¥400; ⊗9am-6pm Thu-Tue Apr-Sep, to 5.30pm
Oct-Mar) Around 4km east of the city centre

Shuri-jō

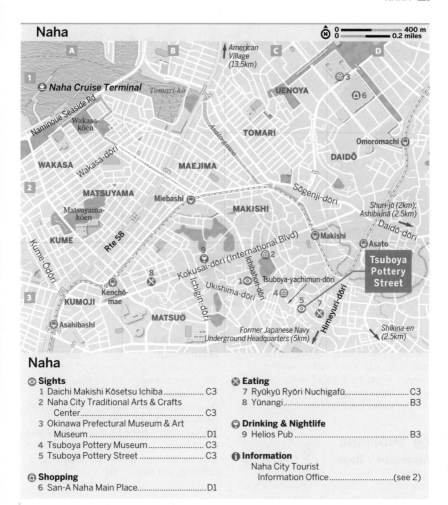

Naha

◎ Sights
1 Daichi Makishi Kōsetsu Ichiba C3
2 Naha City Traditional Arts & Crafts
   Center C3
3 Okinawa Prefectural Museum & Art
   Museum D1
4 Tsuboya Pottery Museum C3
5 Tsuboya Pottery Street C3

◎ Shopping
6 San-A Naha Main Place D1

✗ Eating
7 Ryūkyū Ryōri Nuchigafū C3
8 Yūnangi B3

◎ Drinking & Nightlife
9 Helios Pub B3

ℹ Information
Naha City Tourist
   Information Office ....(see 2)

is a Chinese-style garden containing stone bridges, a viewing pavilion and a villa that belonged to the Ryūkyū royal family. Despite its flawless appearance, everything here was painstakingly rebuilt after WWII. To reach the garden, take bus 2, 3 or 5 to the Shikinaen-mae stop (¥230, 20 minutes).

Former Japanese Navy Underground Headquarters Museum
(旧海軍司令部壕; Kyūkaigun Shireibu-gō; ☎098-850-4055; http://kaigungou.ocvb.or.jp;

236 Tomishiro, Tomigusuku; ¥440; ⊗8.30am-5pm Oct-Jun, to 5.30pm Jul-Sep) Directly south of Naha in Kaigungo-kōen is the Former Japanese Navy Underground Headquarters, where 4000 men committed suicide or were killed as the Battle of Okinawa drew to its bloody conclusion. Only 250m of the tunnels are open, but you can wander through the maze of corridors, see the commander's final words on the wall of his room, and inspect the holes and scars in other walls from the grenade blasts that killed many of the men.

RICHIE CHAN/SHUTTERSTOCK ©

American Village

To reach the site, take bus 55 or 98 from Naha Bus Terminal to the Uebaru Danchi-mae stop (¥220, 10 minutes, several hourly). From there it's a five-minute walk – follow the English signs (the entrance is near the top of the hill).

🔒 SHOPPING

American Village   Concept Store
(☏098-926-5678; www.okinawa-american village.com; 15-69 Mihama, Chatan-cho) This amusement-park-esque, American-themed shopping mall is as kitsch as they come, but closer exploration will provide a fascinating glimpse into modern Okinawan life, where off-duty GIs shop for memories of home alongside Chinese tourists on the hunt for Americana. There are some excellent vintage-clothing stores, a bunch of fun dining options and a big-ass Ferris wheel to boot.

Take the 20, 28 or 29 bus from Naha to the Kuwae stop (40 minutes, ¥720).

**San-A Naha
Main Place**   Shopping Centre
(サンエー那覇メインプレイス; ☏098-951-3300; www.san-a.co.jp/nahamainplace; 4-4-9 Omoromachi; ◷9am-11pm) Naha's busiest downtown mall is always a hive of activity for its many duty-free stores (including Tokyū Hands – great for, well, anything you can think of), cinema complex and array of enticing eateries where you should expect to queue, any time of day.

🍴 EATING & DRINKING

Ashibiunā   Okinawan ¥
(あしびうなぁ; ☏098-884-0035; www.ryoji-family.co.jp/ryukyusabo.html; 2-13 Shuri Tonokura-chō; lunch sets ¥800-1280; ◷11.30am-3pm & 5.30pm-midnight) Perfect for lunch after touring Shuri-jō, Ashibiunā has a traditional ambience and picturesque garden. Set meals feature local specialities such as *gōyā champurū*, *okinawa-soba* and *ikasumi yaki-soba*. On the road leading away from Shuri-jō, Ashibiunā is located

on the right, just before the intersection to the main road.

Yūnangi
Okinawan ¥¥

(ゆうなんぎい; ☎098-867-3765; 3-3-3 Kumoji; dishes ¥750-1400; ⊙noon-3pm & 5.30-10.30pm Mon-Sat) You'll be lucky to get a seat here, but if you do, you'll be treated to some of the best Okinawan food around, served in traditional but bustling surroundings. Try the *okinawa-soba* set (¥1400), or choose from the picture menu. It's on a side street off Kokusai-dōri – look for the wooden sign with white lettering above the doorway.

Helios Pub
Pub

(ヘリオスパブ; ☎098-863-7227; www.helios -food-service.co.jp; 1-2-25 Makishi; ⊙11.30am-11pm Sun-Thu, to midnight Fri & Sat) Craft-beer lovers who tire of Orion can perk up bored palates with a sample flight of four house brews (¥900) and pints for ¥525. Edibles cover the pub-menu gamut, all very reasonably priced.

ℹ INFORMATION

Naha City Tourist Information Office (那覇市観光案内所; ☎098-868-4887; www.visit okinawa.jp; 3-2-10 Makishi; ⊙9am-8pm) Located in the Tenbus Building, it provides free maps and information.

ℹ GETTING AROUND

The Yui Rail monorail runs from Naha International Airport in the south to Shuri in the north.

💬 Kokusai-dōri

The city's main artery is **Kokusai-dōri** (国際通り), a riot of neon, noise, souvenir shops, bustling restaurants and Japanese young things out strutting their stuff. It's a festival of tat and tackiness, but it's good fun if you're in the mood for it.

Many people prefer the atmosphere of the three covered shopping arcades that run south off Kokusai-dōri: **Ichibahon-dōri** (市場本道り), **Mutsumibashi-dōri** (むつみ橋通り) and **Heiwa-dōri** (平和通り).

Prices range from ¥200 to ¥290; a one-day pass costs ¥700. Kenchō-mae Station sits at the western end of Kokusai-dōri, while Makishi Station is at its eastern end.

Driving here can be quite the nightmare: despite its size, Naha's traffic jams make for slow going.

KEELUNG
& TAIPEI

Keelung & Taipei at a Glance

Keelung, home to the famous Miaokou Night Market, is perfectly placed for forays to Taipei, and to the impressive natural and historic sights of Taiwan's northeast coast. Taipei is a tough little city whose beauty lies in its blend of Chinese culture with a curious fusion of Japanese, Southeast Asian and American influences. Taoist temples buzz with the prayers of the hopeful, the wooden boards of Japanese-era mansions creak under the feet of visitors and, best of all, nature is knitted into the city's very fabric.

Clinging to hillsides overlooking the sea, the former mining towns of Jiufen and Jinguashi serve up a captivating mix of yesteryear charm, industrial heritage, whimsical teahouses and enough snacks to feed half the country.

With a Day in Port

In Taipei, follow Taiwan's path to democracy at **Chiang Kai-shek Memorial Hall** (p222), then glimpse some of the treasures of the **National Palace Museum** (p224), if it's open – fingers crossed! Or, tap into the richness of **Jiufen** and **Jinguashi's** (p227) mining heritage, followed by food, drink, entertainment and local life at Keelung's **Miaokou Night Market** (p228), right by the cruise port.

Best Places for...

Signature dishes Yongkang Beef Noodles (p226)

A city stroll Dihua Street (p224)

Small wonders Miniatures Museum of Taiwan (p224)

Souvenirs Lin Hua Tai Tea Company (p225) and Lao Mian Cheng Lantern Shop (p225)

Tea and coffee Jiufen Teahouse (p228) and Lugou Cafe (p226)

Taipei Map (p225)

Getting from the Port

A 700m (10-minute) walk from Keelung port brings you to Keelung Station, from where regular trains depart for Taipei Main Station (NT$65, 50 minutes).

Bus 788, departing just before Keelung Station, runs to Jiufen and Jinguashi (NT$30, 45 minutes).

Fast Facts

Currency New Taiwanese dollar (NT$)

Language Mandarin, Taiwanese

Money There are ATMs and currency exchange at Keelung port. ATMs almost always have the option of choosing an English-language service.

Tourist information The Keelung Visitor Centre is a short walk from the port, on the right-hand side of Keelung Station. Jiufen also has an office (p229).

Wi-fi Free at Keelung port, and in Taipei at many cafes, restaurants and malls. The government's free service, iTaiwan (itaiwan.gov.tw/en), has hotspots at MRT stations and major tourist sites.

ASIASTOCK/SHUTTERSTOCK ©

Chiang Kai-shek Memorial Hall

This vast public square is an imposing sight, flanked on three sides by neoclassical structures – Chiang Kai-shek's memorial in front and the National Theatre and Concert Hall on either side. It's a must-see for all visitors to Taiwan, not only for the spectacle itself but because it opens a window to the political history of Taiwan.

Great For...

☑ Don't Miss

The changing of the guards – every hour, on the hour.

This grandiose monument to authoritarian leader Chiang Kai-shek is a popular attraction, and rightly so. It is a sobering feeling standing in the massive courtyard. Chiang's blue-roofed hall is a prime example of the neoclassical style, favoured by Chiang Kai-shek as a counterpoint to the Cultural Revolution's destruction of real classical culture in China.

Entrance to the main hall is made via a series of 89 steps (the age of Chiang when he died). Inside the cavernous hall is an artefact museum with Chiang's two Cadillacs, various documents and articles from daily life. The hourly changing of the honour guard is probably the most popular sight with most visitors. Note the colour of the guards' uniforms, which change every three months: blue is the air force, green is the land army and white is the navy.

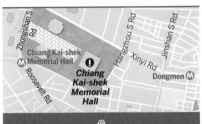

⚓

Explore Ashore

Take the train from Keelung port to Taipei Main Station, then the MRT to Chiang Kai-shek Memorial Hall station.

ⓘ Need to Know

中正紀念堂; Zhōngzhèng Jìniàn Táng; 📞02-2343 1100; www.cksmh.gov.tw; 21 Zhongshan S Rd; 中山南路21號; ⏱9am-6pm; 🅿; MChiang Kai-shek Memorial Hall

At night the locals take over and the whole area really comes to life. Joggers lap the square, teenagers practise dance steps and the two halls buzz with activity as people arrive to watch a concert. In 2007 the surrounding park was renamed 'Liberty Square' in honour of Taiwan's long road to democracy. Many democracy protests in the 1980s took place here, and it is fitting that the public has changed the nature of this space.

For a time it was conceivable that the memorial itself would be renamed and the Chiang sculpture removed. That didn't happen, and the reasons (which will vary depending on who you ask) pretty much summarise where modern Taiwan is at, both politically and socially.

What's Nearby?

The long-running and often hectic **Jinfeng Braised Meat Rice** (金峰滷肉飯; Jīnfēng Lǔròu Fàn; 10 Roosevelt Rd; 羅斯福路10號; dishes NT$30-60; ⏱8am-1am; MChiang Kai-shek Memorial Hall) serves Taiwanese comfort food quickly and cheaply, without fuss or atmosphere. Try the *lǔròu fàn* (滷肉飯; rice and meat strips), *kòng ròu fàn* (焢肉飯; slow-braised pork belly and rice) or *fènglí kǔguā jī* (鳳梨苦瓜雞; bitter melon pineapple chicken).

The pearl milk tea (NT$85) at **Chun Shui Tang** (春水堂; Chūnshuǐ Táng; www.chunshuitang.com.tw; ground fl, National Concert Hall; ⏱11.30am-8.50pm; MChiang Kai-shek Memorial Hall) is supposed to be the best in the city – pink, frothy and creamy with smaller, firmer pearls and only lightly sweetened. There are branches across the city, but this one on the ground floor of the National Concert Hall is one of the nicest. Traditional light noodle dishes and Chinese desserts are also available.

Taipei

◎ SIGHTS

National Palace Museum   Museum

(故宮博物院; Gùgōng Bówùyuàn; ☑02-6610
3600; www.npm.gov.tw/en; 221 Zhishan Rd,
Sec 2; 至善路二段221號; NT$350; ◷8.30am-
6.30pm Sun-Thu, to 9pm Fri & Sat; P; 🚇R30)
Home to the world's largest and arguably
finest collection of Chinese art, this vast
museum covers treasures in painting,
calligraphy, statuary, bronzes, lacquerware,
ceramics, jade and religious objects. The
historical range is truly outstanding.

There are controversial plans to partially
or even wholly close the museum in 2020
for three years while the building is renovated, with exhibits to move to the Southern
Branch in Chiayi in the meantime. Check
for the latest before visiting.

Taipei 101   Tower

(台北101; Táiběi Yīlíngyī; ☑02-8101 8800; www.
taipei-101.com.tw; adult/child NT$600/540;
◷9am-10pm, last ticket sale 9.15pm; P; 🚇Taipei
101) Towering above the city like the gigantic
bamboo stalk it was designed to resemble,
508m-tall Taipei 101 is impossible to miss.
The observation deck on the 89th floor
(head to the 5th floor to buy tickets and
ascend) offers 360-degree views of the
city. The tower itself has several floors of
luxury brands and a very busy and decent
food court in the basement.

The 4th-floor atrium is full of light and
space and offers a nice break from the
sightseeing hordes. Budget around an hour
(or two if you plan to eat).

A money changer (the only non-Asian
currencies exchanged are US dollars and
euros) and a helpful information desk are in
the basement.

Dihua Street   Historic Site

(迪化街; Díhuà Jiē; 🚇Beimen, 🚇Daqiaotou) This
former 'Centre Street' has long been known
for its Chinese medicine shops, fabric
market and lively Lunar New Year sundry
market. In recent years it has attracted
numerous restoration and cultural projects

and it's now a magnet for young entrepreneurs eager to breathe new life into the
neighbourhood with cafes, restaurants, art
studios and antique shops.

Thankfully, this gentrification hasn't
squashed the original atmosphere –
fancy ceramic shops sit side-by-side with
long-term tenants selling sacks of dried
mushrooms and agricultural produce.

Bao'an Temple   Taoist Temple

(保安宮; Bǎoān Gōng; www.baoan.org.tw/
english; 61 Hami St; 哈密街61號; ◷7am-10pm;
🚇Yuanshan) FREE Recipient of a Unesco
Asia-Pacific Heritage Award for both its
restoration and its revival of temple rites
and festivities, the Bao'an Temple is a
must-visit when in Taipei. This exquisite
structure is loaded with prime examples
of the traditional decorative arts, and the
yearly folk arts festival is a showcase of
traditional performance arts.

Miniatures Museum of Taiwan   Museum

(袖珍博物館; Xiùzhēn Bówùguǎn; ☑02-2515
0583; www.mmot.com.tw; 96 Jianguo N Rd, Sec
1; 建國北路一段96號; adult/child NT$200/160;
◷10am-6pm Tue-Sun; 🚼; 🚇Songjiang Nanjing)
Whimsical, wondrous and fantastically
detailed are the creative works at this
private museum located in the basement of
a nondescript tower block. On display are
dozens of doll-house-sized replications of
Western houses, castles, chalets, palaces
and villages, as well as scenes from classic
children's stories such as *Pinocchio* and
Alice in Wonderland. If you're coming by
MRT, take exit 5.

🔒 SHOPPING

With its endless markets, back-alley empo-
riums and glittering shopping malls, Taipei
offers the complete gamut of shopping
experiences. Taiwan has a rich tradition of
wood, ceramic, metal and glass production
and young designers are now pushing the
envelope with everything from clothing
to furniture. Good gift ideas are packaged

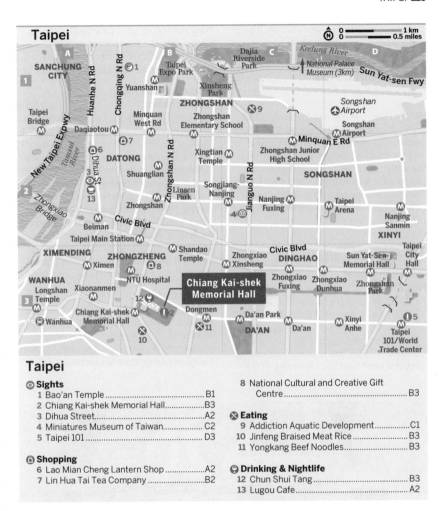

Taipei

organic teas, ceramic decorative tiles and the iconic pineapple cake.

Lin Hua Tai Tea Company   Tea
(林華泰茶行; Línhuátài Cháháng; ☑02-2557 3506; 193 Chongqing N Rd, Sec 2; 重慶北路二段193號; ☉7.30am-9pm; ⓜDaqiaotou) This is the oldest tea-selling shop in Taipei, and dates back to 1883. The current fourth-generation merchants are more than happy to talk tea and let you sample the wares, which sit in large metal drums. Prices per *jin* (600g) are clearly written on the top of each drum. Ask for a tour of the tea factory in the back.

Lao Mian Cheng Lantern Shop   Arts & Crafts
(老綿成, Lǎomiànchéng; 298 Dihua St, Sec 1; 迪化街一段298號; ☉9am-7.30pm; ⓜDaqiaotou) Handmade lamps with painted dragons, bold flowers, bamboo and calligraphy – as big as a gym ball or as small as a fist. There are also concertinaed paper lanterns, purses and cushion covers. This tumbledown marvel of a shop was opened back in 1915

by the current owner's grandfather. It's sometimes closed on Sunday.

National Cultural and Creative Gift Centre
Gifts & Souvenirs

(國家文創禮品館; Guójiā Wénchuàng Lǐpǐn Guǎn; www.handicraft.org.tw; 1 Xuzhou Rd; 徐州路1號; ⏰9am-6pm; 📶; MNTU Hospital) Four floors of jade, ceramics, tea sets, jewellery, scrolls, Kinmen knives, Kavalan whisky and handmade soap are just highlights of the variety on offer here. Colourful Franz porcelain is featured in a special section. There's a money-changing facility and a selection of National Palace Museum Shop products.

🍴 EATING & DRINKING

Yongkang Beef Noodles
Noodles $$

(永康牛肉麵; Yǒngkāng Niúròumiàn; 📞02-2351 1051; 17, Lane 31, Jinshan S Rd, Sec 2; 金山南路二段31巷17號; small/large bowl NT$220/240; ⏰11am-3.30pm & 4.30-9pm; ❄; MDongmen) Open since 1963, this is one of Taipei's top spots for beef noodles, especially of the

hóngshāo (紅燒; red spicy broth) variety. Beef portions are generous, and melt in your mouth. Other worthwhile dishes include steamed ribs. Expect queues.

Addiction Aquatic Development
Seafood $$$

(上引水產; Shàng Yǐn Shuǐchǎn; www.addiction. com.tw; 18, Alley 2, Lane 410, Minzu E Rd; 民族東路410巷2弄18號; ⏰10am-midnight, fish market opens at 6am; ❄; MXingtian Temple) Housed in the former Taipei Fish Market – you can't miss it, it's a huge blue-and-slate-grey building – is this collection of chic eateries serving the freshest seafood imaginable. There's a stand-up sushi bar, a seafood bar (with wine available), hotpot, an outdoor grill, a wholesale area for take-home seafood and a lifestyle boutique. This place is popular and doesn't take reservations.

Lugou Cafe
Cafe

(爐鍋咖啡; Lúguō Kāfēi; 📞02-2555 8225; www. facebook.com/luguocafeartyard; 1, 2nd fl, Lane 32, Dihua St, Sec 1; 迪化街一段32巷1號2樓; ⏰11am-7pm; 📶; MBeimen) Speciality coffees (including some local choices such as Alis-

Addiction Aquatic Development

han) on the 2nd floor of a heritage building (originally the chemist AS Watson & Co) on Dihua St. Mismatched furniture, eclectic decor, Frank Sinatra jazz – grab a window seat and slip back in time. The coffee is a pleasure, the sandwiches not so much.

ℹ INFORMATION

Taiwan Tourism Bureau Runs information booths all over the city, provides maps and pamphlets, and is staffed by friendly English-speaking workers.

Tourist Hotline (☎0800-011 765) Useful 24-hour, toll-free service in English, Japanese and Chinese.

ℹ GETTING AROUND

Bus Great network but routes on timetables are written in Chinese only; can be slow when they get stuck in traffic. Fares are NT$15 on most short routes within the city centre.

MRT Quickest way to get around; super reliable. Runs from 6am to midnight. Fares vary from NT$20 to NT$65.

Taxi Yellow cabs are fairly inexpensive and ubiquitous, but traffic can be frustrating.

Walk If you stick to one or two neighbouring districts, Taipei is a very walkable city.

EASYCARD

◦ EasyCard is the stored-value card of the Taipei Rapid Transit Association (TRTA) and can be bought in most MRT stations for a returnable deposit of NT$100.

◦ EasyCards can be used for the MRT, buses, some local trains, nonreserved HSR rides, some taxis, the YouBike shared-bicycle program (http://taipei.youbike.com.tw/en) and purchases at all convenience stores, Starbucks and dozens of other shops.

Jiufen & Jinguashi

Nestled against the mountains and hemmed in by the sea are Jiufen (九份; Jiǔfèn) and its neighbour Jinguashi (金瓜石;

 Yehliu Geopark

Stretching far out into the East China Sea, the limestone cape of **Yehliu Geopark** (野柳地質公園; Yěliǔ Dìzhí Gōngyuán; ☎02-2492 2016; www.ylgeopark. org.tw; 167-1 Gangdong Rd, Wanli District, 野柳里港東路167-1號; adult/child NT$80/40; ⏰7.30am-6pm May-Sep, to 5pm Oct-Apr, visitor centre 8am-5pm) has long attracted people to its delightfully odd rock formations. It's a geologist's dreamland but also a fascinating place for the day tripper. Aeons of wind and sea erosion can be observed first-hand in hundreds of pitted and moulded rocks with quaint (but accurate) names such as **Fairy's Shoe** (仙女鞋; Xiānnǚ Xié) and **Queen's Head** (女王頭; Nǚwáng Tóu), which truly looks just like a silhouette of the famous Nefertiti bust.

The visitor information centre has an informative English brochure explaining the general conditions that created the cape and also the specific forces that formed different kinds of rock shapes, such as the mushroom rocks, marine potholes and honeycomb rocks. Tourism shuttle buses stop directly outside the park entrance.

The park gets very crowded on weekends and during holidays, with many tourists swarming around Queen's Head waiting to take pictures. Try to visit early morning, if possible on a weekday.

Frequent bus 790 runs between Keelung and Yehliu (NT$30, 40 minutes).

🍽 Miaokou Night Market

Mere steps from the port at Keelung, **Miaokou Night Market** (基隆廟口夜市; Jīlóng Miàokǒu Yèshì; www.miaokow.org; Rensan Rd; 仁三路) is probably the most famous night market in Taiwan. Miaokou became known for its great food during the Japanese era, when a group of merchants started selling snacks at the mouth of the **Dianji Temple** (奠濟宮). Nowadays, Miaokou is considered the best place in Taiwan for street snacks, especially seafood.

The market covers several streets; stalls on the main street are all numbered and have signs in English, Japanese and Chinese explaining what's on the menu.

Despite the name, there's plenty to eat and do here all day long.

LIU YU SHAN/SHUTTERSTOCK ©

Jīnguāshí), 10 minutes by bus away from Jiufen's main road. Both were mining centres during the Japanese era; by the 1930s Jiufen was so prosperous it was known as 'Little Shanghai'.

◎ SIGHTS

Jishan Street   Area
(基山街; Jīshān Jiē; Jiufen Old Street) Countless snack stalls and souvenir shops line the narrow 'old street' threading through Jiufen. Hugely popular, the street can become intolerably crowded by the afternoon, so plan accordingly. Shuqi St, with its famously

steep steps, Japanese-era theatre and teahouses, intersects a few hundred meters along Jishan St.

Grazing on local snacks is the de rigueur pastime here. Look for *yùyuán* (芋圓; taro balls), *yúwán* (魚丸; fish balls), *cǎozǐ gāo* (草仔糕; herbal cakes) and *hēitáng gāo* (黑糖糕; molasses cake). If the crowds get too much, you can take refuge in a teahouse.

Jishan St begins beside the 7-Eleven on the main road.

🍷 DRINKING

Jiufen Teahouse   Teahouse
(九份茶坊; Jiǔfèn Cháfǎng; ☏02-2496 9056; www.jioufen-teahouse.com.tw; 142 Jishan St, 基山街142號; ☺10.30am-9pm; ☎) Step back in time at this century-old wooden teahouse full of antique furnishings and cosy nooks to hunker down in. The tea selection includes aged pu'ers, roasted Oriental Beauty and Tieguanyin. A pot (with unlimited water refills) starts at NT$600, plus NT$100 per guest, so it's an expensive place to drink solo. Find it just west of the Shuqi St steps on Jishan St.

Sweet snacks include pineapple cake and oolong tea cheesecake. In the basement is a ceramic studio and exhibition area, with high-quality pieces for sale.

Shu-ku Tea Store   Teahouse
(樹窟奇木樓; Shùkū Qímùlóu; ☏02-2497 9043; 38 Fotang Ln, 佛堂巷38號; teas/snacks from NT$300/50; ☺10am-10pm Sun-Wed & Fri, to midnight Sat; ☎) This creaking two-storey teahouse from the Japanese era has the look and feel of a frontier gambling den. Inside you can almost picture the miners squatting on makeshift benches, shuffling cards and warming their hands on a metal teapot. There's no minimum order, making it a good spot for an evening beer. Grab a terrace table for views over the twinkling illuminations of Jiufen.

To get here follow Jishan Rd past the main tourist area until it starts to descend steeply. Just past a couple of homestays look for the English sign to the teahouse on the left.

Jiufen Teahouse

ℹ️ INFORMATION

The **Jiufen Visitor Information Centre** (九份旅遊服務中心; ☑02-2406 3270; 89 Qiche Rd, 車路89號; ⊙9am-6pm) is worth a visit for the informative history sections (in English). It's just down the street on the opposite side from the Jiufen Kite Museum.

ℹ️ GETTING THERE & AROUND

Bus 788, departing just before Keelung Station, runs to Jiufen and Jinguashi (NT$30, 45 minutes). Buses pass the Jiufen bus stop near the 7-Eleven first and then proceed to Jinguashi (the final stop). The two towns are 3km apart and are served by buses every 20 minutes or so.

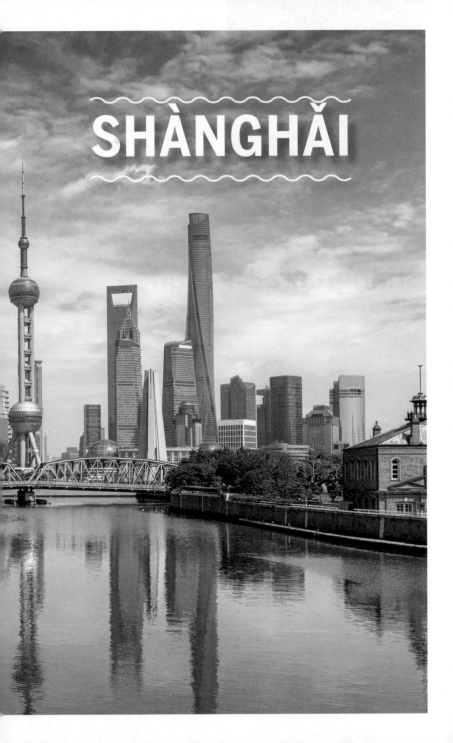

SHÀNGHǍI

Shànghǎi at a Glance

Rapidly becoming a world metropolis, Shànghǎi typifies modern China while being unlike anywhere else in the nation. Awash with cash, ambition and economic vitality, Shànghǎi is, for the movers and shakers of business, the place to be. For all its modernity and cosmopolitanism, however, Shànghǎi is part and parcel of the People's Republic of China, and its challenges are multiplying as fast as cocktails are mixed and served on the Bund.

With a Day in Port

People-watch while strolling along **the Bund** (p234), a gorgeous curve of larger-than-life heritage architecture. Following this, take some time to contemplate and reflect among the harmonious compositions of **Yùyuán Gardens** (p238) – then join the hectic throng in the attached bazaar. If you're in the mood for shopping, browse the boutiques of the **French Concession** (p240).

Best Places for...

Street art and galleries M50 (p243) and Beaugeste (p240)

Views Shanghai Tower (p243)

Street food Huanghe Road Food Street (p247) and Yùyuán Bazaar (p237)

Families Shànghǎi Disneyland (p243)

Previous page: Shànghǎi cityscape
SVEN HANSCHE/SHUTTERSTOCK ©

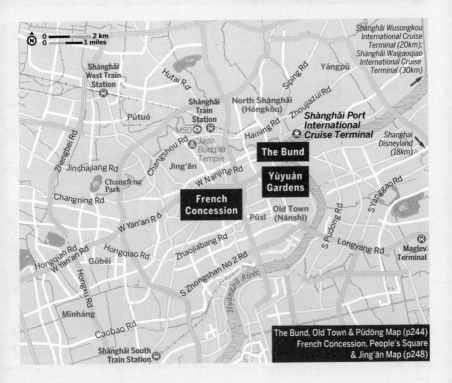

The Bund, Old Town & Pǔdōng Map (p244)
French Concession, People's Square
& Jìng'ān Map (p248)

Getting from the Port

Shànghǎi Port International Cruise Terminal (上海港国际客运中心; Shànghǎi Gǎng Guójì Kèyùn Zhōngxīn; Gaoyang Rd), 1km north of the Bund, is a short walk from the International Cruise Terminal metro station. For small and medium-sized ships.

Shànghǎi Waigaoqiao International Cruise Terminal (aka Haitong Pier) No public transport; take a taxi to the city (¥95, 50 minutes). Little used.

Shànghǎi Wusongkou International Cruise Terminal (aka Baoshan Cruise Terminal) For larger ships. Nearest metro station is Baoyang Road, 3km west (¥25, 12 minutes); take a taxi to the city centre (¥100, 50 minutes).

Fast Facts

Curreny Yuán (元; ¥)

Language Mandarin, Cantonese

Money ATM at Shànghǎi Port International Cruise Terminal; moneychanger at Wusongkou.

Tourist information Shànghǎi Port International Cruise Terminal has a tourist information service. See also p252.

Wi-fi Available at many cafes and throughout the subway system. Note that some popular sites, such as Facebook and Gmail, are blocked in China.

Fairmont Peace Hotel

DENIS LININE/GETTY IMAGES ©

Exploring the Bund

Symbolic of colonial Shànghǎi, the Bund was once the city's Wall St, a place of feverish trading and fortunes made and lost. Today, it's the bars, restaurants and hypnotising views that pull the crowds.

Great For...

☑ Don't Miss

The astonishing views across the Huángpǔ River to Pǔdōng.

Peace Hotel

Lording it over the corner of East Nanjing and East Zhongshan Rds is the most famous building on the Bund, the landmark **Fairmont Peace Hotel** (费尔蒙和平饭店, Fèi'ěrméng Hépíng Fàndiàn; Map p244; ☏021 6321 6888; www.fairmont.com; 20 East Nanjing Rd; 南京东路20号; d¥2500-4000; ☻❄🛜🅿; Ⓜ Line 2, 10 to East Nanjing Rd), constructed between 1926 and 1929. It was originally built as Sassoon House, with Victor Sassoon's famous Cathay Hotel on the 4th to 7th floors. It wasn't for the hoi polloi, with a guest list running to Charlie Chaplin, George Bernard Shaw, and Noel Coward, who penned *Private Lives* here in four days in 1930 when he had the flu.

Sassoon himself spent weekdays in his personal suite on the top floor, just beneath

Custom House

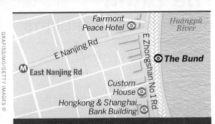

Explore Ashore

Shànghǎi Port International Cruise Terminal is an interesting, 1km walk from the Bund. In a taxi it's just a few minutes away. From Wusongkou port, a taxi is easiest (¥100, 50 minutes); otherwise, take the metro to East Nanjing Road.

ℹ Need to Know

外滩, Wàitān; Map p244; 3 East Zhongshan No 1 Rd; 3 中山东一路; Ⓜ Line 2, 10 to East Nanjing Rd

the green pyramid. The building was renamed the Peace Hotel in 1956.

Custom House

The neoclassical **Custom House** (自订的房子, Zì Dìng De Fángzi; Map p244; 13 East Zhongshan No 1 Rd; 中山东一路13号; Ⓜ Line 2, 10 to East Nanjing Rd, exit 1), established at this site in 1857 and rebuilt in 1927, is one of the most important buildings on the Bund. Capping it is Big Ching, a bell modelled on London's Big Ben. Clocks were by no means new to China, but Shànghǎi was the first city in which they gained widespread acceptance and the lives of many became dictated by a standardised, common schedule.

Hongkong & Shanghai Bank Building

Adjacent to the Custom House, the **Hongkong & Shanghai Bank Building** (HSBC Building, 汇丰大厦; Map p244; 12 East Zhongshan No 1 Rd; 中山东一路12号; Ⓜ Line 2, 10 to East Nanjing Rd) was constructed in 1923. The bank was first established in Hong Kong in 1864 and in Shànghǎi in 1865 to finance trade, and soon became one of the richest in Shànghǎi, arranging the indemnity paid after the Boxer Rebellion. The magnificent mosaic ceiling inside the entrance was plastered over until its restoration in 1997 and is therefore well preserved.

Promenade

The Bund offers a host of things to do, but most visitors head straight for the riverside promenade to pose for photos in front of Pǔdōng's ever-changing skyline.

The Bund

ARCHITECTURAL HIGHLIGHTS

The best way to get acquainted with Shànghǎi is to take a stroll along the Bund.

This illustration shows the main sights along the Bund's central stretch, beginning near the intersection with East Nanjing Rd. The Bund is 1km long and walking it should take around an hour.

Head to the area south of the Hongkong & Shanghai Bank Building to find the biggest selection of drinking and dining destinations.

FACT FILE

➡ Number of remaining heritage buildings on the Bund: 22

➡ Date the first foreign building on the Bund was constructed: 1851

➡ The year in which M on the Bund, the first high-profile Bund restaurant, opened: 1999

➡ Approximate number of wooden piles supporting the Fairmont Peace Hotel: 1600

Hongkong & Shanghai Bank Building (1923)
Head into this massive bank to marvel at the beautiful mosaic ceiling, featuring the 12 zodiac signs and the world's (former) eight centres of finance.

Custom House (1927)
One of the most important buildings on the Bund, Custom House was capped by the largest clock face in Asia and 'Big Ching', a bell modelled on London's Big Ben.

Former Bank of Communications (1947)

Bund Public Service Centre (2010)

TOP TIP

The promenade is open around the clock, but it's at its best in the early morning, when locals are out practising taichi, or in the early evening, when both sides of the river are lit up and the majesty of the waterfront is at its grandest.

North China Daily News Building (1924)

Known as the 'Old Lady of the Bund'. The *News* ran from 1864 to 1951 as the main English-language newspaper in China. Look for the paper's motto above the central windows.

Fairmont Peace Hotel (1929)

Originally built as the Cathay Hotel, this art deco masterpiece was *the* place to stay in Shànghǎi and the crown jewel in Victor Sassoon's real-estate empire.

Russo-Chinese Bank Building (1902)

Former Bank of Taiwan (1927)

Former Chartered Bank Building (1923)

Reopened in 2004 as the upscale entertainment complex Bund 18; the building's top-floor Bar Rouge is one of the Bund's premier late-night destinations.

Former Palace Hotel (1906)

Now known as the Swatch Art Peace Hotel (an artists' residence and gallery, with a top-floor restaurant and bar), this building was completed in 1908 and hosted Sun Yatsen's victory celebration in 1911 following his election as the first president of the Republic of China.

Bank of China (1942)

This unusual building was originally commissioned to be the tallest building in Shànghǎi but, probably because of Victor Sassoon's influence, wound up being 1m shorter than its neighbour.

DOVE LEE/GETTY IMAGES ©

Yùyuán Gardens & Bazaar

With its shaded corridors, glittering pools and whispering bamboo, the Yùyuán Gardens are a delightful escape from Shànghǎi's glass-and-steel modernity. Aim to arrive at 8.30am; from 10am onwards the crowds get increasingly dense.

Great For...

☑ Don't Miss

Hunting out the delightfully ornate inner garden stage.

The Gardens

The Yùyuán Gardens were founded by the Pan family, who were rich Ming-dynasty officials. The gardens took 18 years (from 1559 to 1577) to be nurtured into existence, only to be ransacked during the Opium War in 1842, when British officers were barracked here, and again during the Taiping Rebellion, this time by the French.

Three Ears of Corn Hall & the Rockeries

As you enter, **Three Ears of Corn Hall** (三穗堂; *Sānsuìtáng*) is the largest of the halls in the gardens. The **rockeries** (假山; *jiǎshān*) attempt to recreate a mountain setting within the flatland of the garden, so when combined with **ponds** (池塘; *chítáng*) they suggest the 'hills and rivers' (*shānshuǐ*) of China's landscapes.

⚓

Explore Ashore

From Shànghǎi Port International Cruise Terminal, it's a short metro ride to Yuyuan Garden metro station, or a 3km walk. From Wusongkou port, a taxi is easiest (¥110, 50 minutes); otherwise, take a taxi to Baoyang Road station and ride the subway.

🛈 Need to Know

豫园、豫园商城, Yùyuán & Yùyuán Shāng-chéng; Map p244; Anren St; 安仁街; high/low season ¥40/30; ◔8.30am-5.15pm, last entry at 4.45pm; ⓜLine 10 to Yuyuan Garden

Hall of Heralding Spring & Inner Garden

In the east of the gardens, keep an eye out for the **Hall of Heralding Spring** (点春堂; Diǎnchūn Táng), which in 1853 was the headquarters of the Small Swords Society, a rebel group affiliated with the Taiping rebels. To the south, the **Exquisite Jade Rock** (玉玲珑; Yù Línglóng) was destined for the imperial court in Běijīng until the boat carrying it sank outside Shànghǎi.

South of the Exquisite Jade Rock is the **inner garden** (内园; nèiyuán), where you can also find the beautiful **stage** (古戏台; gǔxìtái) dating from 1888, with a gilded, carved ceiling and fine acoustics, as well as the charming **Hall for Watching Waves** (观涛楼; Guāntāo Lóu).

Take a Break

Grab a tray of dumplings from the famed **Nánxiáng Steamed Bun Restaurant** (南翔 馒头店; Map p244; 85 Yuyuan Rd, Yùyuán Bazaar; 豫园商城豫园路85号; 12 dumplings on 1st fl ¥22; ◔1st fl 10am-9pm, 2nd fl 7am-8pm, 3rd fl 9.30am-7pm; ⓜLine 10 to Yuyuan Garden).

The Bazaar

Next to the Yùyuán Gardens entrance rises the **Mid-Lake Pavilion Teahouse** (湖心亭, Húxīntíng; Map p244; Yùyuán Bazaar; 豫园商城; tea ¥50; ◔9am-9pm; ⓜLine 10 to Yuyuan Garden), one of the most famous teahouses in China.

Surrounding all this is the restored bazaar area, where scores of speciality shops and restaurants jostle over narrow laneways and small squares in a mock 'ye olde Cathay' setting.

At the heart of the melee, south of the Yùyuán Gardens exit, is the venerable **Temple of the Town God** (城隍庙, Chénghuáng Miào; Map p244; Yùyuán Bazaar, off Middle Fang-bang Rd; 豫园商城方浜中路; ¥10; ◔8.30am-4.30pm; ⓜLine 10 to Yuyuan Garden), dedicated to the protector of the city of Shànghǎi.

Tiánzǐfáng

MAOYUNPING/SHUTTERSTOCK ©

The French Concession

For local boutiques, head along leafy backstreets such as Nanchang, Changle, Fumin or Xinle Rds. Xīntiāndì has high-end brands, while Tiánzǐfáng is home to a number of cool gift stores.

Great For...

☑ Don't Miss

Getting thoroughly lost down the disorientating alleyways of Tiánzǐfáng.

Tiánzǐfáng

A shopping complex housed within a grid of tiny alleyways, Tiánzǐfáng is probably the most accessible, authentic, charming and vibrant example of Shànghǎi's trademark traditional back-lane architecture. A community of design studios, cafes and boutiques, it's a much-needed counterpoint to Shànghǎi's mega-malls and skyscrapers.

There are three main north–south lanes (Nos 210, 248 and 274) criss-crossed by irregular east–west alleyways, which makes exploration disorienting and fun. Most shops and boutiques are slim and bijoux. One gallery to seek out is **Beaugeste** (比极影像, Bǐjí Yǐngxiàng; Map p248; ☑ 021 6466 9012; www.beaugeste-gallery.com; 5th fl, No 5, Lane 210, Taikang Rd; 泰康路210弄5号520室田子坊; ⊙10am-6pm Sat & Sun; ⓂDapuqiao) **FREE**, which has thought-provoking contemporary photography exhibits.

Xīntiāndì

L.M.SPENCER/SHUTTERSTOCK ©

⚓ Explore Ashore

From Wusongkou port, a taxi is easiest (¥125, 55 minutes): otherwise, take a taxi to Baoyang Road station and ride the subway. From the Shànghǎi Port International Cruise Terminal, make the short walk to the International Cruise Terminal metro station. For Xīntiāndì, head to South Huangpi Rd or Xintiandi station. For Tiánzǐfáng, take the metro to Dapuqiao.

☑ Top Tip

Eccentric, unconventional **Bell Bar** (Map p248; http://bellbar.cn; Tianzifang, back door No 11, Lane 248, Taikang Rd; 泰康路248弄11号 后门田子坊; ◷10am-2am; 🛜; MDapuqiao) is a delightful Tiánzǐfáng hideaway. It's in the second alley on the right.

Just outside the complex on Taikang Rd, an enormous peony bloom covers the exterior of the **Líulí China Museum** (琉璃艺术博物馆, Líulí Yìshù Bówùguǎn; Map p248; www. liulichinamuseum.com; 25 Taikang Rd; 泰康路25号; adult/child under 18yr ¥20/free; ◷10am-5pm Tue-Sun; MDapuqiao), dedicated to glass sculpture.

Xīntiāndì

With its own namesake metro station, Xīntiāndì has been a Shànghǎi icon for a decade or more. An upscale entertainment and shopping complex modelled on traditional *lòngtáng* (alleyway) homes, this was the first development in the city to prove that historic architecture makes big commercial sense.

The heart of the complex, cleaved into a pedestrianised north and south block, consists of largely rebuilt traditional *shíkùmén* (stone-gate houses), brought bang up to date with a modern spin. But while the layout suggests a flavour of yesteryear, don't expect too much historic magic or cultural allure. Serious shoppers – and diners – will eventually gravitate towards the malls at the southern tip of the south block. Beyond the first mall, which holds some top-notch restaurants on the 2nd floor – including **Din Tai Fung** (鼎泰丰; Map p248; www.dintaifung.com.cn; Xīntiāndì South Block, 2nd fl, Bldg 6; 兴业路123弄新天地南里6号楼2楼; 10 dumplings ¥60-96; ◷10am-midnight; MSouth Huangpi Rd, Xintiandi) and **Shanghai Min** (小南国, Xiǎo Nán Guó; Map p248; Xīntiāndì South Block, 2nd fl, Bldg 6; 兴业路123弄新天地南里6号楼2楼; dishes ¥35-198; ◷11am-10pm; MSouth Huangpi Rd, Xintiandi) – is the **Xīntiāndì Style mall** (新天地时尚, Xīntiāndì Shíshàng; Map p248; 245 Madang Rd; 马当路245号; ◷10am-10pm; MXintiandi) showcasing local brands and chic pieces.

SIGHTS
The Bund & People's Square

West of the Bund, People's Square is ground central for Shànghăi sightseeing, with world-class museums, art galleries and a beautiful park.

Yuanmingyuan Road
Area

(圆明园路, Yuánmíngyuán Lù; Map p244; Ⓜ Line 2, 10 to East Nanjing Rd) Like a smaller, more condensed version of the Bund, the pedestrianised, cobblestone Yuanmingyuan Rd is lined with a mishmash of colonial architecture. Running parallel with the Bund, just one block back, some fine examples of renovated red-brick and stone buildings dating from the 1900s include the art-deco YWCA Building (No 133) and Chinese Baptist Publication building (No 209), the ornate 1907 red-brick Panama Legation building (No 97) and the 1927 neoclassical Lyceum Building.

Shanghai Museum
Museum

(上海博物馆, Shànghăi Bówùguǎn; Map p248; www.shanghaimuseum.net; 201 People's Ave; ⊙9am-5pm Tue-Sun, last entry 4pm; ⊞; Ⓜ Line 1, 2, 8 to People's Square) **FREE** This must-see museum escorts you through the craft of millennia and the pages of Chinese history. It's home to one of the most impressive collections in the land: take your pick from the archaic green patinas of the Ancient Chinese Bronzes Gallery through to the silent solemnity of the Ancient Chinese Sculpture Gallery; from the exquisite beauty of the ceramics in the Zande Lou Gallery to the measured and timeless flourishes captured in the Chinese Calligraphy Gallery.

Jìng'ān

Jade Buddha Temple
Buddhist Temple

(玉佛寺, Yùfó Sì; cnr Anyuan & Jiangning Rds; 安远路和江宁路街口; ¥20; ⊙8am-4.30pm; Ⓜ Line 7, 13 to Changshou Rd, exit 5) One of Shànghăi's few active Buddhist monasteries, this temple was built between 1918 and 1928. The highlight is a transcendent Buddha crafted from pure jade, one of five shipped back to China by the monk Hui Gen at the turn of the 20th century.

Views from Shanghai Tower

MICHAEL GORDON/SHUTTERSTOCK ©

M50 — Arts Centre

(M50创意产业集聚区, M50 Chuàngyì Chǎnyè Jíjùqū; www.m50.com.cn/en; 50 Moganshan Rd; 莫干山路50号; MLine 13 to Jiangning Rd) FREE Shànghǎi may be known for its glitz and glamour, but it's got an edgy subculture too. The industrial M50 art complex is one prime example, where galleries have been set up in disused factories and cotton mills, utilising the vast space to showcase contemporary Chinese emerging and established artists. There's a lot to see, so plan to spend half a day poking around the site.

Shanghai Natural History Museum — Museum

(上海自然博物馆, Shànghǎi Zìrán Bówùguǎn; Map p248; 021 6862 2000; www.snhm.org. cn; 510 West Beijing Rd; 北京西路510号; adult/senior/teen/under 13yr ¥30/25/12/free; 9am-5.15pm Tue-Sun; MLine 1 to Shanghai Natural History Museum) Perhaps not quite on the same scale as the Smithsonian, this new sleek space would nevertheless be a fitting choice for a *Night at the Museum* movie. As comprehensive as it is entertaining and informative, the museum is packed with displays of taxidermied animals, dinosaurs and cool interactive features. Its architecture is also a highlight, with a striking design that is beautifully integrated in its art-filled **Jìng'ān Sculpture Park** (静安雕塑公园, Jìng'ān Diāosù Gōngyuán; Map p248; 128 Shimen 2nd Rd; 石门二路128号; 6am-8.30pm; MLines 2, 12, 13 to West Nanjing Rd, Line 13 to Shanghai Natural History Museum) FREE setting.

⊙ Pǔdōng

Shanghai Tower — Notable Building

(上海中心大厦, Shànghǎi Zhōngxīn Dàshà; Map p244; www.shanghaitower.com.cn; cnr Middle Yincheng & Huayuanshiqiao Rds; ¥180; 8.30am-9.30pm, last admission 8.30pm; MLujiazui) China's tallest building dramatically twists skywards from its footing in Lùjiāzuǐ. The 121-storey, 632m-tall, Gensler-designed tower topped out in August 2013 and opened in mid-2016. The observation deck on the 118th-floor is the world's highest.

 Shànghǎi Disneyland

After a decade of planning and diplomatic wrangling, the Magic Kingdom finally arrived in the Middle Kingdom in 2016, offering up a spectacular serving of **Disney** (上海迪士尼乐园, Shànghǎi Díshìní Lèyuán; 021 3158 0000; www. shanghaidisneyresort.com; Shanghai Disney Resort, Pudong; adult/child 1.0-1.4m & senior from ¥499/375; 8.30am-10pm; MDisney Resort) seasoned with a dash of Chinese culture. 'Main Street USA' has become the locally inspired yet rather sterile 'Gardens of the Imagination', and you can gnaw the ears off a steamed Mickey Mouse pork bun at snack vendors throughout the park.

Much has been said about the queues; if you're serious about packing in all the big rides in a day, aim to arrive at least 30 minutes before the park opens, and play a tactical Fast Pass game (the longest lines are at Roaring Rapids, Soaring Over the Horizon and TRON). Alternatively, for groups of three, a cool ¥6300 (¥9000 at peak times) gets you a 'Premier Tour' with fast access to all the rides.

With younger kids in tow you can takes things at a more leisurely pace, and there are plenty of roving musical performances, costumed characters to meet and the excellent parades (12pm and 3.30pm) and fireworks display (8.30pm), which don't require any waiting.

The Bund, Old Town & Pǔdōng

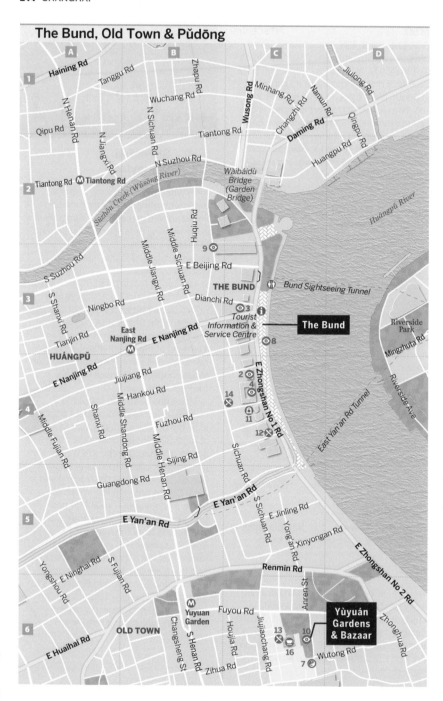

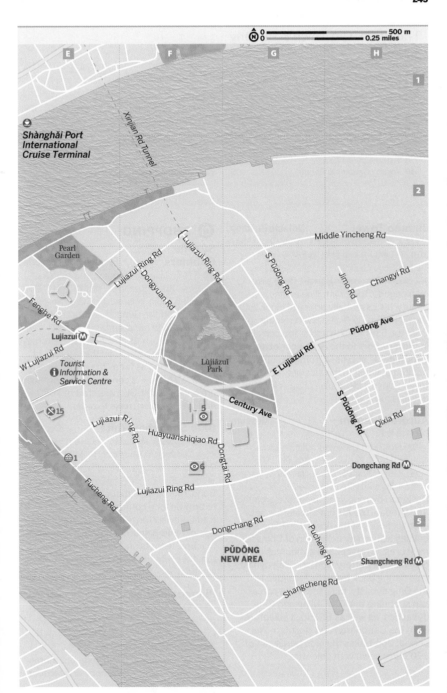

0   500 m
0   0.25 miles

Shànghǎi Port International Cruise Terminal

Xinjian Rd Tunnel

Pearl Garden

Lujiazui Ring Rd

Dongyuan Rd

Lujiazui Ring Rd

Middle Yincheng Rd

S Pǔdōng Rd

Jimo Rd

Changyi Rd

Fenghe Rd

Pǔdōng Ave

Lujiazui Ⓜ

W Lujiazui Rd

E Lujiazui Rd

Lùjiāzuǐ Park

Tourist ⓘ Information & Service Centre

Century Ave

S Pǔdōng Rd

Qixia Rd

Ⓧ 15

Lujiazui Ring Rd

Huayuanshiqiao Rd

Dongtai Rd

🔺 5
◎

Dongchang Rd Ⓜ

🏛 1

◎ 6

Lujiazui Ring Rd

Fucheng Rd

Dongchang Rd

Pucheng Rd

PǓDŌNG NEW AREA

Shangcheng Rd Ⓜ

Shangcheng Rd

The Bund, Old Town & Pǔdōng

Jīnmào Tower   Notable Building

(金茂大厦, Jīnmào Dàshà; Map p244; ☑021 5047 5101; 88 Century Ave; 世纪大道88号; adult/student/child ¥120/90/60; ⏰8.30am-10pm; Ⓜ Lujiazui) Resembling an art-deco take on a pagoda, this crystalline edifice is a beauty. It's essentially an office block with the high-altitude Grand Hyatt renting space from the 53rd to 87th floors. You can zip up in the elevators to the 88th-floor **observation deck**, accessed from the separate podium building to the side of the main tower (aim for clear days at dusk for both day and night views).

Aurora Museum   Museum

(震旦博物馆, Zhèn Dàn Bówùguǎn; Map p244; ☑021 5840 8899; www.auroramuseum.cn; Aurora Bldg, 99 Fucheng Rd; 富城路99号震旦大厦; ¥60; ⏰10am-5pm Tue-Thu, Sat & Sun, to 9pm Fri, last entry 1hr before closing; Ⓜ Lujiazui) Designed by renowned Japanese architect, Andō Tadao, the Aurora Museum is set over six floors of the Aurora building and houses a stunning collection of Chinese treasures. Artefacts and antiquities on display include pottery from the Han dynasty; jade dating back from the Neolithic to the Qing dynasty; blue and white porcelain spanning the Yuan, Ming and Qing dynasties; as well as Buddhist sculptures from the Gandharan and Northern Wei period. Don't miss the jade burial suit of 2903 tiles sewn with gold wire.

🛍 SHOPPING

Sūzhōu Cobblers   Fashion & Accessories

(摩登绣鞋; Map p244; www.suzhou-cobblers. com; Unit 101, 17 Fuzhou Rd; 福州路17号101室; ⏰10am-6.30pm; Ⓜ Line 2, 10 to East Nanjing Rd) Right off the Bund, this cute boutique sells exquisite hand-embroidered silk slippers, bags, hats and clothing. Patterns and colours are based on the fashions of the 1930s, and as far as the owner, Huang 'Denise' Mengqi, is concerned, the products are one of a kind. Slippers start at ¥650 and the shop can make to order.

Blue Shanghai White   Ceramics

(海晨, Hǎi Chén; Map p244; ☑021 6323 0856; www.blueshanghaiwhite.com; Unit 103, 17 Fuzhou Rd; 福州路17号103室; ⏰10.30am-6.30pm; Ⓜ Line 2, 10 to East Nanjing Rd) Just off the Bund, this little boutique is a great place to browse for a contemporary take on a traditional art form. It sells a tasteful selection of hand-painted Jīngdézhèn porcelain teacups, teapots and vases, displayed together with the shop's ingeniously de-signed wooden furniture.

Pilingpalang   Ceramics

(噼呤啪唥; Map p248; ☑021 6219 5020; www. pilingpalang.com; Shanghai Centre, Shop 116, 1376 West Nanjing Rd; 上海商城南京西路1376号东峰116; ⏰10am-9.30pm; Ⓜ Lines 2, 12 & 13 to West Nanjing Rd) You'll find gorgeous vibrant coloured ceramics, cloisonné and lacquer, in pieces that celebrate traditional Chinese forms while adding a modern and deco-inspired slant. Tea caddies and decorative trays make for great gifts or souvenirs.

❌ EATING

As much an introduction to regional Chinese cuisine as a magnet for talented chefs from around the globe, Shànghǎi has staked a formidable claim as the Middle Kingdom's hottest dining destination.

Huanghe Road
Food Street
Chinese $

(黄河路美食街, Huánghé Lù Měishí Jiē; Map p248; M Line 1, 2, 8 to People's Square) With a prime central location near People's Park, Huanghe Rd covers all the bases from cheap lunches to late-night post-theatre snacks. You'll find large restaurants, but it's best for dumplings – get 'em fried at **Yang's** (小杨生煎馆, Xiǎoyáng Shēngjiān Guǎn; Map p248; 97 Huanghe Rd; 黄河路97号; dumplings from ¥9; ⏰6.30am-8pm; M Line 1, 2, 8 to People's Square) or served up in bamboo steamers across the road at **Jiājiā Soup**

Dumplings (佳家汤包, Jiājiā Tāngbāo; Map p248; 90 Huanghe Rd; 黄河路90号; 12 dumplings ¥25; ⏰7am-8pm; M Lines 1, 2, 8).

Shanghai
Grandmother
Shanghai $

(上海姥姥, Shànghǎi Lǎolao; Map p244; ☎021 6321 6613; 70 Fuzhou Rd; 福州路70号; dishes ¥25-150; ⏰10.30am-9.30pm; M Line 2, 10 to East Nanjing Rd) This packed eatery is within easy striking distance of the Bund and cooks up all manner of home-style dishes. You can't go wrong with the classics here: braised aubergine in soy sauce, Grandmother's braised pork, crispy duck, three-cup chicken and *mápó dòufu* (麻婆豆腐; tofu and pork crumbs in a spicy sauce) rarely disappoint.

Jian Guo 328
Shanghai $

(建国, Jiànguó; Map p248; ☎021 6471 3819; 328 West Jianguo Rd; 建国西路328号; mains ¥22-58; ⏰11am-2pm & 5-9.30pm; M Jiashan Rd) Frequently crammed, this boisterous, narrow, two-floor spot tucked away on Jiàn-guó Rd does a roaring trade on the back of excellent well-priced Shanghainese

Xiǎolóngbāo at Jiājiā Soup Dumplings

French Concession, People's Square & Jìng'ān

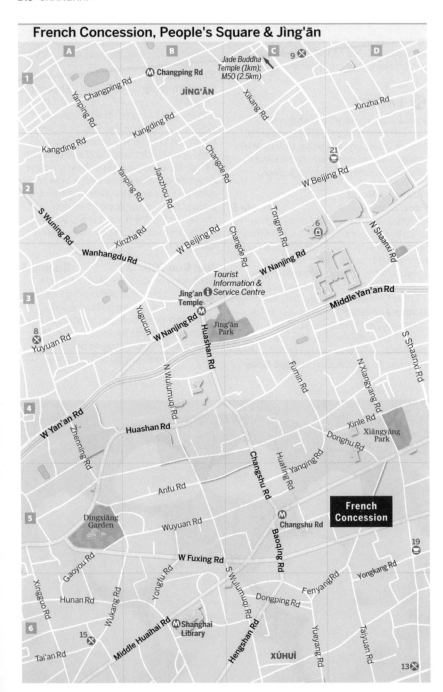

Jade Buddha Temple (1km); M50 (2.5km)

JÌNG'ĀN

French Concession

XÚHUÌ

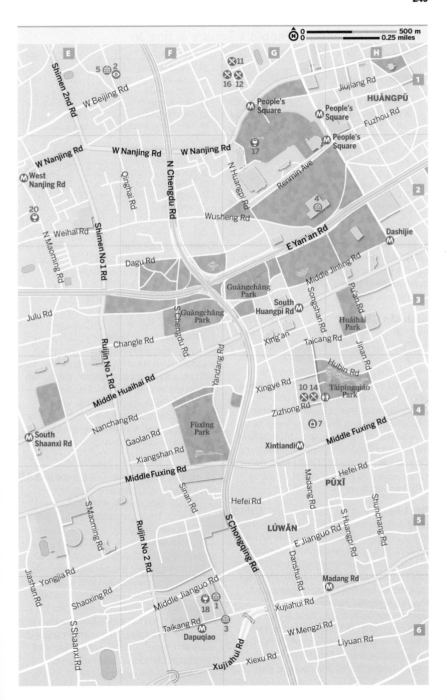

0 500 m
0 0.25 miles

Shimen 2nd Rd

5 2

11
16 12

W Beijing Rd

People's
Square

People's
Square

Jiujiang Rd

HUÁNGPǓ

Fuzhou Rd

W Nanjing Rd

W Nanjing Rd

W Nanjing Rd

N Chengdu Rd

People's
Square

West
Nanjing Rd

Qinghai Rd

17

20

N Weihai Rd

Shimen No 1 Rd

N Maoming Rd

N Huangpi Rd

Renmin Ave

Wusheng Rd

E Yan'an Rd

4

Dashijie

Dagu Rd

Middle Jinling Rd

Julu Rd

S Chengdu Rd

Guǎngchǎng
Park

Guǎngchǎng
Park

South
Huangpi Rd

Songshan Rd

Puan Rd

Jinan Rd

Huáihǎi
Park

Ruijin No 1 Rd

Changle Rd

Xing'an

Taicang Rd

Middle Huaihai Rd

Yandang Rd

Xingye Rd

Hubin Rd

10 14

Tàipíngqiáo
Park

South
Shaanxi Rd

Nanchang Rd

Gaolan Rd

Fùxīng
Park

Zizhong Rd

7

Xiangshan Rd

Xintiandi

Middle Fuxing Rd

Middle Fuxing Rd

S Maoming Rd

Sinan Rd

Hefei Rd

Madang Rd

Hefei Rd

PǓXĪ

S Huangpi Rd

Shunchang Rd

Ruijin No 2 Rd

S Chongqing Rd

LÚWĀN

E Jianguo Rd

Danshui Rd

Jiashan Rd

Yongjia Rd

Shaoxing Rd

Middle Jianguo Rd

18 1

Xujiahui Rd

Madang Rd

S Shaanxi Rd

Taikang Rd

3

Dapuqiao

W Mengzi Rd

Liyuan Rd

Xujiahui Rd

Xiexu Rd

French Concession, People's Square & Jìng'ān

cuisine. You can't go wrong with the MSG-free menu, but highlights include the deep-fried duck legs, eggplant casserole, scallion oil noodles and yellow croaker fish spring rolls. Reserve.

Sìchuān Citizen   Sichuan $
(龙门阵茶屋, Lóngménzhèn Cháwū; Map p248; ☑021 54041235; 378 Wukang Rd; 武康路378号; dishes ¥26-98, set lunch ¥38-68; ☺11am-10.30pm; �🖉; ⓂShanghai Library) The subdued evening lighting and welcoming service concocts a warm and homely atmosphere at this popular outpost of Sìchuān cuisine in Shànghǎi. The extensive photo menu is foreigner friendly and includes a sizeable vegetarian selection. The *dàndàn* noodles (担担面) are textbook spicy, while the pork wontons in hot oil (¥10) are spot on.

Brut Eatery   Cafe $
(悦璞食堂; Map p248; 698 Yuyuan Rd, 愚园路698号; mains from ¥46; ☺8am-10pm; ⓂLine 2 & 11 to Jiangsu Rd) An extremely popular cubby hole casual eatery with half a dozen tables, plus steps with cushions and mini-side tables out front. Diners queue and then sit shoulder to shoulder with other patrons for Californian Chinese chef Jun Wu's creations. The waffles and chicken is a winner – with six-spice fried chicken, a large bouncy waffle, pickled watermelon radish, jujube honey and candied walnuts.

Commune Social   Tapas $$
(食社; Shíshè; Map p248; ☑021 6047 7638; www.communesocial.com; 511 Jiangning Rd; 江宁路511号; tapas ¥38-238, 9-course tasting menu per person ¥629; ☺noon-2.30pm Tue-Sun, 6-10.30pm Tue-Thu, 5.30-10.30pm Fri & Sat, 11.30am-10pm Sun; Ⓜ Line 7 to Changping Rd) A venture by UK celebrity chef Jason Atherton, this natty Neri & Hu–designed restaurant blends a stylish, yet relaxed, vibe with sensational tasting dishes, exquisitely presented by chef Scott Melvin. It's divided neatly into upstairs cocktail bar with terrace, downstairs open-kitchen tapas bar and dessert bar. It's the talk of the town, but has a no-reservations policy, so prepare to queue.

M on the Bund   European $$$
(米氏西餐厅, Mǐshì Xīcāntīng; Map p244; ☑021 6350 9988; www.m-restaurantgroup.com/mbund; 7th fl, 20 Guangdong Rd; 广东路20号7楼; mains ¥200-400, 2-course set lunch ¥198, weekend brunch 2-/3-courses ¥298/328; ☺11.30am-2.30pm & 6-10.30pm; ⓂLine 2, 10 to East Nanjing Rd) M exudes a timelessness and level of sophistication that eclipses the razzle-dazzle of many other upscale Shànghǎi restaurants. The menu ain't radical, but that's the question it seems to ask you – is breaking new culinary ground really so crucial? Crispy suckling pig and tajine with saffron are, after all, simply delicious just the way they are.

Yi Cafe
Cafe $$$

(怡咖啡; Yí Kāfēi; Map p244; ☎021 6882 8888; www.shangri-la.com; 2nd fl, Pudong Shangri-La, 33 Fucheng Rd; 富城路33号2楼; buffet meals from ¥218; ⏰breakfast 6-10.30am, lunch 11.30am-2.30pm, dinner 5.30-10pm; 🛜; Ⓜ Lujiazui) If you're squabbling over what to eat for lunch, brunch or dinner, settle your differences at smart-casual Yi Cafe. With 12 open kitchens and a walk-through layout, it's a veritable Asian–Southeast Asian–international food fest with endless menus. Be sure to cultivate a real hunger before you stop by. The buffet breakfasts easily match Pǔdōng's sightseeing calorific demands.

🍷 DRINKING

Sumerian
Cafe

(苏美尔人, Sū Měi Ěr Rén; Map p248; www.sumeriancoffee.com; 415 North Shaanxi Rd; 陕西北路415号; coffee from ¥28; ⏰7.30am-6pm Mon, to 7.30pm Tue-Sun; 🛜; Ⓜ Line 2, 12, 13 to West Nanjing Rd, exit 1) Run by a bright and sunny team of staff, good-looking Sumerian packs a lot into a small space. The real drawcard here is the coffee – the cafe roasts its own single-origin beans sourced seasonally from Ethiopia, El Salvador and China. It does good pour-overs and lattes, as well as a nitro and eight-hour cold drip. The homemade bagels are also a standout, with a delicious selection of toppings and spreads.

Café del Volcán
Cafe

(Map p248; www.cafevolcan.com; 80 Yongkang Rd; 永康路80号; coffee ¥26-46; ⏰8am-8pm Mon-Fri, 10am-8pm Sat & Sun; 🛜; Ⓜ South Shaanxi Rd) Tiny Café del Volcán offers a pit stop from the bustle of bar-heavy Yongkang Rd. The minimalist cafe has just a few wooden box tables sharing the space with the roasting machine. The coffee here is excellent and its signature beans come from the owner's coffee plantation in Guatemala – in the family for 120 years – while other single-origin beans are from Ethiopia, Kenya, Panama and Yúnnán.

🍽 Dumplings

Shànghǎi's favourite dumpling is the *xiǎolóngbāo* (小笼包; 'little steamer buns'), copied everywhere else in China but only true to form here. *Xiǎolóngbāo* are normally bought by the *lóng* (笼; steamer basket) and dipped in vinegar.

There's an art to eating them, as they're full of a delicious but scalding gelatinous broth: the trick is to avoid both burning your tongue and staining your shirt (not easy), while road-testing your chopstick skills.

Tradition attributes the invention of the dumpling – filled with pork, or in more upmarket establishments with pork and crab – to Nánxiáng, a village north of Shànghǎi city.

Another Shanghainese speciality is *shēngjiān* (生煎), scallion-and-sesame-seed-coated dumplings that are fried in an enormous flat-bottomed wok, which is covered with a wooden lid. These are also pork-based; again, watch out for the palate-scorching, scalding oil, which can travel.

Top dumpling joints:

Yang's Fry Dumplings (p247) Simply scrumptious.

Din Tai Fung (p241) Outstanding *xiǎolóngbāo*.

Nánxiáng Steamed Bun Restaurant (p239) Round-the-block lines.

Jiājiā Soup Dumplings (p247) Humble spot serving some of the city's best *xiǎolóngbāo*.

Chef at Nánxiáng Steamed Bun Restaurant (p239)
BOGOSHIPDA/SHUTTERSTOCK ©

Tea Tasting

It may be a rather clichéd choice, but there's no doubt that a Yíxīng teapot and a package of oolong tea makes for a convenient gift. But how do you go about a purchase? Two things to remember: first of all, be sure to taste (品尝; *pǐncháng*) and compare several different teas – flavours vary widely, and there's no point in buying a premium grade if you don't like it.

Tasting is free (免费; *miǎnfèi*) and fun, but it's good form to make some sort of purchase afterwards. Second, tea is generally priced by the *jīn* (斤; 500g), which may be more tea than you can finish in a year. Purchase several *liǎng* (两; 50g) instead – divide the list price by 10 for an idea of the final cost. Some of the different types of tea for sale include oolong (乌龙; *wūlóng*), green (绿; *lǜ*), flower (花茶; *huāchá*) and *pu-erh* (普洱; *pǔ'ěr*) – true connoisseurs have a different teapot for each type of tea.

Tea for sale
ZVONIMIR ATLETIC/SHUTTERSTOCK ©

Barbarossa   Bar

(芭芭露莎会所, Bābālùshā Huìsuǒ; Map p248; www.barbarossa.com.cn; People's Park, 231 West Nanjing Rd; 南京西路231号人民公园内; ⊗11am-2am; 🛜; Ⓜ Line 1, 2, 8 to People's Square, exit 11) Set back in People's Park alongside a pond, Barbarossa is all about escapism. Forget Shànghǎi, this is Morocco channelled by Hollywood set designers. The action gets steadily more intense as you ascend to the roof terrace, via the cushion-strewn 2nd floor, where the hordes puff on fruit-flavoured hookahs. At night, use the park entrance just east of the former Shànghǎi Race Club building (上海跑马总会; Shànghǎi Pǎomǎ Zǒnghuì).

Happy hour (from 2pm to 8pm) is a good time to visit for two-for-one cocktails.

Patio Lounge   Lounge

(Map p244; http://shanghai.grand.hyatt.com; Grand Hyatt, Jīnmào Tower, 88 Century Ave; 世纪大道88号君悦大酒店; afternoon tea for 4 ¥368; ⊗11.30am-11pm Sun-Thu, to midnight Fri & Sat; Ⓜ Lujiazui) Have a drink or indulge in afternoon tea with the spectacular 33-floor atrium of the Grand Hyatt soaring above you in the Jīnmào Tower.

Goose Island Brewhouse   Brewery

(Map p248; ☑021 6219 0268; www.gooseisland. com; 209 Maoming Bei Lu, 茂名北路209号; ⊗11.30am-midnight Sun-Thu, 11.30am-2am Fri & Sat; Ⓜ Line 2, 12, 13 to West Nanjing Rd) You'll likely spot this beer brand all over town – this warehouse-style space over two floors is where it's brewed in enormous vats. Choose from dozens of white, blonde, amber and brown ales, poured from taps shaped like goose heads. A full food menu includes hearty oxtail soup, hickory smoked pork ribs, IPA fried chicken and roasted kimchi nachos. A few patio tables are available in the alley outside.

ⓘ INFORMATION

Shànghǎi has about a dozen or so rather useless **Tourist Information & Service Centres** (旅游咨询服务中心; Lǚyóu Zīxún Fúwù Zhōngxīn) where you can at least get free maps and (sometimes) information. Locations include the following:

Jìng'ān (Map p248; ☑021 6248 3259; Shop 19, Lane 1678, 18 West Nanjing Rd; 南京西路1678弄18号; ⊗10am-6pm; Ⓜ Line 2, 7 to Jing'an Temple)

Pǔdōng (Map p244; 168 West Lujiazui Rd; 陆家嘴西路168号; ⊗9am-5pm)

The Bund (Map p244; ⊗9.30am-9.30pm; Ⓜ East Nanjing Rd)

Barbarossa

ℹ GETTING AROUND

Bicycle Good for small neighbourhoods, but distances are too colossal for effective transport about town.

Bus With a wide-ranging web of routes, buses may sound tempting, but that's before you try to decipher routes and stops or attempt to squeeze aboard during the crush hour. Buses also have to contend with Shànghǎi's traffic, which can slow to an agonising crawl.

Metro The rapidly expanding metro and light railway system works like a dream; it's fast, effi-cient and inexpensive. Rush hour on the metro operates at overcapacity, however, and you get to savour the full meaning of the big squeeze.

Taxi Ubiquitous and cheap, but flagging one down during rush hour or during a rainstorm requires staying power of a high order.

Walking This is only really possible within neigh-bourhoods, and even then the distances can be epic and tiring.

JEJU ISLAND

Jeju Island at Glance

Jeju-do (제주도), South Korea's largest island, has long been the country's favourite domestic holiday destination thanks to its beautiful beaches, lush countryside and seaside hotels designed for rest and relaxation.

Explore tangerine-trimmed country roads, jagged coasts and narrow lanes dotted with cottage-style homes made from black lava rock. The ocean is never far away, so plunge into blue seas to view coral as colourful as the sunsets and dig into Jeju-do's unique cuisine, including seafood caught by haeneyo (female free divers).

With a Day in Port

Find Buddha in **Sanbanggul-sa** (p258), a cave at the top of a mountain, or go underground in **Manjang-gul** (p260), part of the world's largest lava-tube cave system. You can also sample gardens, lava tubes and a folk village at **Hallim Park** (p261).

Best Places for...

Climbing a volcano Seongsan Ilchul-bong (p260)

Coastal walks Yongmeori Coast (p259)

Local culture Jeju Folk Village (p260)

Waterfalls Cheonjiyeon Pokpo (p260)

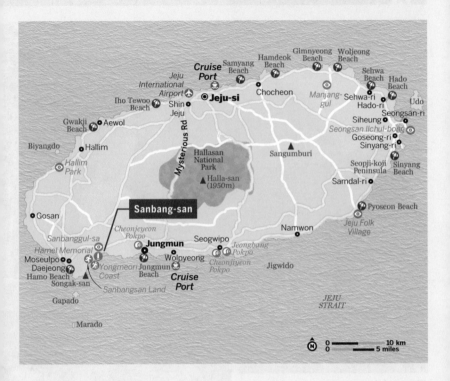

Getting from the Port

Most cruise ships dock at Jeju-do's capital, **Jeju-si** (제주시), on the island's north side; from here it's about 2km into the city. There is usually a shuttle service and taxis waiting. Others dock at the new **Jeju Naval Base** near Gangjeong in the south, not far from atmospheric Seogwipo.

Both make convenient bases for exploring the small island. Inexpensive buses run from the ports into Jeju-si and Seogwipo, and head out all over the island. If you plan on visiting more than one sight, then all-day taxi hire is a good investment.

Fast Facts

Currency Korean won (₩)

Language Korean

Money Jeju-si terminal has an ATM that accepts foreign-issued cards. At the time of research there was only currency exchange, not an ATM, at the southern port. Bring currency, or look for an ATM in Seogwipo. Most ATMs on Jeju-do do not accept foreign-issued cards: bring currency with you to be sure.

Tourist information There is a tourist office (p263) at Jeju-si terminal.

Wi-fi There is free service at the Jeju-si terminal, on public buses and at many public buildings and tourist sites on the island.

Sanbanggul-sa

Sanbang-san

Hugging the southwest corner of the island, the sleepy village of Sagye-ri boasts a number of terrific sights, including dramatic coastlines and incredible rock formations, but most attractive is the imposing Sanbanggul-sa (395m). Its temples peer out to sea, and at the top of a short hike, a cave holds the dramatic spectacle of a stone Buddha in a cave dripping with water.

Great For...

☑ **Don't Miss**
Gorgeous views out across the sea.

Sanbanggul-sa

A steep, 20-minute walk up the south face of the craggy Sanbang-san is a small stone Buddha in a 5m-high cave called Sanbanggul-sa. From Sagye-ri, the walk up looks more daunting than it really is, but after reaching the cave you'll be delighted because of the powerful 'wow' factor. Lower down, by the defunct ticket office and cafe, are more-modern shrines and statues with free admission. There is a separate ticket office just before the cave.

Hamel Memorial

The **Hamel Memorial** (하멜상선전시관; combo ticket with Sanbanggul-sa adult/youth/ child ₩2500/2000/1500) is housed in a replica of a Dutch ship. Hendrick Hamel (1630–92), one of the survivors of a shipwreck near Jeju in 1653, was forced to

LOES KIEBOOM/SHUTTERSTOCK ©

Yongmeori coast

LOESKIEBOOM/GETTY IMAGES ©

Explore Ashore

Buses (₩1200, every 20 minutes) travel between Sanbanggul-sa and Jeju-si Intercity Bus Terminal (bus 250 or 251, 75 minutes) and Jungang Rotary (bus 202, one hour) in Seogwipo.

ⓘ Need to Know

산방굴사; 218-10 Sanbang-ro, Andeok -myeon; adult/youth/child ₩1000/700/ 500, parking ₩1000; ☺sunrise-sunset; ℗

stay in Korea for 13 years before escaping in a boat to Japan. Later he was the first Westerner to write a book on the 'hermit kingdom'.

Yongmeori Coast

A short walk from Sanbanggul-sa towards the ocean brings you to the **Yongmeori coast** (용머리해안; combo ticket with Sanbanggul-sa adult/youth/child ₩2500/2000/1500; ☺8am-5.30pm), a spectacular seaside trail with soaring cliffs pockmarked by erosion into catacombs, narrow clefts and natural archways. Some say the rock formation looks like a dragon's head, hence the name (dragon, 용, *yong*, and head, 머리, *meori*).

From the temple entrance, cross the street and walk towards the shipwreck. Note: the walk along the cliffs closes during very high seas.

Sanbangsan Land

This 'viking' **pirate ship ride** (산방산 랜드; ☎064-794 1425; 24-32 Sagyenam-ro 216beon-gil; ride ₩2000; ☺9am-6pm; ⊞) sits between Sanbang-san and the coast. You'll hear the screams of visitors as they are launched higher than any other similar ship in Korea. The ride was made mildly famous when it inspired the song 'Viking' by K-Indie group Peppertones.

Take a Break

If you like seafood, check out the restaurants along the road from Sanbang-san to the port.

◉ SIGHTS

Jeju Folk Village   Village
(제주민속촌; ☎064-787 4501; http://jejufolk.
com; 631-34 Minsokhaean-ro, Pyoseon-myeon;
adult/youth/child ₩11,000/8000/7000;
☻8.30am-6pm, to 5pm Oct-Feb; ☐201, Pyeosolli
Office stop) The educational Jeju Folk Village
gathers together traditional buildings from
across the island (some reconstructions,
others hundreds of years old) in an attractively designed park. Various sections cover
Jeju's culture from shamans to *yangban*
(aristocrats), and the differences between
mountain, hill-country and fishing villages.

Seongsan Ilchul-bong   Volcano
(성산일출봉; ☎064-783 0959; http://jejuwnh.
jeju.go.kr; 284-12 Ilchul-ro, Seongsan-eup; adult/
youth ₩2000/1000; ☻1hr before sunrise-8pm;
☐201, 210, Seongsan Ilchulbong Tuff Cone Entrance stop) This majestic 182m-high, extinct
tuff volcano, shaped like a giant punchbowl,
is one of Jeju-do's most impressive sights
and a Unesco World Heritage Site. The
forested crater is ringed by jagged rocks,
though there's no lake because the rock is
porous. From the entrance, climbing the
steep stairs to the crater rim only takes 20
minutes.

Buses run to adjacent Seongsan-ri
village from Jeju-si Intercity Bus Terminal
(201 and 210, 70 to 90 minutes, every 20
minutes).

Cheonjiyeon Pokpo   Waterfall
(천지연폭포; adult/child ₩2000/1000; ☻7am-
10pm) This popular 22m-high waterfall is
reached after a 10-minute walk through
a beautifully forested, steep gorge. The
waterfall can be impressive following heavy
rain; at other times it's more noisy than
wide. Well worth visiting in the evening,
too, when the illuminated gorge takes on a
romantic atmosphere. The falls are on Olle
Trail 6; you can easily walk here from town
or take the Seogwipo City Tour Bus.

Manjang-gul   Cave
(만장굴; ☎064-710 7905; http://jejuwnh.jeju.
go.kr; 182 Manjanggul-gil, Gujwa-eup; adult
₩2000, youth & child ₩1000; ☻9am-6pm;
☐711, Manjang-gul stop) Manjang-gul is
the main access point to the lava-tube

Hallim Park

caves. In total the caves are 7.4km long, with heights between 2m and 23m. In this section you can walk around 1km underground to a 7m-high lava pillar, the cave's outstanding feature. The immense black tunnel with swirling walls looks like the lair of a giant serpent and it's hard to imagine the geological forces that created it aeons ago, moulding rock as if it were play dough.

Take a jacket and good shoes, as the cave ceiling drips, the ground is wet and uneven and the temperature inside is a chilly 10°C, regardless of the weather outside.

Hallim Park   Gardens
(한림공원; ☑064-796 0001; www.hallimpark. co.kr; 300 Hallim-ro, Hallim-eup; adult/youth/ child ₩11,000/8000/7000; ⊗8.30am-7pm Mar-Sep, to 6pm Oct-Feb; ℗⏾; ☒202, Hallim Park stop) Hallim Park offers a botanical and bonsai garden, a mini folk village and walks through a lava-tube cave. The caves are part of a 17km-long lava-tube system and are said to be the only lava caves in the world to contain stalagmites and stalactites.

TOURS

Jeju City Tour Bus   Bus
(☑064-748 3211; www.jejugoldenbus.com; day pass adult/child ₩12,000/8000; ⊗9 departures 9am-7pm, closed 3rd Mon of month) A day pass on the blue, white and orange Jeju City Tour Bus is a convenient way to explore multiple sights on a 22-stop hop-on, hop-off circuit in and around Jeju-si, including the ferry terminal.

Seogwipo City Tour Bus   Bus
(www.seogwipo.go.kr/group/culture/tourism/ electricity.htm; rides with/without T-money card ₩1150/1200; ⊗9am-9.35pm, every 35-40min; ⏶) The 880 bus makes it easy to see all of Seogwipo's main sights in and around downtown in one day. Using a T-money card, you get two free transfers within 40 minutes of tapping off one ride and making another.

Tourism Controversy

Home to barely 600,000, Jeju Island receives some 15 million visitors each year. To help cope with the increasing arrivals, a second (controversial) port was built in the island's south. Some welcome the additional income tourism brings to the island, but there are also concerns about the sustainability of the industry, which brings increasing litter, traffic and demand on the island's freshwater supplies. As a visitor you're unlikely to see much evidence of Jeju's struggles to adapt to increasing visitor numbers (beyond the traffic). Where you can, spend money in local and traditional businesses. Be respectful. Don't litter, and try to minimise waste by bringing your own reusable water bottle and tote bag.

Seogwipo

Yeha Bus Tours   Bus
(☑064-713 5505; www.yehatour.com; adult/ youth ₩109,000/89,000; ⊗8.30am-5.30pm) You get bus travel, sight entrance fees, lunch and a guide to explain everything on this one-day excursion. The company operates three routes that run to some of the most popular destinations on the island.

⊗ EATING & DRINKING

In Jeju-si, Black Pork Street (*heukdwaeji geori* on Gwandeong-ro 15-gil) is a string of barbecue restaurants serving the island's speciality, black-skinned pig. Plenty of

DANIELVFUNG/GETTY IMAGES ©

Dongmun Market

regular Korean and seafood restaurants run behind the Tapdong promenade on Jungang-ro 2-gil and 1-gil.

In Seogwipo, the art street Lee Jung Seop-ro and surrounds is the best area for interesting, ever-changing restaurants. The southern and eastern side of the harbour is promoted as 'Chilsimni Food Street' with traditional Korean seafood and black-pork restaurants.

Dasoni   Vegan $

(다소니; ☎064-753 5533; 24 Onam-ro 6-gil, Jeju-si; mains from ₩6000, set lunch from ₩11,000; ⊗11am-10pm; ☐312, Ora 1 Dong stop) Sit cross-legged at rustic wooden tables, peering out into the wild garden of this meat-free restaurant. Local Jeju produce is used for dishes such as sticky rice wrapped in lotus leaves, or acorn jelly, delighting even non-vegetarians. The lunch photo menu has ample interesting *banchan*, such as green chive *pajeon*. Mention if you don't eat fish as it's used in a couple of dishes.

Haejin Seafood
Restaurant   Seafood $$

(해진횟집; ☎064-757 4584; 1435-2 Geonip-dong, Jeju-si; mains ₩12,000-50,000; ⊗10.30am-midnight) Of the many restaurants overlooking the harbour, Haejin is the largest and one of the most popular places to try Jeju-do's seafood specialities such as cuttlefish, eel, squid, octopus, sea cucumber and abalone. The set meal (₩30,000) feeds two people.

Dongmun Market   Market $$

(동문재래시장; 20 Gwandeong-ro 14-gil, Jeju-si; mains ₩10,000-25,000, snacks from ₩500; ⊗8am-9pm) This traditional Korean food market is fun for a wander and a peek at local seafood for sale, which you can have cooked up on the spot at small restaurants. It's also a good place to stock up on *gamgyul*, Jeju's traditional citrus fruit, or to snack on *mandu* (dumplings), *hotteok* (fried, syrup-filled pancakes) and black-pork cabbage rolls.

Saesom Galbi
Barbecue $$

(새섬 갈비; ☎064-732 4001; 32 Soldongsan-ro
10beon-gil, Seogwi-dong, Seogwipo; mains
₩12,000-30,000; ⏰11.30am-10.30pm) Perched
on a cliff overlooking the harbour, this is
the place for barbecued beef or pork. The
atmosphere is informal and boisterous
thanks to the weathered floors, open dining
concept and giddy staff. Side dishes are
modest, but the meat is top-notch. Look for
a black and white building.

Nilmori Dong Dong
Bar

(닐모리동동; ☎064-745 5008; www.nilmori.
com; 2396 Yongdamsam-dong, Jeju-si; ⏰10am-
11pm, to 10pm Nov-Mar) On the coastal
road behind the airport is this eclectic
cafe-bar-restaurant that often stages
craft exhibitions and other arty events.
A ₩6000 taxi ride from Shin Jeju, it's
a worthwhile stop if you're looking for
a place to eat (pizza and pasta from
₩15,000), drink and sample the local arts
scene before or after strolling the ocean-
front promenade.

ℹ INFORMATION

**Tourist Information Centre Ferry Termi-
nal** (☎064-758 7181; Jeju-si Ferry Terminal;
⏰6.30am-8pm) At Jeju-si's ferry terminal.

www.visitjeju.net/en Packed with useful info,
and offers a live chat service.

ℹ GETTING AROUND

BUS

It is possible to travel by bus across the whole
island from Jeju-si, with the furthest destinations
between one and two hours away.

Streams of city and round-island buses
originate from the **Intercity Bus Terminal**
(제주시외버스터미널; ☎064-753 1153; 174
Seogwang-ro, Orail-dong); tourist information of-
fices can provide a timetable. All regular fares are
₩1200. Most stops have convenient screens with
live departure information and maps in English.

TAXI

The charge is ₩2800 for the first 2km; a 15km
journey costs about ₩10,000. You can hire a taxi
for around ₩150,000 a day.

BUSAN

In This Chapter

Busan at a Glance

Home to majestic mountains, glistening beaches, steaming hot springs and fantastic seafood, South Korea's second-largest city is a rollicking port town with tonnes to offer. From casual tent bars and chic designer cafes to fish markets teeming with every species imaginable, Busan (부산) has something for all tastes. Rugged mountain ranges slice through the urban landscape, and events such as the Busan International Film Festival underscore the city's desire to be a global meeting place.

With a Day in Port

Explore serene **Beomeo-sa** (p268), Busan's most magnificent temple, then select fresh seafood for lunch at **Jagalchi Fish Market** (p270). Top it off by bathing with the locals at **Spa Land** (p272).

Best Places for...

City views Geumgang Park Cable Car (p269)

Tea break Maru (p272)

Photo ops Gamcheon Culture Village (p270)

Shopping Shinsegae Centum City (p272)

Beomeo-sa

Busan Map (p271)

Getting from the Port

The **International Passenger Terminal** (부산항 국제여객터미널; ☑051 400 1200; www.busanpa.com; 45-39 Choryang-dong; ⊗8am-11.30pm; Ⓜ Line 1 to Choryang, Exit 6) is about a 15-minute walk from Choryang subway station; cruise operators often offer a shuttle service to the station. From here it's a short ride to central Nampo-dong metro station.

Larger ships often dock at the **International Cruise Terminal** at Yeongdo; a free shuttle takes about 30 minutes to reach Nampo-dong station.

Fast Facts

Currency Korean won (₩)

Language Korean

Money ATMs that accept foreign cards are common: look for one that has a 'Global' sign or the logo of your credit-card company. Portable ATMs are often brought in to greet cruise ships.

Tourist information The international passenger terminal has a tourist information service. There is also an office at Busan station (p273).

Wi-fi Busan is a wired city – many public areas and tourist attractions have open wi-fi networks and most cafes and restaurants have password-protected access.

Beomeo-sa

*Busan's most magnificent temple
and one of Korea's five great temples,
Beomeo-sa temple complex sits high
above Busan. It's not close to the port,
but the interesting temple buildings,
hiking trails and serene atmosphere
make it worth the journey.*

Great For...

☑ **Don't Miss**

Before heading back to the city, visit
the *pajeon* (파전; green onion pancake)
restaurants near the bus stop.

The Temple

This magnificent,1300-year-old temple is
Busan's best sight. Despite its city location,
Beomeo-sa is a world away from the
urban jungle, with impressive architecture
set against an extraordinary mountain
backdrop. The temple complex features
several beautiful buildings, gates and steles
sprinkled around paths and courtyards. In
spring the masses of wisteria bloom laven-
der; autumn brings spectacular foliage.

Beomeo-sa can be a busy place on
weekends and holidays, as the path leading
to the temple is the northern starting point
for trails across Geumjeong-san.

Buddhism in Korea

When first introduced during the Koguryo
dynasty in AD 370, Buddhism in Korea
coexisted with shamanism. Buddhism

Explore Ashore

Take a shuttle to Nampo-dong or Cho-ryang station, then take Line 1 straight up to Beomeo-sa station. At street level from the station, spin 180 degrees, turn left at the corner and walk 200m to the terminus. Catch bus 90 (₩1200, 20 minutes, every 15 minutes) or take a taxi (₩5000) to the temple entrance.

ℹ Need to Know

범어사; ☑051 508 3122; www.beomeo.kr; 250 Beomeosa-ro; ⏱8.30am-5.30pm; Ⓜ Line 1 to Beomeosa, Exit 5

was persecuted during the Joseon period, when temples were tolerated only in remote mountains. The religion suffered another sharp decline after WWII as Koreans pursued worldly goals. But South Korea's success in achieving developed-nation status, coupled with a growing interest in spiritual values, is encouraging a Buddhist revival. Temple visits have increased and large sums of money are flowing into temple reconstruction. According to 2015 data from Statistics Korea, 15% of the population claims to be Buddhist.

Geumjeong Fortress

Trails from the temple complex lead uphill to **Geumjeong-san** (금정산; Geumjeong Mountain), home to **Geumjeong Fortress** (금정산성) FREE. Travellers expecting to see a fortress here will be disappointed; the 'fortress' consists of four gates and 17km of stone

walls encircling 8 sq km of mountaintop. Not all is lost, though, because this is where you'll find some of the city's best hiking, and the opportunity to see Korean hikers sporting the very latest in alpine fashion.

For those with leftover time and energy, there's a steep walk up to the main ridge, heading from the left side of Beomeo-sa, which takes about an hour. Follow the trail left and head to Bukmun (북문; North Gate). The 8.8km hike from Beomeo-sa to Nammun (남문; South Gate) is a comfortable walk with a couple of steep stretches. From here you can continue on to the **Geumgang Park Cable Car** (금강공원 케이블카; http://geumgangpark.bisco.or.kr; one way/return adult ₩5000/8000, child ₩4000/6000; ⏱9am-5pm; Ⓜ Line 1 to Oncheonjang, Exit 1) – the panoramic view is breathtaking. All up the walk from the temple to the top of the cable car takes around four hours. The cable car is a 15-minute walk from Oncheonjang station.

◎ SIGHTS & ACTIVITIES

Jagalchi Fish Market — Market

(자갈치 시장; ☑051 245 2594; http://jagalchi
market.bisco.or.kr; 52 Jagalchihaean-ro; ◷8am-
10pm, closed 1st & 3rd Tue of month; Ⓜ Line 1 to
Jagalchi, Exit 10) Anyone with a love of seafood and a tolerance for powerful odours
could easily spend an hour exploring the
country's largest fish market. Narrow
lanes outside the main building teem with
decades-old stalls and rickety food carts
run by grannies who sell an incredible
variety of seafood, including red snapper,
flounder and creepy-crawly creatures with
undulating tentacles.

Inside the main building, dozens of
1st-floor vendors sell just about every
edible sea animal, including crabs and
eels, two Busan favourites. After buying
a fish, the fishmonger will point you to a
2nd-floor seating area where your meal
will be served (service charge per person
₩4000).

Gamcheon Culture Village — Architecture

(감천문화마을; ◷24hr; Ⓜ Line 1 to Toseong-
dong, Exit 8) **FREE** This historically rich,
mountainside slum became a tourist
destination after an arty makeover in 2009,
when students decided to brighten up the
neighbourhood with clever touches up
the stairs, down the lanes and around the
corners. Today it's a colourful, quirky community of Lego-shaped homes, cafes and
galleries, ideal for an hour or two of strolling
and selfies. Buy a map (₩2000) and join
the scavenger hunt. Comfortable walking
shoes recommended.

From the metro station, cross the street
and walk to the bus stop in front of the
hospital. Catch minibus 2 or 2-2 (₩900, 10
minutes) up the steep hill to the village. A
taxi from the hospital (₩3000) is faster.

Haedong Yonggungsa — Temple

(해동 용궁사; ☑051 722 7744; www.yongkung
sa.or.kr/en; 86 Yonggung-gil, Gijang-eup; 🚌181
to Yonggungsa Temple stop, Ⓜ Line 2 to Haeun-
dae, Exit 7) **FREE** One of the country's few

Haedong Yonggungsa

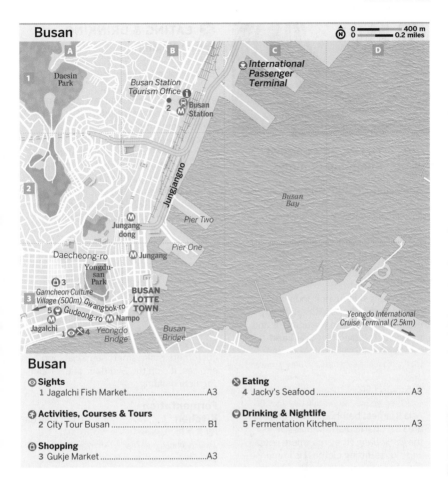

Busan

⊛ **Sights**
1 Jagalchi Fish Market.....................................A3

⊛ **Activities, Courses & Tours**
2 City Tour Busan B1

🏠 **Shopping**
3 Gukje Market...A3

⊗ **Eating**
4 Jacky's Seafood A3

🍷 **Drinking & Nightlife**
5 Fermentation Kitchen...............................A3

temples situated on the coast, there are spectacular views of the temple grounds and surrounding ocean. Located quite north of the city, it gets congested on the weekends – but the vistas, elaborate altars, and statues of towering zodiac animals and a giant gold Buddha make the venture well worth it.

City Tour Busan
Bus

(부산 시티 투어버스; ☑051 464 9898; www. citytourbusan.com; 206 Jungang-daero, Busan Station; adult/child ₩15,000/8000; ☉tour times vary; ⓂLine 1 to Busan station, Exit 1) City Tour runs six daytime routes with different

themes. Buy a Loop Tour ticket and you can jump on and off the bus all day. All buses start at Busan station.

🏠 SHOPPING

Gukje Market
Market

(국제시장; ☑051 245 7389; Sinchang-dong 4(sa)-ga; ☉8.30am-8.30pm; ⓂLine 1 to Jagalchi, Exit 7) West of Nampo-dong, this traditional market has hundreds of small booths with a staggering selection of items, from leather goods to Korean drums.

The World's Largest Shopping Complex

Shinsegae Centum City (신세계 센텀 시티; ☑1588 1234; www.shinsegae.com; 35 Centumnam-daero; ⊗10.30am-8pm; MLine 2 to Centum City, Shinsegae Exit) is the world's largest shopping complex – bigger than Macy's in New York – with everything you'd expect in a temple of commerce.

There's a skating rink, indoor golf driving range, shops with seemingly every brand name in the universe and a place to recuperate – **Spa Land** (☑051 745 2900; www.shinsegae.com; 1st fl, Shinsegae Centum City; adult/youth weekdays ₩13,000/10,000, weekends ₩15,000/12,000; ⊗6am-midnight, last entry 10.30pm; MLine 2 to Centum City, Exit 3), Asia's largest bathhouse. The bathing area isn't particularly impressive, but the *jjimjil-bang* (the area where people wear loose-fitting clothes) is immense – there's a panoply of relaxation rooms of various temperatures and scents. Kids under 13 are not permitted.

Shinsegae Centum City
CHANAWAT PHADWICHIT/SHUTTERSTOCK ©

Bujeon Market   Market
(부전시장; ☑051 818 1091; 23 Jungang-daero 783beon-gil; ⊗4am-8pm; MLine 1 to Bujeon, Exit 5) You could easily spend an hour getting lost in this enormous traditional market specialising in produce, seafood and knick-knacks.

✖ EATING & DRINKING

Yetnal Jjajang   Korean $
(옛날짜장; ☑051 809 8823; 15 Gaya-daero 784beon-gil; meals from ₩4000; ⊗11am-10pm; MLine 1 or 2 to Seomyeon, Exit 7) A sterling example of a successful restaurant owner who won't update the interior. According to superstition, the good fortune a successful shop enjoys can be lost if the interior were changed. Consequently, some shoddy-looking restaurants, like this one, serve great food. See noodles get hand-pulled as you enjoy the excellent *jjajangmyeon* (짜장면; black bean-paste noodles) and *jjambbong* (짬뽕; spicy seafood soup).

Jacky's Seafood   Seafood $$
(돼지초밥 횟집; ☑051 246 2594; 52 Jagal-chihaean-ro, 2F; ⊗9am-10pm, closed 1st & 3rd Tue of month; MLine 1 to Jagalchi, Exit 10) Buying a raw-fish dinner couldn't be easier thanks to Jacky, the affable owner of this seafood restaurant. He speaks fluent English and uses signboards to help customers make smart seasonal food choices. It's on the 2nd floor of the main Jagalchi building.

Fermentation Kitchen   Cocktail Bar
(발효주방, Barhyo Kitchen; ☑010 3041 1320; www.facebook.com/barhyokitchen; 2F, 83 Gwangbok-ro jung-gu; makgeolli from ₩16,000; ⊗noon-12.30am Sun-Thu, to 1.30am Fri & Sat; 🛜; MLine 1 to Nampo, Exit 3) Fermentation Kitchen is a great place to sample *makgeolli* (traditional Korean rice wine). The restaurant-bar serves special carbonated *makgeolli* in wine glasses alongside modern takes on Korean dishes. While *makgeolli* purists might not prefer the venue's high-end feel, the prices here are reasonable.

Maru   Teahouse
(마루; ☑051 803 6797; Saesak-ro 17-1, Jin-gu; ⊗10am-10pm; MLine 1 or 2 to Seomyeon, Exit 9) Splendid herbal teas and a warm interior make this an excellent alternative

Soup at Bujeon Market

to the sterile sameness of chain coffee shops. The dark and earthy twin flower tea (쌍화차) is a speciality.

ℹ INFORMATION

Busan Station Tourism Office (부산역 관광 안내소; ☑051 441 6565; 206 Jungang-daero; ⊙9am-8pm; Ⓜ Line 1 to Busan station, Exit 8 or 10) Maps and helpful staff, located on the 2nd floor.

ℹ GETTING AROUND

Bus Busan's bus system is extensive; adult cash fares are ₩1300/1800 for regular/express buses.

Subway Busan's four-line subway uses a two-zone fare system that costs ₩1400 per ride for one zone and ₩1600 for longer trips if using single-journey paper tickets; a one-day pass costs ₩4500.

Taxi Plentiful and easy to hail on the street. Basic fares start at ₩3300 (with a 20% night premium). Avoid black-and-red deluxe taxis if possible, because the fares can run high.

In Focus

Shànghǎi (p231)

DOVE LEE/GETTY IMAGES ©

Northeast Asia Today

Ageing populations, booming tourist numbers, riding the tech boom, regional geopolitical tensions (old and new) and money, money, money. Northeast Asia is diverse and complex, but the same themes emerge across the region.

Japan

Japan's stubbornly stagnant economy and dramatically declining population may well be harbingers of the kinds of problems other developed nations will face as their populations taper off. And while many developed countries have recently focused inwards, Japan is taking tentative steps towards looking out. Will the country grow to embrace a new, yet-to-be-defined kind of cosmopolitanism, setting a model for others to follow?

Japan has long hoped to boost its underdeveloped inbound-tourism industry. Then it got real by relaxing visa regulations for visitors from its Asian neighbours. Along with the periodically weak yen, this has resulted in a dramatic uptick of foreign visitors. Inbound numbers have more than doubled since 2010; in 2017 the country logged 28.7 million visitors, already overshooting the target of 20 million set for 2020 – the year Tokyo holds the Summer Olympics.

There is hand wringing, of course. How do we please these tourists? Where are we going to park all the tour buses? And will we ever be able to visit Kyoto in peace again?

But there is also intense fascination. What, exactly, do foreigners find interesting about Japan? There has been an explosion of TV shows trying to figure that out, interviewing tourists and even sending TV personalities to check out places listed in the Lonely Planet guide.

Shànghǎi

The Shanghainese may natter about traffic gridlock and chat about the latest celebrity faux pas or political scandal, but what they really talk about is cash. Labelled *xiǎozī* – 'little capitalists' – by the rest of the land, the Shànghǎi Chinese know how to make *qián* (money) and, equally importantly, how to flaunt it. Ever since Shànghǎi first prospered under foreign control, wealth creation has been indivisible from the Shànghǎi psyche. Whether it's the stock market, apartment price tags or the latest Dior evening bag, money's the talk of the town.

South Korea

Plagued with high youth unemployment, growing social welfare liabilities, old-age poverty and a rapidly declining birth rate, South Korea today faces multiple challenges. Relations with China and Japan have been uncertain.

Yet South Korea is today, by any measure, one of the world's star performers. Its top companies, such as Samsung, LG and Hyundai, make products the world wants. South Korea is now possibly the most wired nation on earth. The talented younger generation has created such a dynamic pop culture that *hallyu* (the Korean Wave) has swept the globe. And a dramatic rapprochement between North and South Korea promises – but does not guarantee – to replace decades of hostility.

Taipei

With the January 2016 victory of the Democratic Progressive Party (DPP) and the 2018 reelection of Taipei mayor Ko Wen-je, a self-styled man of the people, the mood in Taipei is a mixture of youthful hope and trepidation. You can see that hope in the blossoming of art districts – Songshan and Huashan Cultural Parks, Dihua St – led by young designers and entrepreneurs. However, many residents feel that old-school corruption continues to blight the city, citing a number of construction projects that are behind schedule, including Taipei Dome and the airport MRT connection.

Wall painting, Bao'an Temple (p224), Taipei

History

The modern cities of Northeast Asia glitter with the promise of tomorrow, but even amid the high-rises and neon, you'll find compelling stories of the region's past at every turn. Age-old power struggles have long defined the region's fortunes, bringing conflict, invasion and rebellion, as well as cultural cross-pollination and economic interdependency.

c 10,000 BC
Ancestors of Taiwan's present-day indigenous people first come to the island by sea and begin settling around the island.

AD mid-5th century
Writing is introduced to Japan by scholars from the Korean kingdom of Baekje and is based on the Chinese system of characters.

1274
With help from Korea, a Mongol army attempts to conquer Japan but is thwarted by a heavy sea storm (kamikaze).

Guardian sculptures, Beomeo-sa (p268), Busan

ISARINT SANGMANEE/SHUTTERSTOCK ©

Japan

Early Japan

The earliest traces of human life in Japan date to around 30,000 years ago, but it is possible that people were here much earlier. The first recognisable culture to emerge was the neolithic Jōmon, from about 13,000 BC.

Agriculture-based settlement led to territories and boundaries being established, and the rise of kingdoms, the most powerful of which was ruled by the Yamato clan in the Kansai region. The Yamato clan would go on to found the court in Nara and then later Heian-kyō (Kyoto), from where the imperial dynasty would rule for over a millennia.

The Rise & Fall of the Heian Court

In Kyoto over the next few centuries courtly life reached a pinnacle of refined artistic pursuits and etiquette, captured famously in the novel *The Tale of Genji,* written by the

1543

Portuguese, the first Westerners, arrive by chance in Japan, bringing firearms and Christianity.

1553

The wall around Shànghǎi Old City is constructed to fend off Japanese pirates. The wall stands until the fall of the Qing dynasty.

1638

The *sakoku* policy of Japanese national isolation is in place.

court-lady Murasaki Shikibu in about 1004. But it was also a world increasingly estranged from the real one. Manipulated over centuries by the politically powerful Fujiwara family, the imperial throne was losing its authority.

Out in the provinces powerful military forces were developing. Some were led by distant imperial family members, barred from succession claims and hostile to the court. Their retainers included skilled warriors known as samurai (literally 'retainer'). An all-out feud developed between the two main clans of disenfranchised nobles, the Minamoto and the Taira.

The Taira initially prevailed, but by 1185 Kyoto had fallen and the Taira had been pursued to the western tip of Honshū. A naval battle ensued, won by the Minamoto.

The Kamakura Shogunate

Minamoto Yoritomo did not seek to become emperor, but wanted the new emperor to give him legitimacy by conferring the title of shogun (generalissimo), which was granted in 1192, and in practice he was in charge. He left many existing offices and institutions in place and set up a base in his home territory of Kamakura (not far from present-day Tokyo) rather than Kyoto. Yoritomo established a feudal system – which would last almost 700 years as an institution – centred on a loyalty-based lord–vassal system.

After Yoritomo died in 1199, Yoritomo's widow, of the Hōjō clan, acted first as regent before claiming the shogunate outright. It was during the Hōjō shogunate that the Mongols, under Kublai Khan (r 1260–94), twice tried to invade, in 1274 and 1281. On both occasions they were ultimately defeated by storms that destroyed much of their fleet. The typhoon of 1281 prompted the idea of divine intervention, with the coining of the term kamikaze (literally 'divine wind'). Later this term was used to describe Pacific War suicide pilots who, said to be infused with divine spirit, gave their lives to protect Japan from invasion.

Despite victory, the Hōjō suffered: their already depleted finances could not cover the payment promised to the warriors enlisted to fight the Mongols. Dissatisfaction towards the shogunate came to a head under the unusually assertive emperor Go-Daigo (1288–1339), who banded together with the promising young general Ashikaga Takauji (1305–58) to overthrow the Hōjō. Ashikaga claimed the mantle of shogun, setting up a base in Kyoto.

The Warring States

With a few exceptions, the Ashikaga shoguns were relatively ineffective. Without strong, centralised government and control, the country slipped into civil war; the period from 1467 to 1603 is known as the Sengoku (Warring States) era. In 1543 the first Europeans arrived – another game changer – bringing with them Christianity and firearms. The warlord Nobunaga Oda (1534–82) was quick to apprehend the advantage of the latter. Starting from a relatively minor power base, his skilled and ruthless generalship produced a series of victories. In 1568 he seized Kyoto and held de facto power until, betrayed by

1853–54	1859	1861–64
US commodore Matthew Perry's 'black ships' arrive off the coast of Shimoda, forcing Japan to open up for trade.	Five international ports are established in Japan: Yokohama, Hakodate, Kōbe, Niigata and Nagasaki.	The Treaty of Tianjin forces open Taiwan ports Anping, Tamsui, Keelung and Kaohsiung to Western trade.

one of his generals, he was killed in 1582. Another of his generals, Hideyoshi Toyotomi (1536–98), took up the torch, disposing of potential rivals among Nobunaga's sons and taking the title of regent.

Hideyoshi's power had been briefly contested by Tokugawa Ieyasu (1543–1616), son of a minor lord allied to Nobunaga. After a brief struggle for power, Ieyasu agreed to a truce with Hideyoshi; in return, Hideyoshi granted him eight provinces in eastern Japan. While Hideyoshi intended this to weaken Ieyasu by separating him from his ancestral homeland Chūbu (now Aichi Prefecture), the upstart looked upon the gift as an opportunity to strengthen his power. He set up his base in a small castle town called Edo (which would one day become Tokyo). On his deathbed, Hideyoshi entrusted Ieyasu, who had proven to be one of his ablest generals, with safeguarding the country and the succession of his young son Hideyori (1593–1615). Ieyasu, however, had bigger ambitions and soon went to war against those loyal to Hideyori, finally defeating them at the legendary Battle of Sekigahara in 1600. He chose Edo as his permanent base and ushered in two and a half centuries of Tokugawa rule.

The Way of the Warrior

Samurai followed a code of conduct that came to be known as *bushidō* (the way of the warrior), drawn from Confucianism, Shintō and Buddhism. Confucianism required a samurai to show absolute loyalty to his lord, possess total self-control, speak only the truth and display no emotion. Since his honour was his life, disgrace and shame were to be avoided above all else, and all insults were to be avenged. Seppuku (ritual suicide by disembowelment), also known as hara-kiri, was an accepted means of avoiding the dishonour of defeat. From Buddhism, the samurai learnt the lesson that life is impermanent – a handy reason to face death with serenity. Shintō provided the samurai with patriotic beliefs in the divine status both of the emperor and of Japan.

Tokugawa Rule

Ieyasu and his successors kept tight control over the provincial *daimyō* (warlords), who ruled as vassals for the regime.

Early on, the Tokugawa shogunate adopted a policy of *sakoku* (seclusion from the outside world). Following the Christian-led Shimabara Rebellion, Christianity was banned and several hundred thousand Japanese Christians were forced into hiding. All Westerners, except the Protestant Dutch, were expelled by 1638. Overseas travel for Japanese was banned (as well as the return of those already overseas). And yet, the country did not remain completely cut off: trade with Asia and the West continued through the Dutch and the Ryūkyū empire (now Okinawa) – it was just tightly controlled and, along with the exchange of ideas, funnelled exclusively to the shogunate. Japan's cities grew enormously during this period: Edo's population topped one million in the early 1700s, dwarfing much older London and Paris.

1876	1895	1910
The Japanese prevail in getting Korea to sign the Treaty of Ganghwa, formally opening up three of the nation's ports to international trade.	The Treaty of Shimonoseki concludes the First Sino-Japanese War, forcing China to cede territories (including Taiwan) to Japan.	Korean Emperor Sunjong refuses to sign the Japan–Korea Annexation Treaty, but Japan effectively annexes Korea in August.

The Meiji Restoration

In 1853 and again the following year, US commodore Matthew Perry steamed into Edo-wan (now Tokyo Bay) with a show of gunships – which the Japanese called *kurofune* (black ships), because they were cloaked in pitch – and demanded Japan open up to trade and provisioning. The shogunate was no match for Perry's firepower and agreed to his demands. Soon other Western powers followed suit. Japan was obliged to sign what came to be called the 'unequal treaties', opening ports and giving Western nations control over tariffs. Anti-shogun sentiment was high and following a series of military clashes between the shogun's armies and the rebels, the last shogun – Yoshinobu (1837–1913) – agreed to retire in 1867.

In 1868, the new teenage emperor Mutsuhito (1852–1912; later known as Meiji) was named the supreme leader of the land, commencing the Meiji period (1868–1912; Enlightened Rule). The institution of the shogun was abolished and the shogun's base at Edo was refashioned into the imperial capital and given the new name, Tokyo (Eastern Capital). In truth, the emperor still wielded little actual power.

Above all, the new leaders of Japan – keen observers of what was happening throughout Asia – feared colonisation by the West. They moved quickly to modernise, as defined by the Western powers, to prove they could stand on an equal footing with the colonisers.

Rise of a Global Power

A key element of Japan's aim to become a world power was military might. Using the same 'gunboat diplomacy' on Korea that Perry had used on the Japanese, in 1876 Japan was able to force on Korea an unequal treaty of its own. Using Chinese 'interference' in Korea as a justification, in 1894 Japan manufactured a war with China; victorious, Japan gained Taiwan and the Liaotung Peninsula. When Japan officially annexed Korea in 1910, there was little international protest. Japan entered WWI on the side of the Allies, and was rewarded with a council seat in the newly formed League of Nations. It also acquired German possessions in East Asia and the Pacific.

Yet as the 1920s rolled around, a sense of unfair treatment by Western powers once again took hold in Japan. The Washington Conference of 1921–2 set naval ratios of three capital ships for Japan to five American and five British; around the same time, a racial-equality clause Japan proposed to the League of Nations was rejected. In the fall of 1931, members of the Japanese army stationed in Manchuria, there to guard rail lines leased by China to Japan, detonated explosives along the track and blamed the act on Chinese dissidents. This ruse, which gave the Japanese army an excuse for armed retaliation, became known as the Manchurian Incident. Within months the Japanese had taken control of Manchuria and installed a puppet government. The League of Nations refused to acknowledge the new Manchurian government; in 1933 Japan left the league.

Skirmishes continued between the Chinese and Japanese armies, leading to full-blown war in 1937. Following a hard-fought victory in Shànghǎi, Japanese troops advanced south

1931–7	**1941**	**1945**
Japan takes control of Manchuria and eventually Shànghǎi, too.	Japan enters WWII by striking Pearl Harbor without warning on 7 December.	Hiroshima and Nagasaki become victims of atomic bombings on 6 and 9 August.

to capture Nanjing. Over several months somewhere between 40,000 and 300,000 Chinese were killed in what has become known as the Nanjing Massacre or Rape of Nanjing. To this day, the number of deaths and the prevalence of rape, torture and looting by Japanese soldiers is hotly debated among historians (and government nationalists) on both sides.

WWII & Occupation

Encouraged by Germany's early WWII victories, Japan signed a pact with Germany and Italy in 1940. With France and the Netherlands distracted and weakened by the war in Europe, Japan quickly moved on their colonial territories – French Indo-China and the Dutch West Indies – in Southeast Asia. Tensions between Japan and the United States intensified, as the Americans, alarmed by Japan's aggression, demanded Japan back down in China. When diplomacy failed, the USA barred oil exports to Japan – a crucial blow. Japanese forces struck at Pearl Harbor on 7 December 1941, damaging much of America's Pacific fleet.

Japan advanced swiftly across the Pacific; however, the tide started to turn in the Battle of Midway in June 1942, when much of its carrier fleet was destroyed. Japan had over-extended itself, and over the next three years was subjected to an island-hopping counter-attack. By mid-1945, Japan, ignoring the Potsdam Declaration calling for unconditional surrender, was preparing for a final Allied assault on its homeland. On 6 August the world's first atomic bomb was dropped on Hiroshima, killing 90,000 civilians. And on 9 August another atomic bomb was dropped, this time on Nagasaki, with another 50,000 deaths. Emperor Hirohito formally surrendered on 15 August.

The terms of Japan's surrender to the Allies allowed the country to hold on to the emperor as the ceremonial head of state, but Hirohito no longer had authority – nor was he thought of as divine – and Japan was forced to give up its territorial claims in Korea and China. In addition, America occupied the country under General Douglas MacArthur, a situation that would last until 1952 (Okinawa would remain occupied until 1972).

The Boom Years

In the 1950s Japan took off on a trajectory of phenomenal growth that is often described as miraculous (jump-started by US procurement for the Korean War). Throughout the 1960s, Japan's GDP grew, on average, 10% a year. The new consumer class, inspired by the images of affluence introduced during the American occupation, yearned for the so-called 'three sacred treasures' of the modern era (a play on the three sacred treasures of the imperial family: the sword, the mirror and the jewel) – a refrigerator, a washing machine and a television. By 1964, 90% of the population had them.

Growth continued through the '70s and reached a peak in the late '80s. Based on the price paid for the most expensive real estate in the late 1980s, the land value of Tokyo exceeded that of the entire US. The wildly inflated real-estate prices and stock specula-tion fuelled what is now known as the 'Bubble economy'. It seemed like things could only go up – until they didn't.

1947	1949	1953
The Taiwanese government suppresses a public uprising, killing thousands of people in what is later known as the 2-28 Incident.	Communist forces take Shànghǎi and the People's Republic of China (PRC) is proclaimed.	The armistice ending the Korean War is signed by the US and North Korea, but not South Korea.

Heisei Doldrums

In 1991, just two years after the Heisei Emperor ascended the throne, the bubble burst and Japan's economy went into a tailspin. The 1990s were christened the 'Lost Decade', but that has since turned into two, and probably three, as the economy continues to slump along, despite government intervention. Long-time prime minister Abe Shinzō's so-called Abenomics plan, which included a devaluing of the yen, has had some positive effects on corporate gains – and also on inbound tourism (making Japan a cheaper place to visit!) – and generated some 'Japan is back!' headlines, but ordinary people have seen little change. By now a whole generation has come of age in a Japan where lifelong employment – the backbone of the middle class – is no longer a guarantee.

With the abdication of the Heisei Emperor in 2019, the era came to a close and so, many hope, will the malaise it came to symbolise.

Shànghǎi

In just a few centuries, Shànghǎi went from being an insignificant walled town south of the mouth of the Yangzi River to becoming China's leading and wealthiest metropolis. A dizzying swirl of opium, trade, foreign control, vice, glamour, glitz, rebellion, restoration and money, Shànghǎi's story is a rags-to-riches saga of decadence, exploitation and, ultimately, achievement.

Up until around the 7th century AD, Shànghǎi was little more than marshland, but by the late 17th century, Shànghǎi supported a population of 50,000 on cotton production, fishing and trade in silk and tea.

By the 18th century, the British passion for Chinese tea was increasingly matched by China's craving for opium (yāpiàn), the drug that would virtually single-handedly create latter-day Shànghǎi and earn the city its bipolar reputation as the splendid 'Paris of the East' and the infamous 'Whore of the Orient'. Trading tensions culminated in war; the Treaty of Nanking, which concluded the First Opium War in 1842, was Shànghǎi's moment of reckoning. Its signing spelled the death of old Shànghǎi and the birth of the new Shànghǎi: an open, lawless and spectacularly prosperous trading city. Years of rebellion, exploitation, and, finally, war and occupation ended with the declaration of the People's Republic of China in 1949.

In 1990 the central government began pouring money into Shànghǎi, beginning the city's stunning turnaround. Obsessively comparing itself to Hong Kong, the Huángpǔ River city closed the gap on the ex-British territory with breathtaking rapidity during the noughties. The process was unparalleled in scale and audacity.

South Korea

Koreans can trace a continuous history on the same territory reaching back thousands of years. The present politically divided peninsula is mirrored by distant eras such as the Three Kingdoms period (57 BC–AD 668), when the kingdoms of Goguryeo, Silla and

1987	2010	2011
After 38 years, martial law is lifted in Taiwan, setting the stage for the island's eventual shift from authoritarian rule to democracy.	China surpasses Japan as the world's second-largest economy after the USA.	The Great East Japan Earthquake strikes off the coast of Tōhoku, generating a tsunami that kills many thousands.

Baekje jockeyed for control of territory that stretched deep into Manchuria. Korea's relationship with powerful neighbours China and Japan has also long defined the country's fortunes, while ties to the West have added further complexity to national self-understanding.

Taiwan

Taipei is an architectural hotpot of temples, run-down walk-ups, colonial finery, and modern skyscrapers and shopping malls. Three hundred years ago it was just a scattering of indigenous settlements; since then it's been a Chinese tea-trading post, a Japanese colony and a Kuomintang (KMT) base.

In 1709, settlers from China's Fujian province received permission from the Qing government to settle and develop the island, and in 1886 Taipei became the capital of the newly founded Taiwan province. China ceded Taiwan to Japan under the Treaty of Shimonoseki in 1895 and Japanese troops entered Taipei that same year. After Japan's defeat in WWII, Taiwan was returned to China.

In 1949, Nationalist forces fled the Communist takeover of mainland China for Taiwan. With the remarkable growth of Taiwan's economy starting in the 1960s, the capital attracted people from all over and architectural anarchy played out in the drive to provide housing for the masses. Since the late '90s and the country's democratisation, the capital has made a remarkable transformation into one of the most liveable and vibrant cities in Asia. Today, Taipei dreams of success and international recognition – a perplexing product of decades of turmoil.

South Korea's Jeju-do

According to legend, Jeju-do was founded by three brothers who came out of holes in the ground and established the independent Tamna kingdom. Early in the 12th century the Goryeo dynasty took over, but in 1273 Mongol invaders conquered the island, contributing a tradition of horsemanship, a special horse (*jorangmal*) and quirks in the local dialect.

The Japanese colonial period of the early 20th century can be traced through abandoned military bases and fortifications on the island. From 1947 to 1954, as many as 30,000 locals were massacred by right-wing government forces in events collectively labelled the 'April 3 Incident'.

Recent decades have seen Jeju-do's economy shift from mainly agriculture to tourism. In 2006 the island was made into a special autonomous province, giving it a level of self-government that is encouraging further economic development. Ambitious carbon-free electricity generation ventures are being tested.

2012	April 2019	May 2019
Anti-Japanese demonstrations are held in Shànghǎi and other cities across China in response to Japanese claims to the Diàoyú Islands.	Emperor Akihito, the first Japanese emperor of the modern age to abdicate, steps down on 30 April, ushering in the new Reiwa era.	Taiwan becomes the first Asian nation to legalise same-sex marriage.

Shànghǎi (p231)

AAAImages/Getty Images © ORIENTAL PEARL TOWER, ARCHITECT: JIANG HUAN CHENG

Arts & Architecture

Centuries of cross-pollination, isolation, migration and trade have gifted this region with a strong and complex artistic tradition. It's fascinating to pick out common trends and unique cultural facets, aesthetics from the West that have been incorporated into the traditions of the region, and vice versa.

Cinema

Golden Age of Japanese Cinema

The Japanese cinema of the 1950s – the era of acclaimed auteurs Ozu Yasujirō, Mizoguchi Kenji and Kurosawa Akira – is responsible for a whole generation of Japanophiles. Ozu (1903–63) was the first great Japanese director, known for his piercing, at times heartbreaking, family dramas. Mizoguchi (1898–1956) began by shooting social realist works in the 1930s but found critical acclaim with his reimagining of stories from Japanese history and folklore.

Kurosawa (1910–98) is an oft-cited influence for film-makers around the world. His films are intense and psychological; the director favoured strong leading men and worked often with the actor Mifune Toshirō. Kurosawa won the Golden Lion at the Venice International

Film Festival and an honorary Oscar for the haunting *Rashōmon* (1950), based on the short story of the same name by Akutagawa Ryūnosuke and starring Mifune as a bandit. Japanese cinema continues to produce directors of merit but has not emerged as the influential cultural force that its heyday seemed to foreshadow.

Anime

Miyazaki Hayao (b 1941), who together with Takahata Isao (1935–2018) founded Studio Ghibli, is largely responsible for anime gaining widespread, mainstream appeal abroad. Thematically, his works are noteworthy for their strong female characters and environmentalism; *Nausicaä of the Valley of the Wind* (1984) is an excellent example. He was given an Academy Honorary Award in 2014.

Among the best-known anime is *Akira* (1988), Ōtomo Katsuhiro's psychedelic fantasy set in a future Tokyo inhabited by speed-popping biker gangs and psychic children. *Ghost in the Shell* (1995) is an Ōshii Mamoru film with a sci-fi plot worthy of Philip K Dick involving cyborgs, hackers and the mother of all computer networks. The works of Kon Satoshi (1963–2010), including the Hitchcockian *Perfect Blue* (1997), the charming *Tokyo Godfathers* (2003) and the sci-fi thriller *Paprika* (2006), are also classics.

One new director to watch is Shinkai Makoto: his 2016 *Your Name* was both a critical and box-office smash – the second-highest-grossing domestic film ever, after *Spirited Away*.

Ang Lee

One of the world's most famous directors, Ang Lee (1954–) is known best for his megahits *The Life of Pi* (2012) and *Crouching Tiger, Hidden Dragon* (2000). Ang's first film was *Pushing Hands* (1992), filmed in New York. His next movie, *The Wedding Banquet* (1993), took a bold step in exploring homosexuality in Chinese culture. Ang then joined Hollywood and filmed *Sense and Sensibility* (1995), *The Ice Storm* (1997), *Brokeback Mountain* (2005), and *Lust Caution* (2007). Lee's accolades have included the Golden Bear (Berlin), the Golden Lion (Venice), and Best Director (Academy Awards).

Shànghǎi Architecture

Jaw-dropping panoramas of glittering skyscrapers are its trump card, but Shànghǎi is no one-trick pony: the city boasts a diversity of architectural styles that will astound most first-time visitors. Whether you're an art deco hound, a neoclassical buff, a fan of English 1930s suburban-style villas, 1920s apartment blocks or Buddhist temple architecture, Shànghǎi has it covered.

Lòngtáng & Shíkùmén

Even though Shànghǎi is typified by its high-rise and uniform residential blocks, near ground level the city comes into its own with its low-rise *lòngtáng* and *shíkùmén* (stone gate) architecture. Here, both Western and Asian architectural motifs were synthesised into harmonious, utilitarian styles that still house a large proportion of Shànghǎi's residents.

Concession Architecture

For many foreign visitors, Shànghǎi's modern architectural vision is a mere side salad to the feast of historic architecture lining the Bund and beyond. Remnants of old Shànghǎi, these buildings are part of the city's genetic code, inseparable from its sense of identity as the former 'Paris of the East'.

Contemporary Korean Cinema

Korean cinema is today embraced by both local audiences (thanks partly to government quotas that mandate a certain amount of screen time for domestic films) and the international festival circuit. Yeon Sang-ho's zombie apocalypse thriller *Train to Busan* (2016) set a record as the first Korean film of the year to reach more than 10 million theatregoers.

Some films worth watching include the jaw-dropping action-revenge flick *Oldboy* (Park Chan-wook; 2003); the critically acclaimed monster epic *The Host* (Bong Joon-ho; 2006); the controversial, and hypersexual, *Pieta* (Kim Ki-duk; 2012), a Golden Lion winner at Venice; and anything by low-budget, shoe-gazer Hong Sang-soo – his 2017 *On the Beach at Night Alone* won a handful of awards.

Building the Bund

The Bund – Shànghǎi's most famous esplanade of concession buildings – was built on unstable foundations due to the leaching mud of the Huángpǔ River. Bund buildings were first built on concrete rafts that were fixed onto wood pilings, which were allowed to sink into the mud. Because of the lack of qualified architects, some of the earliest Western-style buildings in Shànghǎi were partially built in Hong Kong, shipped to Shànghǎi, then assembled on-site.

Modern Architecture

Charm and panache may ooze from every crevice of its concession-era villas, *shíkùmén* buildings and art deco marvels, but for sheer wow factor, look to the city's modern skyline. Shànghǎi's tall towers get all the media attention, but many of the city's most iconic and noteworthy contemporary buildings are low-rise.

K-Pop

K-Pop, with its catchy blend of pop R&B, hip hop and EDM – complete with synchronised dance moves – shows no sign of fading away. As soon as critics declare it over, new groups emerge to capture hearts (and endorsements) around Asia and, more recently, the United States. In 2018 one of the top groups of the moment, BTS – which stands for *'bangtan sonyeondan'* or 'bulletproof boy scouts' – became the first-ever K-Pop act to take the number-one spot on the *Billboard* 200 with the album *Love Yourself: Tear*. The group of seven young men are acclaimed for speaking out on subjects that are especially taboo in Korean culture, such as LGBTQ rights, mental health and the pressure to succeed.

But it's not just about covetable hairstyles and infectious tunes. According to the Korea Creative Content Agency, K-Pop was responsible for a record ₩5.3 trillion in revenue based on album, concert ticket, merchandise and music-streaming sales generated overseas in 2016.

K-Indie is the artist-driven alternative to K-Pop. Hunt for new underground bands at Korean Indie (www.koreanindie.com).

Traditional Japanese Arts

Gardens

Flowering plants are only one component of the Japanese garden, which may be composed of any combination of vegetation (including trees, shrubs and moss), stones of varying sizes, and water. Some gardens are not limited to that which falls within their walls, but take into account the scenery beyond (a technique called *shakkei* or 'borrowed scenery'). Often they are meant to evoke a landscape in miniature, with rocks standing in for famous mountains of myth or Chinese literature; raked gravel may represent flowing water. Garden elements are arranged asymmetrically and shapes, such as the outline of a pond, are often irregular. The idea is that the garden should appear natural, or more like nature in its ideal state; in reality most gardens are meticulously maintained – and entirely by hand.

Gardens may be designed as spaces of beauty, for leisure and entertainment purposes, or they might be a designation of sacred space (most fall somewhere in between). The white gravel that appears in some temple gardens is rooted in Shintō tradition: there are gravel courtyards at Ise-jingū, which dates to the 3rd century and is considered Japan's most sacred spot.

You'll encounter four major types of gardens during your horticultural explorations.

Funa asobi Meaning 'pleasure boat' and popular in the Heian period, such gardens feature a large pond for boating and were often built around nobles' mansions.

Shūyū These 'stroll' gardens are intended to be viewed from a winding path, allowing the design to unfold and reveal itself in stages and from different vantages. Popular during the Heian, Kamakura and Muromachi periods, a celebrated example is the garden at Ginkaku-ji in Kyoto.

Kanshō Zen rock gardens (also known as *kare-sansui* gardens) are an example of the type of 'contemplative' garden intended to be viewed from one vantage point and designed to aid meditation. Kyoto's Ryōan-ji is perhaps the most famous example.

Kaiyū The 'varied pleasures' garden features many small gardens with one or more teahouses surrounding a central pond. Like the stroll garden, it is meant to be explored on foot and provides the visitor with a variety of changing scenes, many with literary allusions. The imperial villa of Katsura Rikyū in Kyoto is the classic example.

The Tea Ceremony

Chanoyu (literally 'water for tea') is usually translated as 'tea ceremony', but it's more like performance art, with each element carefully designed to articulate an aesthetic experience. It's had a profound and lasting influence on the arts in Japan, one that has percolated through all the divergent arts wrapped up in it: architecture, landscape design, ikebana (flower arranging), ceramics and calligraphy.

The culture of drinking *matcha* (powdered green tea) entered Japan along with Zen Buddhism in the 12th century. Like everything else in monastic life – the sweeping of the temple grounds and the tending of the garden, for example – the preparation of tea was approached as a kind of working meditation. The practice was later taken up by the ruling class, and in the 16th century the famous tea master Sen no Rikkyū (1522–1591) is credited with laying down the foundations of *wabi-sabi* – and with raising tea to an art form.

More than just a place to drink tea, a Japanese teahouse is a distillation of an artistic vision; even today, no architect would turn down a commission to work on one. Visitors to a teahouse approach via the *roji* ('dewy' path), formed by irregular stepping stones. The path represents a space of transition – a place to clear one's mind and calm one's spirit before entering the teahouse. The doorway is purposely low, causing those who enter to stoop, and thus humble themselves. All are considered equal inside the teahouse (swords were to remain outside). Gardens all over Japan have *chashitsu* (teahouses).

Wabi-sabi

Wabi-sabi is a Japanese aesthetic that embraces the notion of ephemerality and imperfection and is Japan's most distinct – though hard to pin down – and profound contribution to the arts. *Wabi* roughly means 'rustic' and connotes the loneliness of the wilderness, while *sabi* can be interpreted as 'weathered', 'waning' or 'altered with age'. Together the two words signify an object's natural imperfections, arising in its inception, and the acquired beauty that comes with the patina of time. It is most often evoked in descriptions of the tea ceremony. Ceramics made for the tea ceremony – and this is where Japanese ceramics finally came into their own – often appeared dented or misshapen or had a rough texture, with drips of glaze running down the side. The teahouses too, small, exceedingly humble and somewhat forlorn (compared to the manors they were attached to) also reflected *wabi-sabi* motifs, as did the ikebana (flower arrangements) and calligraphy scrolls that would be placed in the teahouse's *tokanoma* (alcove).

Painting

Traditionally, paintings were done in black ink or mineral pigments on *washi* (Japanese handmade paper; itself an art form), scrolls (that either unfurled horizontally or were designed to hang vertically), folding screens or sliding doors.

Paintings of the Heian era (794–1185) depicted episodes of court life, like those narrated in the novel *Genji Monogatari (The Tale of Genji),* or seasonal motifs, often on scrolls. Works such as these were later called *yamato-e* (Yamato referring to the imperial clan), as they distinguished themselves thematically from those that were mere copies of Chinese paintings. Gradually a series of style conventions evolved to further distinguish *yamato-e;* one of the most striking is the use of a not-quite-bird's-eye perspective peering into palace rooms without their roofs (the better to see the intrigue!).

With the rise of Zen Buddhism in the 14th century, minimalist monochrome ink paintings came into vogue; the painters themselves were priests and the quick, spontaneous brush strokes of this painting style were in harmony with their guiding philosophies.

It was during the Muromachi period (1333–1573) that the ruling class became great patrons of Japanese painters, giving them the space and the means to develop their own styles. Two styles emerged at this time: the Tosa school and the Kano school.

The Tosa clan of artists worked for the imperial house, and were torch-bearers for the now classic *yamato-e* style, using fine brushwork to create highly stylised figures and elegant scenes from history and of the four seasons; sometimes the scenes were half-cloaked in washes of wispy gold clouds.

The Kano painters were under the patronage of the Ashikaga shogunate and employed to decorate their castles and villas. It was they who created the kind of works most associated with Japanese painting: decorative polychromatic depictions of mythical Chinese creatures and scenes from nature, boldly outlined on large folding screens and sliding doors.

Preparation of dumplings (p251), Shànghǎi

DFLC PRINTS/SHUTTERSTOCK ©

Food & Drink

Eating is a highlight of any trip to Northeast Asia.
Each region and town has its own signature dishes
and preparations, and while there's no shortage
of fine-dining options, your most memorable bites
are likely to be found at a streetside noodle bar,
aromatic market or tiny teahouse.

Japan

At its best, Japanese food is highly seasonal, drawing on fresh local ingredients coaxed into goodness with a light touch. Rice is central: the word for 'rice' and for 'meal' are the same – *gohan*. Miso soup and pickled vegetables often round out the meal. But from there Japanese food can vary tremendously; it can be light and delicate (as it is often thought to be), but it can also be hearty and robust.

Dining Out

When you enter a restaurant in Japan, you'll be greeted with a hearty *irasshaimase* (Welcome!). In all but the most casual places, the waiter will next ask you *nan-mei sama* (How many people?). Indicate the answer with your fingers, which is what the Japanese do. More

Signature Drinks

Japan Microbrews, *nihonshū* (sake), *o-cha* (green tea), *ryokucha* (leaf tea) and *matcha* (powdered tea).

Shànghǎi Coffee and craft cocktails.

South Korea *Nokcha* (green tea) and *soju* (local vodka).

Taiwan Bubble tea *(boba cha)*, oolong tea and third-wave coffee.

and more restaurants these days (especially in touristy areas) have English menus.

Often the bill will be placed discreetly on your table. If not, you can ask for it by catching the server's eye and making an 'x' in the air with your index finger. You can also say *o-kanjō kudasai*. At some restaurants, you can summon the server by pushing a call bell on the table. On your way out, if you were pleased with your meal, give your regards to the staff or chef with the phrase, *gochisō-sama deshita*, which means 'it was a real feast'.

There's no tipping, though higher-end restaurants usually tack on a 10% service fee. During dinner service, some restaurants may instead levy a kind of cover charge (usually a few hundred yen); this will be the case if you are served a small appetiser (called *o-tsumami*, or 'charm') when you sit down. Payment is usually settled at the register near the entrance.

Eat Like a Local

All but the most extreme type-A chefs will say they'd rather have foreign visitors enjoy their meal than agonise over getting the etiquette right. Still, a few points to note if you want to make a good impression: there's nothing that makes a Japanese chef grimace more than out-of-towners who over-season their food – a little soy sauce and wasabi goes a long way (and heaven forbid, don't pour soy sauce all over your rice; it makes it much harder to eat with chopsticks). It's perfectly OK, even expected, to slurp your noodles. They should be eaten at whip speed, before they go soggy (letting them do so would be an affront to the chef); that's why you'll hear diners slurping, sucking in air to cool their mouths.

Don't stick your chopsticks upright in a bowl of rice or pass food from one pair of chopsticks to another – both are reminiscent of Japanese funeral rites. When serving yourself from a shared dish, it's polite to use the back end of your chopsticks (ie not the end that goes into your mouth) to place the food on your own small dish.

Lunch is one of Japan's great bargains; however, restaurants can only offer cheap lunch deals because they anticipate high turnover. Spending too long sipping coffee after finishing your meal might earn you dagger eyes from the kitchen.

Shànghǎi

Brash, stylish and forward-thinking, Shànghǎi's culinary scene typifies the city's craving for foreign trends and tastes. As much an introduction to regional Chinese cuisine as a magnet for talented chefs from around the globe, Shànghǎi has staked a formidable claim as the Middle Kingdom's hottest dining destination.

Local Shànghǎi cuisine has been heavily influenced by the culinary styles of neighbouring provinces, and many of the techniques, ingredients and flavours originated in the much older cities of Yángzhōu, Sūzhōu and Hángzhōu. Broadly speaking, dishes tend to be sweeter and oilier than in other parts of China. Spiciness is anathema to Shànghǎi cooking.

Many places have English and/or picture menus, although they aren't always as comprehensive (or comprehensible) as the Chinese version. In any case, if you see a dish on someone else's table that looks absolutely delicious, just point at it when the waiter comes – no one will think you're being rude.

South Korea

Options range from casual bites at a market stall to elaborate multicourse meals at lavish restaurants. While the basic building blocks of the cuisine are recognisably Asian (garlic, ginger, green onion, black pepper, vinegar and sesame oil), Korean food combines them with three essential sauces: *ganjang* (soy sauce), *doenjang* (fermented soybean paste) and *gochujang* (hot red-pepper paste). The main course is nearly always served with *bap* (boiled rice), soup, kimchi and a procession of *banchan* (side dishes).

Seafood and black pork are Jeju-do specialities, but you'll also find horse meat and more regular Korean dishes. You'll see the island's citrus fruit *gamgyul* everywhere, from juices in stalls at remote sights to crates of the mandarin fruit in markets.

Taiwan

The Taiwanese love to eat out so much that many apartments, especially studios, don't even come with a kitchen. You've got local food at all budget levels – from big bowls of noodle soup for little more than NT$50 to fine dining that requires reservations days in advance. Gourmands know that some of Asia's best street eats are found in markets in and around Taiwan's cities.

Taiwanese cuisine can be divided into several styles of cooking, though the boundaries are often blurred: there's Taiwanese, Hakka, Fujianese and the gamey fare of the indigenous peoples. Most regional Chinese cuisines can also be found as well, the most popular being Cantonese. A healthy influx of Southeast Asian immigrants has 'tanged' up taste buds too, and the Japanese legacy has given the capital some of the best Japanese food outside of Tokyo.

Top Dining Experiences

Markets Visit any market in Taipei for a filling meal that's light on your wallet.

Ramen Your basic Japanese ramen is a big bowl of crinkly egg noodles in broth, served with toppings such as *chāshū* (sliced roast pork), *moyashi* (bean sprouts) and *menma* (fermented bamboo shoots). The broth can be made from pork or chicken bones or dried seafood; usually it's a top-secret combination of some or all of the above. Well-executed ramen is a complex, layered dish – though it rarely costs more than ¥1000 a bowl.

Hoe A Busan speciality, a typical *hoe* (sounds like 'when' without the 'n') dinner starts with appetisers such as raw baby octopus still wiggling on the plate. For the main course, sliced raw fish is dipped into a saucer of *chogochujang*, a watery red-pepper sauce, or soy sauce mixed with wasabi. Finish with rice and a boiling pot of *maeuntang* (spicy fish soup).

Shànghǎi street food Excellent and usually quite safe to eat. It generally consists of tiny dumpling and noodle shops along with vendors selling snacks such as *cōngyóu bǐng* (green onion pancakes), *bāozi* (steamed buns), *chòu dòufu* (stinky tofu) and *dìguā* (baked sweet potatoes).

Okonomiyaki This Japanese savoury pancake is stuffed with cabbage plus meat or seafood (or cheese or kimchi...), which you grill at the table and top with *katsuo bashi* (bonito flakes), nori (seaweed), mayonnaise and Worcestershire sauce.

Sushi At an average *sushi-ya* (sushi restaurant) in Japan a meal should run between ¥2000 and ¥5000 per person. You can order à la carte – often by just pointing to the fish in the refrigerated glass case on the counter. But the most economical way to eat sushi is to order a set, usually of around 10 to 12 pieces, which may be served all at once or piece by piece.

Performance at Hyakumangoku Matsuri (p21), Kanazawa

The People of Northeast Asia

Each new port brings with it a chance to meet new people and experience a new culture. Knowing a little about the lifestyles and beliefs of locals gives background and context to these experiences.

Japan

The people of Japan are depicted as inscrutable. Or reticent. Or shy. They can be, but often they're not. Japan is typically considered a homogeneous nation, and ethnically this is largely true (though there are minority cultures). But there are also deep divides between urban and rural, stubbornly persistent gendered spheres and growing social stratification. Increasingly, the Japanese are grappling with the problems faced by developed nations the world over.

Population

The population of Japan is approximately 126.5 million. That alone makes Japan a densely populated nation. But the population is unevenly distributed: about nine out of 10 people live in an area classified as urban. Roughly 36 million live within the Greater Tokyo Metro-

Shinjuku (p53), Tokyo

politan Area, which encompasses the cities of Tokyo, Kawasaki and Yokohama, plus the commuter towns stretching deep into the suburbs; it's the most heavily populated metropolitan area in the world. Nearly 20 million live in the Kyoto–Osaka–Kōbe conurbation (often called Keihanshin). Japan has 13 cities in which the population exceeds one million.

But the population, in general, is shrinking and getting older: for the last two decades the country's birth rate has hovered consistently around 1.4 – among the lowest in the world. The population peaked at 128 million in 2007 and has been in decline since; the latest estimates see a decline of 20 million (roughly one sixth of the total population) in the next 25 years. Currently over one in four Japanese is over the age of 65; in 25 years, if current trends hold, the number will be one in three and less than one in 10 will be a child under the age of 15.

Work Life

Over 70% of Japanese work in the service industry, a broad category that covers white-collar jobs, retail, care-giving and so on. A quarter of the population works in manufacturing, though these jobs are on the decline. Just 3.4% of Japanese today still work full-time in agriculture, forestry and fishing. It's a huge shift: until the beginning of last century, the majority of Japanese lived in close-knit rural farming communities.

For much of the 20th century, the backbone of the middle class was the Japanese corporation, which provided lifetime employment to the legions of blue-suited, white-collar workers, almost all of them men (nicknamed 'salarymen'), who lived, worked, drank, ate and slept in the service of the companies for which they toiled. Families typically consisted of a salaryman father, a housewife mother, kids who studied dutifully to earn a place at one of Japan's elite universities, and an elderly in-law who had moved in.

We Japanese

It's common to hear Japanese begin explanations of their culture by saying, *ware ware nihonjin*, which means, 'we Japanese'. There's a strong sense of national cohesion, reinforced by the media, which plays up images of Japan as a unique cultural Galapagos; TV programs featuring foreign visitors being awed and wowed by the curious Japanese way of doing things are popular with viewers. The Japanese, in turn, are often fascinated (and intimidated) by what they perceive as the otherness of outside cultures.

Since the recession of the 1990s (which plagues the economy to this day), this system has faltered. Today, roughly 37% of employees are considered 'nonregular', meaning they are on temporary contracts, often through dispatch agencies. In many cases they are doing work that once would have been done by full-time, contract-ed staff – only now with lower pay, less stability and fewer benefits.

Minority Cultures

Hidden within the population stats are Japan's invisible minorities – those who are native-born Japanese, who appear no different from other native-born Japa-nese but who can trace their ancestry to historically disenfranchised peoples. Chief among these are the descendants of the Ainu, the native people of Hokkaidō, and Okinawans. Prior to being annexed by Japan in the 19th century, Hokkaidō and Okinawa (formerly the Ryūkyū Empire) were independent territories. Following annexation, the Japanese government imposed assimilation policies that forbade many traditional customs and even the teaching of native languages.

The number of Japanese who identify as Ainu is estimated to be around 20,000, though it is likely that there are many more descendants of Hokkaidō's indigenous people out there – some who may not know it, perhaps because their ancestors buried their identity so deep (for fear of discrimination) that it became hidden forever. There are maybe 10 native speakers of Ainu left; however, in recent decades movements have emerged among the younger generation to learn the language and other aspects of the culture.

Today's Okinawans have a strong regional identity, though it is less about their ties to the former Ryūkyū Empire and more about their shared recent history since WWII. The Okinawans shouldered an unequal burden, both of casualties and of occupation.

Religion

Shintō and Buddhism are the main religions in Japan. They are not mutually exclusive: for much of history they were intertwined. Only about one-third of Japanese today identify as Buddhist and the figure for Shintō is just 3%; however, many Japanese participate in rituals rooted in both, which they see as integral parts of their culture and community ties. Generally it is said in Japan that Shintō is concerned with this life: births and marriages, for example, are celebrated at shrines. Meanwhile, Buddhism deals with the afterlife: funerals and memorials take place at temples.

Shintō

Shintō, or 'the way of the gods', is the native religion of Japan. Its innumerable *kami* (gods) are located mostly in nature (in trees, rocks, waterfalls and mountains, for example), but also in the mundane objects of daily life, like hearths and wells. *Kami* can be summoned through rituals of dance and music in the shrines the Japanese have built for them, where they may be beseeched with prayers for a good harvest or a healthy pregnancy, for exam-ple, and in modern times for success in business or school exams.

Shintō's origins are unclear. For ages it was a vague, amorphous set of practices and beliefs. It has no doctrine and no beginning or endgame; it simply is. One important concept is *musubi,* a kind of vital energy that animates everything (*kami* and mortals alike). Impurities *(tsumi)* interfere with *musubi,* so purification rituals are part of all Shintō rites and practices. For this reason, visitors to shrines first wash their hands and mouth at the *temizu* (font). Some traditional rites include fire, which is also seen as a purifying force. In the late 19th and early 20th centuries, Shintō was reconfigured by the imperialist state into a national religion centred on emperor worship. This ended with Japan's defeat in WWII, when Emperor Hirohito himself publicly renounced his divinity. It's unclear what those who today identify as Shintō actually believe.

Regardless of belief, there are customs so ingrained in Japanese culture that many continue to perform them anyway, as a way of carrying on family and community traditions. Shrines are still the place to greet the New Year, a rite called Hatsu-mōde; to celebrate the milestones, such as Coming-of-Age Day and Shichi-go-san; and where the lovelorn come to pray for a match. At the very least, many would say, doing such things can't hurt.

Buddhism

Buddhism in Japan is part of the Mahāyāna (Great Vehicle) tradition, which teaches that anyone (as opposed to just monks) can attain salvation in this lifetime. A key figure in Mahāyāna Buddhism is the bodhisattva, a compassionate being who, on the cusp of achieving Buddha-hood, delays transcendence in order to help others. By the time Buddhism arrived in Japan in the 6th century, having travelled from India via Tibet, China and Korea, it had acquired a whole pantheon of deities. More importantly, it didn't so much supplant Shintō as elaborate on it. Over time, Shintō *kami* became integrated into the Buddhist cosmology while many new deities were adopted as *kami;* those with similar aspects were seen as two faces of the same being.

Over the centuries, several distinct sects developed in Japan. Zen is the most well-known internationally, for its meditative practice *zazen* (seated meditation), but there are others, too, like the older esoteric Shingon sect (which shares similarities with Tibetan Buddhism) and the populist Pure Land sect (which has the greatest number of adherents). Regardless of sect, the most popular deity in Japan is Kannon, a bodhisattva who embodies mercy and compassion and is believed to have the power to alleviate suffering in this world.

Given its association with the afterlife, many turn to Buddhism later in life. (And because of its role in funeral rites, many young Japanese have a dour view of the religion). But, like Shintō, there are certain practices carried out by believers and non-believers alike. The Buddhist festival of O-Bon, in midsummer, is when the souls of departed ancestors are believed to pay a short visit. Families return to their hometowns to sweep gravestones, an act called *ohaka-mairi,* and welcome them. Only the most staunch non-believer could avoid the creeping sense that skipping such rituals would be tempting fate.

Women in Japan

Women have historically been viewed as keepers of the home, responsible for overseeing the household budget, monitoring the children's education and taking care of the day-to-day tasks of cooking and cleaning. Of course this ideal was rarely matched by reality: labour shortfalls often resulted in women taking on factory work and, even before that, women often worked side by side with men in the fields.

As might be expected, the contemporary situation is complex. There are women who prefer the traditionally neat division of labour. They tend to opt for shorter college courses, often at women's colleges. They may work for several years, enjoying a period of

Identity & the Shànghǎi Dialect

Older Shanghainese are highly conscious of the disappearance of the Shànghǎi dialect (Shanghaihuà), under assault from the increased promotion of the Mandarin (Pǔtōnghuà) dialect and the flood of immigrant tongues. It's a deeply tribal element of Shànghǎi culture and heritage, so the vanishing of the dialect equals a loss of identity. Fewer and fewer young Shanghainese and children are now able to speak the pure form of the dialect, or can understand it, and prefer to speak Mandarin. Youngsters might not care, but older Shanghainese agonise over the tongue's slow extinction. The most perfectly preserved forms of Shanghaihuà survive in rural areas around Shànghǎi, where Mandarin has less of a toehold. The Shanghainese may remind themselves of the Chinese idiom – *jiùde bù qù, xīnde bù lái* ('If the old doesn't go, the new doesn't arrive') – but it may offer scant consolation.

independence before settling down, leaving the role of breadwinner to the husband and becoming full-time mums.

While gender discrimination in the workforce is illegal, it remains pernicious. And while there is less societal resistance to women working, they still face enormous pressure to be doting mothers. Most women see the long hours that Japanese companies demand as incompatible with child-rearing, especially in the early years; few fathers are willing or, given their own work commitments, able to pick up the slack. Attempts at work-life balance, such as working from home, can result in guilt trips from colleagues or bosses. Working women have coined the phrase 'maternity harassment' to describe the remarks they hear in the office after announcing a pregnancy, the subtle suggestions that she quit so as not to cause trouble. Six out of 10 women quit work after having their first child.

And yet many return: women do in fact make up over 40% of the workforce – not far off the global average; however, over half of them are working part-time and often menial, low-paying jobs. They hold only 9.3% of managerial positions. Women in full-time positions make on average 73% of what their male counterparts make; up from 60% in the 1990s. Women also continue to spend far more time on unpaid labour (including childcare and housework duties): 3¾ hours per day, compared to men's 40 minutes. These are among the most dramatic imbalances in the developed world.

South Korea

Once divided strictly along nearly inescapable social-class lines, South Koreans today are comparatively better off in terms of economic opportunities and are more individualistic in their world view. Nuclear rather than extended families have become the norm, and birth rates are among the lowest in the developed world. Still, strong traces linger of Korea's particular identity; remnants of its Confucian past coexist alongside 'imported' spiritual beliefs and a striking devotion to displays of material success.

Contemporary & Traditional Culture

Driven by the latest technology and fast-evolving trends, Korea can sometimes seem like one of the most cutting-edge countries on the planet. People tune into their favourite TV shows via their smart phones. In PC-*bang* (computer-game rooms) millions of diehard fans battle at online computer games.

General fashions too tend to be international and up to the moment. However, it's not uncommon to see some people wearing *hanbok,* the striking traditional clothing that follows the Confucian principle of unadorned modesty. Women wear a loose-fitting short blouse with long sleeves and a voluminous long skirt, while men wear a jacket and baggy trousers.

Today *hanbok* is worn mostly at weddings or special events, and even then it may be a more comfortable 'updated' version. Everyday *hanbok* is reasonably priced, but formal styles, made of colourful silk and intricately embroidered, are objects of wonder and cost a fortune.

Mono-Culturalist South Korea

South Korea is a monocultural society. As of 2016, *foreigners* (the local name given to foreign nationals) numbered 2 million or 3.9% of the population. Much like a foreigner among any homogenous group of people, you can expect to get stared at in public. This can be more intense depending on how melanin-rich your skin is, and often lingers most unabashedly from people of older generations.

Taiwan

First-time visitors to Taiwan often expect to find a completely homogenised society, with little difference in thinking, customs and attitudes from one generation to the next, from city to countryside, or even from person to person. In fact, the country is a multiethnic melting pot. Customs and traditions go back and forth between groups and evolve over time; these days, family background and life experience are far more indicative of a person's attitudes and beliefs than simple ethnicity.

Lifestyle

Despite the low birth and marriage rate, family still remains central to Taiwanese life. Both young and old are generally deeply committed to each other.

Most people in Taiwan live in crowded urban conditions. However, with low taxes, cheap utilities, fresh local foods, to say nothing of excellent low-cost universal medical care, people enjoy a good balance between the cost of living and quality of life. (On the other hand, stagnating wages are a major problem for young people.) Life expectancy is 83 years for women and 77 years for men.

The Taiwanese Character

Taiwanese have often been characterised as some of the friendliest people in the world. Reports from Western travellers and officials in Taiwan in the 1930s read like modern accounts, which suggests friendliness is a deep long-standing quality. Some claim this is likely due to Taiwan's immigrant background, in which trust among strangers was paramount.

Taiwan's Modernity

Just as traditional rites are used to celebrate the opening of businesses and honour the passing of lives, in Taiwan, pop culture is part and parcel of many religious processions. It is not uncommon to spot scantily clad pole dancers busting moves on large vehicles at these events, or dance music pumping out of converted cars with gull-wing doors and badass lights, not to mention bros sporting tats and trainers strutting along to the temple dressed as deities. Whatever one's opinion of such modern manifestations of faith, they're not meant to be disrespectful of tradition. If anything, they show how deeply ingrained faith is in the lives of Taiwanese of all ages. And for outsiders, the ease with which the Taiwanese sashay in and out of tradition and modernity is what makes this country so fascinating.

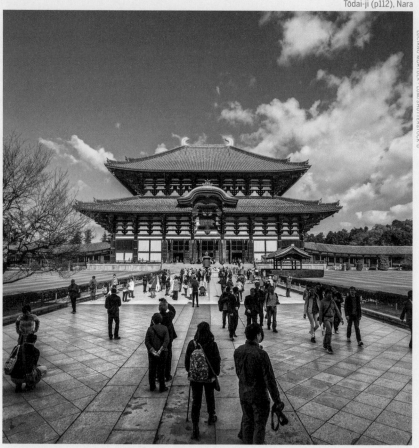

Tōdai-ji (p112), Nara

LUCIANO MORTULA - LGM/SHUTTERSTOCK ©

Survival Guide

Directory A–Z

Accessible Travel

Accessibility throughout the region is improving, but has some way to go.

On the plus side, many buildings have access ramps, major train stations have lifts, traffic lights have speakers playing melodies when it is safe to cross, and train platforms have raised dots and lines to provide guidance for the visually impaired. You'll find most service staff will go out of their way to be helpful, even if they don't speak much English. Major sights take great pains to be wheelchair friendly and many have wheelchairs you can borrow for free.

On the negative side, many city streets are still rather difficult to negotiate – streets can be narrow and busy, and pavements cluttered, uneven or non-existent. In Shànghǎi, the city's traffic, overpasses and underpasses are the greatest challenges to travellers with disabilities. Try to take a lightweight chair for navigating around obstacles and for collapsing into the back of taxis.

○ Download Lonely Planet's free Accessible Travel guide

from http://lptravel.to/AccessibleTravel.

○ Japan Accessible Tourism Center (www.japan-accessible.com) is a good resource.

○ Taiwan Access for All Association (twaccess4all.wordpress.com) provides advice and assistance.

Discount Cards

Seniors over the age of 65 are frequently eligible for discounts, and in Taipei and China, 70-and-overs often get

free admission, so make sure you take your passport when visiting sights as proof of age.

Health

○ Health is generally of high standard throughout the region.

○ Treatment can be expensive; make sure you are fully insured for your trip. Note, though, the only insurance accepted at Japanese

Climate

Shanghai

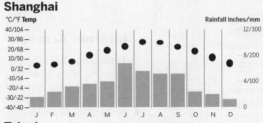

Taipei

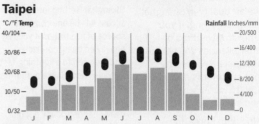

Tokyo

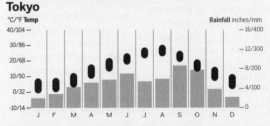

Japan Helpline

English-speaking operators at **Japan Helpline** (☏0570-000-911) are available 24 hours a day to help you negotiate tricky situations. If you don't have access to mobile service, use the contact form on the website (http://jhelp.com/english/index.html).

hospitals is Japanese insurance. You'll have to pay up front and apply for a reimbursement when you get home.

○ In Japan, most hospitals do not have doctors and nurses who speak English.

○ Expect to pay from around ¥20,000 and upwards for emergency care.

○ Health concerns for travellers to Shànghǎi include worsening atmospheric pollution, traveller's diarrhoea and winter influenza. The air quality in Shànghǎi can be appalling. If you suffer from asthma or other allergies you should anticipate a worsening of your symptoms and may need to increase your medication.

○ In South Korea, the language barrier will be the biggest obstacle. International clinics in hospitals in large cities will likely have English-speaking doctors, but expect to pay between ₩40,000 to ₩80,000 for the consultation alone.

○ Many Taiwanese doctors have trained in Western countries and speak at least some English.

Insurance

A travel-insurance policy to cover theft, loss and medical problems is essential. Worldwide travel insurance is available at www.lonelyplanet.com/travel-insurance. You can buy, extend and claim online anytime – even if you're already on the road.

For health insurance information, see p301.

Internet Access

Japan Many cities in Japan (including Tokyo, Osaka and Kyoto) have free wi-fi networks for travellers, though the system is still clunky in areas.

Shànghǎi Getting internet access will be one constant source of frustration if you rely heavily on being connected, and are used to a lightning-fast service. The Chinese authorities remain mistrustful of the internet, and censorship is heavy-handed. Many popular social networking sites and email providers are blocked – the list changes regularly, so check before you arrive.

South Korea With the world's fastest connections and one of the highest rates of internet usage, you'll find abundant free internet access, either via

a computer or wi-fi in cafes, public streets and tourist information centres.

Taiwan Free wi-fi is widely accessible in cafes, restaurants, and in some shopping malls.

Language

Japan English use is not widespread, though cities and popular destinations are well-signposted in English and will have Tourist Information Centres (TICs) with English-speaking staff; restaurants in these areas will also often have English menus. Most Japanese are more comfortable with written than spoken English, so whenever possible, email is often the best means of communicating.

Shànghǎi Outside hotels, English is not widely spoken. You'll be able to get by in tourist areas, but it's useful to learn a few basic phrases. Some restaurants may not have an English menu. You'll find yourself surrounded by written Chinese wherever you travel, so a Pleco app (www.pleco.com) or phrasebook is useful.

South Korea It's relatively easy to find English speakers in the big cities, but not so easy in smaller towns and the countryside. Learning a few key phrases will help you enormously in being able to decode street signs, menus and timetables.

Taiwan Although on the street you will hear Mandarin and Taiwanese, plenty of young and middle-aged Taiwanese speak reasonable English, especially anyone working in the tourist trade. You might have some trouble, though, with taxi drivers. MRT announcements are also in English, and many signs are in English too. Any restaurant that is midrange or above is very likely to have an English menu. Saying all that, a few polite phrases in Mandarin will go a long way.

LGBT+ Travellers

Japan Gay and lesbian travellers are unlikely to encounter problems in Japan. There are no legal restraints on same-sex sexual activities in Japan apart from the usual age restrictions.

Shànghǎi Local law is ambiguous in its attitude to LGBT people; generally the authorities take a dim view of same-sex couples but there's an increasingly confident scene, as indicated by gay bars and the annual event-stuffed Shanghai Pride (www.shpride. com). Shànghǎi heterosexuals are not, by and large, particularly homophobic, especially the under-40s. Young Chinese men sometimes hold hands; this carries no sexual overtones.

South Korea Korea has never passed any laws that mention homosexuality, but this shouldn't be taken as a sign of tolerance or acceptance. Attitudes are changing, especially among young people, but virtually all local gays and lesbians choose to stay firmly

Tap Water

Japan Tap water is fine to drink.

Shànghǎi Don't drink tap water or eat ice. Bottled water is readily available. Boiled water is OK.

South Korea Some of the cleanest tap water in the world. Filtered or bottled water is served free in most restaurants and machines with free purified hot and cold water are at most shopping plaza entrances.

Taiwan Tap water here is supposed to be drinkable, but nobody does. There are drinking water dispensers in major tourist sites, temples, some MRT stations and hospitals.

in the closet. Gay and lesbian travellers who publicise their sexual orientation tend to receive less than positive reactions.

Taiwan In 2019, Taiwan became the first Asian nation to legalise same-sex marriage. Foreign-born gay and lesbian travellers will find Taipei friendly, open-minded and exciting. It's common to see LGBT couples holding hands on the streets, though not common to see them kissing.

Money

ATMs

o ATMs are widespread throughout the region, though they may not be open 24 hours.

o Many ATMs in Japan and South Korea do not accept foreign-issued cards. In Japan, most Seven Bank ATMs at 7-Eleven convenience stores (open 24 hours) and Japan Post Bank ATMs

at post offices accept most overseas cards and have instructions in English. In South Korea, look for one that has a 'Global' sign or the logo of your credit-card company.

o In Shànghǎi and Taipei, ATMs generally accept Visa, MasterCard, Cirrus and Maestro cards, as well as JCB and Plus in Taipei. Most operate 24 hours. Bank of China and the Industrial & Commercial Bank of China are the best bets in Shànghǎi.

Cash

Many places in Japan – particularly outside the cities – don't accept credit cards. Smaller restaurants and shops are common cash-only places, so it's wise to keep cash on hand.

Credit Cards

Credit cards are increasingly accepted, but plenty of places, including budget or smaller restaurants, stalls and shops still require cash. Always check before deciding to order in a restaurant. It's also always wise to carry some cash to be sure.

Exchanging Money

The best rates are given by banks. Note that not all banks will change money and many will only change US dollars. In Japan and China, you will need your passport in order to change money.

Exchange rates in China are uniform wherever you change money, so there's little need to shop around. Whenever you change foreign currency into Chinese currency you will be given a money-exchange voucher recording the transaction. You need to show this to change your yuán back into any foreign currency. Changing Chinese currency outside China is a problem, though it's quite easily done in Hong Kong.

Note that you receive a better exchange rate when withdrawing cash from ATMs than when exchanging cash or travellers cheques in Japan.

Tipping

○ Tipping is not customary throughout the region.

○ There's no need to tip in bars or taxis.

○ Japanese high-end restaurants usually add a 10% service fee to the bill, as do some in Shànghǎi.

○ Guides don't require a tip, but a small gift is appreciated. In Taipei, a 10%

addition to the fee if you are happy with the service is common.

Opening Hours

Japan

Some outdoor attractions (such as gardens) may close earlier in the winter. Standard opening hours:

Banks 9am to 3pm (some to 5pm) Monday to Friday.

Bars From around 6pm to late.

Department stores 10am to 8pm.

Museums 9am to 5pm, last entry by 4.30pm; often closed Monday (if Monday is a national holiday then the museum will close on Tuesday instead).

Post offices 9am to 5pm Monday to Friday; larger ones have longer hours and open Saturday.

Restaurants Lunch 11.30am to 2pm; dinner 6pm to 10pm; last orders taken about half an hour before closing.

Shànghǎi

Businesses in China close for the week-long Chinese New Year (usually in February) and National Day (beginning 1 October).

Bank of China Branches 9.30am to 11.30am and 1.30pm to 4.30pm Monday to Friday. Some also open Saturday and Sunday. Most have 24-hour ATMs.

Bars Around 5pm to 2am (some open in the morning).

China Post Most major offices 8.30am to 6pm daily; some-

times open until 10pm. Local branches closed weekends.

Museums Most open weekends; a few close Monday. Ticket sales usually stop 30 or 60 minutes before closing.

Offices and government departments Generally 9am to noon and 2pm to 4.30pm Monday to Friday.

Restaurants Most 11am to 10pm or later; some 10am to 2.30pm and 5pm to 11pm or later.

Shops Malls and department stores generally 10am to 10pm.

South Korea

Banks 9am to 4pm Monday to Friday; ATMs 7am to 11pm (or 24 hours).

Bars 6pm to 1am, longer hours Friday and Saturday.

Cafes 7am to 10pm.

Restaurants 11am to 10pm.

Shops 10am to 8pm.

Taiwan

Some restaurants and cafes and many museums are closed on Mondays. Bars and some restaurants often close an hour or so later on Fridays and Saturdays.

Banks 9am to 3.30pm Monday to Friday.

Cafes Noon to 8pm (often closed Monday).

Convenience stores Most are 24 hours.

Department stores 11am to 9.30pm.

Government offices 8.30am to 5.30pm Monday to Friday.

Museums 9am to 5pm Tuesday to Sunday.

Night markets 5pm to midnight.

Offices 9am to 5pm Monday to Friday.

Post offices 8am to 5pm Monday to Friday; larger offices may open till 9pm and have limited hours on weekends.

Restaurants 11.30am to 2pm and 5pm to 9pm.

Shops 10am to 9pm.

Supermarkets Until at least 8pm; sometimes 24 hours.

Safe Travel

Northeast Asia is generally a very safe region for travel – urban streets are safe and muggings or violent assaults uncommon. Still, it's wise to keep up the same level of caution and common sense that you would back home.

In Shànghǎi, crossing the road is probably the greatest danger: develop avian vision and a sixth sense to combat the shocking traffic. Don't end up in an ambulance: Chinese drivers never give way.

Likewise traffic is your biggest risk in South Korea and Taipei. In South Korea, drivers almost never stop for pedestrian crossings that are not protected by traffic lights, and they routinely jump red lights late at night, so take care on pedestrian crossings even if they are protected by lights. In Taipei and South Korea, watch out for 'wayward' scooters on the roads (or pedestrian crossings, or pavements...).

Smoking

Japan In many cities (including Tokyo, Osaka and Kyoto) smoking is banned in public spaces but allowed inside bars and restaurants. Designated smoking areas are set up around train stations.

Shànghǎi From 2010, antismoking legislation in Shànghǎi required a number of public venues (including bars and restaurants) to have designated nonsmoking areas and to install signs prohibiting smoking. However, you'll often find this rule flouted in bars and some restaurants.

South Korea Nationwide ban on smoking in public enclosed spaces such as bars and restaurants, on train platforms and 10m from station exits. Smoking is not allowed on many tourist streets.

Taiwan Not allowed in public facilities, public transport, shopping malls and restaurants and this is strictly enforced. Even some parks are marked smoke-free.

Telephone

● Japan operates on the 3G network, so overseas phones with 3G technology should work. Prepaid SIM cards that allow you to make voice calls are not available in Japan. Data-only SIM cards for unlocked smartphones are available at large electronics stores (such as Bic Camera, Yodobashi Camera etc) in major cities. You'll need to download and install an APN profile; ask staff to help you if you are unsure how to do this (they usually speak some English).

● In Shànghǎi, a mobile phone should be the first choice for calls, but ensure your mobile is unlocked

for use in China if taking your own.

● Most networks in South Korea use the WCDMA 2100 MHz network, as well as one of five different 4G LTE bands. Most unlocked recent smartphones will work with a Korean SIM. Mobile phones and portable wi-fi eggs can be hired.

● Local SIM cards in Taipei should fit most overseas-bought mobiles. They come with prepaid plans.

Time

Japan & South Korea Nine hours ahead of Greenwich Mean Time (GMT); do not have daylight saving time.

Shànghǎi & Taiwan Eight hours ahead of GMT/UTC. There is no daylight-saving time.

Toilets

• Public toilets in the region are generally plentiful, free and clean.

• The exception is in Shànghǎi. Often charging a small fee, toilets here run from the sordid to coin-operated portaloos and modern conveniences. The best bet is to head for a top-end hotel, where someone will hand you a towel, pour you some aftershave or exotic hand lotion and wish you a nice day.

• You will come across both Western-style toilets and traditional squat toilets. When you are compelled to squat, the correct position is facing the hood, away from the door.

• In Japan, the katakana for 'toilet' is トイレ, and the kanji is お手洗い. Also good to know: the kanji for female (女) and male (男).

• In Shànghǎi and Taiwan, look for the Chinese characters for men (男) and women (女).

• In Korean, public toilets are hwajangsil (화장실).

• Toilet paper is usually provided (except in Shànghǎi), but it is still a good idea to carry tissues with you. In South Korea, toilet paper is usually outside the cubicles.

• Many places in Taiwan ask you not to flush toilet paper but to put it in the waste-paper basket beside the toilet.

Tourist Information

Japan

Tourist information offices (*kankō annai-sho;* 観光案内所) can be found inside or in front of major train stations. Staff may not speak much English; however, there are usually English-language materials and staff are accustomed to the usual concerns of travellers. Many have free wi-fi.

Japan National Tourism Organization (JNTO; www.jnto.go.jp) is Japan's government tourist bureau. It produces a great deal of useful literature in English, which is available from its overseas offices as well as its **TIC** (Map p52; ☑03-3201-3331; 1st fl, Shin-Tokyo Bldg, 3-3-1 Marunouchi, Chiyoda-ku; ☺9am-5pm; ☞; ⓢChiyoda line to Nijūbashimae, exit 1) in Tokyo.

Shànghǎi

Shànghǎi has about a dozen or so rather useless Tourist Information & Service Centres. For competent English-language help, call the **Shànghǎi Call Centre** (☑021 962 288), a free 24-hour English-language hotline that can respond to cultural or transport enquiries (and even provide directions for your cab driver).

South Korea

If you need interpretation help or information on practically any topic, any time of the day or night, you can call **BBB** (☑1588 5644; www.bbbkorea.org).

Taiwan

Visitor information centres are present in most city train stations and popular scenic areas. They stock English-language brochures, maps, and train and bus schedules, and usually staff can speak some English. Welcome to Taiwan (http://eng.taiwan.net.tw/) is the official site of the Taiwan Tourism Bureau; the **Tourist Hotline** (☑0800-011 765) is a useful 24-hour service in English, Japanese and Chinese.

Visas

Japan

Citizens of 67 territories, including Australia, Canada, Hong Kong, Korea, New Zealand, Singapore, the UK, the USA, and almost all European nations will be automatically issued a *tanki-taizai* (temporary-visitor visa) on arrival. Typically this visa is good for 90 days. For a complete list of visa-exempt territories, consult www.mofa.go.jp/j_info/visit/visa/short/novisa.html#list.

For additional information on visas and regulations, contact your nearest Japanese embassy or consulate, or visit the website of the Ministry of Foreign Affairs of Japan (www.mofa.go.jp).

Shànghǎi

Citizens from a number of countries including the USA, Australia, Canada, New Zealand, Germany, Sweden and France, can transit through Shànghǎi for up to 144 hours without a visa as long as they have visas for their onward countries and proof of passage out of China. Your departure point and destination should not be in the same country. Note also that you are not allowed to visit other cities in China during your transit.

South Korea

With a confirmed onward ticket, visitors from the USA, nearly all Western European countries, New Zealand, Australia and around 30 other countries receive 90-day permits on arrival. About 30 countries do not qualify for visa exemptions. Citizens from these countries must apply for a tourist visa, which allows a stay of 90 days.

As rules are always changing, see www.hikorea.go.kr for more visa information.

Taiwan

Tourists from most European countries, Canada, the US, Australia (until December 2019; see Taiwan's Ministry of Foreign Affairs website for updates), New Zealand, South Korea and Japan are

given visa-free entry for stays of up to 90 days.

Transport

Flights, cars and tours can be booked online at lonely planet.com/bookings.

Getting There & Away

Air

Japan

Japan's major international airports include the following:

Narita International Airport (www.narita-airport.jp) About 75 minutes east of Tokyo by express train, Narita gets the bulk of international flights to Japan; most budget carriers flying to Tokyo arrive here.

Haneda Airport (www.tokyo-airport-bldg.co.jp) Tokyo's more convenient airport – about 30 minutes by train or monorail to the city centre – Haneda, also known as Tokyo International Airport, is getting an increasing number of international arrivals; domestic flights to/from Tokyo usually arrive/depart here.

Kansai International Airport (www.kansai-airport.or.jp) Serves the key Kansai cities of Kyoto, Osaka, Nara and Kōbe.

Shànghǎi

Pǔdōng International Airport (PVG; 浦东国际机场; Pǔdōng Guójì Jīchǎng; ☎021 6834 7575, flight information 96990; www.shairport.com) Located 30km southeast of Shànghǎi, near the East China Sea. Most international flights operate from here.

Hóngqiáo International Airport (SHA; 虹桥国际机场; Hóngqiáo Guójì Jīchǎng; ☎021 5260 4620, flight information 021 6268 8899; www.shairport. com; Ⓜ Hongqiao Airport Terminal 1, Ⓜ Hongqiao Airport Terminal 2) Located 18km west of the Bund.

South Korea

International travellers can fly directly to **Gimhae International Airport** (김해 국제 공항; Map p267; ☎051 974 3114; www.airport.co.kr/ gimhaeeng/index.do; Ⓜ Busan-Gimhae LRT, Exit Airport), 27km west of Busan's city centre.

Taiwan

Taiwan Taoyuan International Airport (☎03-273 3728; www.taoyuan-airport. com) is about 40km west of Taipei, while **Taipei Songshan Airport** (松山機場; Sōngshān Jīchǎng; Map p221; www.tsa.gov.tw/tsa; 340-9 Dunhua N Rd; 敦化北路340-9; Ⓜ Songshan Airport) is just north of the city centre and services direct international flights to China, Japan and South Korea, plus domestic routes.

Getting Around

Car & Motorcycle
Japan

• Driving in Japan is quite feasible, even for the mildly adventurous. Most roads are signposted in English; roads are in excellent condition; road rules are generally adhered to; and petrol, while expensive, is not prohibitively so.

• Typical rates for a small car are ¥5000 to ¥7000 per day, with reductions for rentals of more than one day. On top of the rental charge, there's about a ¥1000-per-day insurance cost. Prices among major agencies are comparable.

• Toyota Rent-a-Car (https://rent.toyota.co.jp) and Nippon Rent-a-Car (www.nrgroup-global.com) have large rental networks and booking in English is possible online.

Shànghǎi

It is possible to hire a car in Shànghǎi, but the bureaucratic hurdles are designed to deter would-be foreign drivers. You will need a temporary or long-term Chinese driving licence. For most visitors, it is more advisable to hire a car and a driver.

South Korea

Driving in South Korea is not recommended for first-time visitors. Korea has an appalling road-accident record, and foreign drivers in large cities are likely to spend most of their time lost, stuck in traffic jams, looking for a parking space or taking evasive action.

Taiwan

By the standards of many countries, driving in Taiwan can be chaotic and dangerous. Not recommended.

Local Transport
Japan

Japan's larger cities are serviced by subways or trams, buses and taxis; indeed, many locals rely entirely on public transport. Note that all public transport except for taxis shuts down between midnight and 5am.

Bus

The city where you'll find yourself relying on public buses is Kyoto. Though the city has a subway system, it is not convenient for all major tourist sites.

Subway & Tram

Kyoto, Osaka, Tokyo and Sapporo have subway systems, which are usually the fastest and most-convenient way to get around the city. Stops and line names are posted in English. Hiroshima has trams.

Fares are typically ¥150 to ¥250, depending on how far your ride (half-price for children). If you plan to zip around a city in a day, an

---

IC Cards in Japan

IC cards are prepaid travel cards with chips that work on subways, trams and buses in the Tokyo, Kansai, Sapporo and Hiroshima metro areas. They save you the trouble of having to purchase paper tickets and work out the correct fare for your journey. Each region has its own card, but they can be used interchangeably in any region where IC cards are used; however, they cannot be used for intercity travel.

The two most frequently used IC cards are **Suica** (www.jreast.co.jp/e/pass/suica.html) from JR East and **Icoca** (www.westjr.co.jp/global/en/ticket/icoca-haruka) from JR West; purchase them at JR travel counters at Narita and Haneda or Kansai airports, respectively. Cards can also be purchased and topped up from ticket-vending machines in any of the cities that support them. Both require a ¥500 deposit, which you get back when you return your card to any JR ticket window.

To use the card, simply swipe it over the reader at the ticket gates or near the doors on trams and buses.

unlimited-travel day ticket (called *ichi-nichi-jōsha-ken*) is a good deal; most cities offer them and they can be purchased at station windows.

Taxi

∘ Taxis are ubiquitous in big cities. They can be found in smaller cities and even on tiny islands, too, though usually just at transport hubs (train and bus stations and ferry ports) – otherwise you'll need to get someone to call one for you.

∘ Transit stations have taxi stands where you are expected to queue. In the absence of a stand, hail a cab from the street by standing on the curb and sticking your arm out.

∘ Fares are fairly uniform throughout Japan and all cabs run by the meter. Flagfall (posted on the taxi windows) is around ¥600 to ¥710 for the first 2km, after which it's around ¥100 for each 350m (approximately). There's also a time charge if the speed drops below 10km/h and a 20% surcharge between 10pm and 5am.

∘ A red light means the taxi is free and a green light means it's taken.

∘ Drivers rarely speak English, though fortunately most taxis now have navigation systems. It's a good idea to have your destination written down in script, or better yet, a business card with an address.

Shànghǎi

The rapidly expanding metro and light railway system works like a dream; it's fast, efficient and inexpensive. Rush hour on the metro operates above capacity, however, and you get to savour the full meaning of the big squeeze.

With a wide-ranging web of routes, buses may sound tempting, but that's before you try to decipher routes and stops or attempt to squeeze aboard during the crush hour. Buses also have to contend with Shanghai's traffic, which can slow to an agonising crawl.

Taxis are ubiquitous and cheap, but flagging one down during rush hour or during a rainstorm requires staying power of a high order.

South Korea

Busan has a subway (metro) system. It's a cheap and convenient way of getting around and station names are in English as well as Korean.

Local city buses provide a frequent and inexpensive service. The main problem with local buses is finding and getting on the right bus. Timetables, stop names and destination signs on buses are rarely in English, and drivers usually don't speak English. The app Naver Map is available in English and has accurate journey planner information for the whole country.

Taxis are numerous almost everywhere and fares are inexpensive. Every taxi has a meter that works on a distance basis but switches to a time basis when the vehicle is stuck in a traffic jam. Tipping is not a local custom and is not expected or necessary.

Since few taxi drivers speak English, plan how to communicate with the driver; if you have a mobile phone you can also use the 1330 tourist advice line to help with interpretation. Ask to be dropped off at a nearby landmark. It can be useful to write down your destination or a nearby landmark in *hangeul* on a piece of paper.

Taiwan

Buses throughout the country are generally reliable, cheap and comfortable. In Taipei, routes on timetables are written in Chinese only, and buses can be slow when they get stuck in traffic.

Taipei has a Mass Rapid Transit (MRT; http://eng lish.metro.taipei/) metro system. It is clean, safe, convenient and reliable. All signs and ticket machines are in English. English signs around stations indicate which exit to take to nearby sights. Posters indicate bus transfer routes.

Taxis are ubiquitous in Taiwan's cities, though traffic can be frustrating and drivers are unlikely to speak much English. Outside urban areas, taxi drivers will either use meters or ask for a flat rate (the smaller the town the more likely the latter).

Language

In Japan

Japanese pronunciation is not difficult as most of its sounds are also found in English. You can read our pronunciation guides as if they were English and you'll be understood just fine. Just remember to pronounce every vowel individually, make those with a macron (ie a line above them) longer than those without, and pause slightly between double consonants.

To enhance your trip with a phrasebook, visit **lonelyplanet.com**. Lonely Planet iPhone phrasebooks are available through the Apple App store.

Basics

Hello.
こんにちは。 konnichiwa

How are you?
お元気ですか? o-genki des ka

I'm fine, thanks.
はい、元気です。 hai, genki des

Excuse me.
すみません。 sumimasen

Yes./No.
はい。/いいえ。 hai/iie

Please. (when asking/offering)
ください。/どうぞ。 kudasai/dōzo

Thank you.
どうも ありがとう。 dōmo arigatō

You're welcome.
どういたしまして。 dō itashimashite

Do you speak English?
英語が話せますか? eigo ga hanasemas ka

I don't understand.
わかりません。 wakarimasen

How much is this?
いくらですか? ikura des ka

Goodbye.
さようなら。 sayōnara

Eating & Drinking

I'd like ..., please.
…をください。 ... o kudasai

What do you recommend?
おすすめは何 o-susume wa nan
ですか? des ka

That was delicious.
おいしかった。 oyshikatta

Bring the bill/check, please.
お勘定をお願い o-kanjō o onegai
します。 shimas

I don't eat ...
…は食べません。 ... wa tabemasen
  chicken 鶏肉 tori-niku
  fish 魚 sakana
  meat 肉 niku
  pork 豚肉 buta-niku

Emergencies

I'm ill.
気分が悪いです。 kibun ga warui des

Help!
たすけて! taskete

Call a doctor!
医者を呼んで! isha o yonde

Call the police!
警察を呼んで! keisatsu o yonde

Directions

I'm looking for (a/the) ...
…を探しています。 ... o sagashite imas
  bank
  銀行 ginkō
  ... embassy
  大使館 taishikan
  market
  市場 ichiba
  museum
  美術館 bijutsukan
  restaurant
  レストラン restoran
  toilet
  お手洗い/トイレ o-tearai/toire
  tourist office
  観光案内所 kankō annaijo

In Shànghǎi

Most of the population speaks Mandarin, so you'll find that knowing a few basics in Mandarin will come in handy. In this chapter we've provided Pinyin alongside the Mandarin script. See p298 for information on the Shànghǎi dialect (Shanghaihuà).

Basics

Hello.
你好。 nǐhǎo.

Goodbye.
再见。 zàijiàn.

How are you?
你好吗? nǐhǎo ma?

Fine. And you?
好。你呢? hǎo. Nǐ ne?

Excuse me.
劳驾。 láojià.

Sorry.
对不起。 duìbùqǐ.

Yes./No.
是。/不是。 shì./bùshì.

Please ...
请...... qǐng ...

Thank you.
谢谢你。 xièxie nǐ.

You're welcome.
不客气。 bù kèqi.

What's your name?
你叫什么名字? nǐ jiào shénme míngzi?

My name is ...
我叫...... Wǒ jiào ...

Do you speak English?
你会说英文吗? nǐ huìshuō Yīngwén ma?

I don't understand.
我不明白。 wǒ bù míngbái.

In South Korea

Korean pronunciation is pretty straightforward for English speakers, as most sounds are also found in English or have a close approximation.

Basics

Hello.
안녕하세요. an·nyŏng ha·se·yo

Goodbye.
안녕히 an·nyŏng·hi
(if leaving/ 계세요/ kye·se·yo/
staying) 가세요. ka·se·yo

How are you?
안녕하세요? an·nyŏng ha·se·yo

Fine, thanks. And you?
네. 안녕하세요? ne an·nyŏng ha·se·yo

Excuse me.
실례합니다. shil·lé ham·ni·da

Sorry.
죄송합니다. choé·song ham·ni·da

Yes.
네. né

No.
아니요. a·ni·yo

Thank you.
고맙습니다./ ko·map·sŭm·ni·da/
감사합니다. kam·sa·ham·ni·da

You're welcome.
천만에요. ch'ŏn·ma·ne·yo

What's your name?
성함을 여쭤봐도 sŏng·ha·mŭl yŏ·tchŏ·bwa·do
될까요? doélk·ka·yo

My name is ...
제 이름은 ...입니다. che i·rŭ·mŭn ...im·ni·da

Do you speak English?
영어 하실 줄 yŏng·ŏ ha·shil·jul
아시나요? a·shi·na·yo

I don't understand.
못 알아 들었어요. mot a·ra·dŭ·rŏss·ŏ·yo

In Taiwan

The official language of Taiwan is referred to in the west as Mandarin Chinese. The Chinese call it Pǔtōnghuà (common speech) and in Taiwan it is known as Guóyǔ (the national language). Taiwanese, often called a 'dialect' of Mandarin, is in fact a separate language and the two are not mutually intelligible. Travellers to Taiwan can get by without using any Taiwanese, as virtually all young and middle-aged people speak Mandarin. See under In Shànghǎi for basics.

Behind the Scenes

Acknowledgements

Cover photograph: Yokohama, Japan; Prisma by Dukas Presseagentur GmbH/ Alamy Stock Photo ©

Climate map data adapted from Peel MC, Finlayson BL & McMahon TA (2007) 'Updated World Map of the Köppen-Geiger Climate Classification', Hydrology and Earth System Sciences, 11, 1633–44.

Illustrations pp40–1 and pp236–7 by Michael Weldon.

This Book

This 1st edition of Lonely Planet's *Cruise Ports Northeast Asia* guidebook was researched and written by Ray Bartlett, Andrew Bender, Jade Bremner, Stephanie d'Arc Taylor, Dinah Gardner, Trent Holden, Craig McLachlan, Rebecca Milner, Kate Morgan, MaSovaida Morgan, Thomas O'Malley, Simon Richmond, Phillip Tang and Benedict Walker. It was curated by Imogen Bannister, William Allen, Jenna Myers and Kathryn Rowan.

This guidebook was produced by the following:

Destination Editor James Smart

Senior Product Editors Kate Chapman, Anne Mason

Product Editor Carolyn Boicos

Senior Cartographer Diana Von Holdt

Book Designer Fergal Condon

Assisting Editors Paul Harding, Lauren O'Connell

Assisting Cartographer Anthony Phelan

Cover Researcher Naomi Parker

Thanks to Ronan Abayawickrema, Andi Jones, Alison Lyall, Akamatsu Naoko, Alison Ridgway, Claire Rourke, Jacqui Saunders, Jaeyoon Adela Shin, Angela Tinson, Guan Yuanyuan

---

Send Us Your Feedback

We love to hear from travellers – your comments keep us on our toes and help make our books better. Our well-travelled team reads every word on what you loved or loathed about this book. Although we cannot reply individually to postal submissions, we always guarantee that your feedback goes straight to the appropriate authors, in time for the next edition. Each person who sends us information is thanked in the next edition, the most useful submissions are rewarded with a selection of digital PDF chapters.

Visit lonelyplanet.com/contact to submit your updates and suggestions or to ask for help. Our award-winning website also features inspirational travel stories, news and discussions.

Note: We may edit, reproduce and incorporate your comments in Lonely Planet products such as guidebooks, websites and digital products, so let us know if you don't want your comments reproduced or your name acknowledged. For a copy of our privacy policy visit lonelyplanet.com/privacy.

A – Z
Index

Symbols & Map Key

Look for these symbols to quickly identify listings:

- ◎ Sights
- ✪ Activities
- ✪ Courses
- ⊙ Tours
- ✪ Festivals & Events
- ✪ Eating
- ✪ Drinking
- ✪ Entertainment
- ✪ Shopping
- ✪ Information & Transport

These symbols and abbreviations give vital information for each listing:

- 🌿 Sustainable or green recommendation
- **FREE** No payment required

- ☎ Telephone number
- ☺ Opening hours
- Ⓟ Parking
- ☺ Nonsmoking
- ✳ Air-conditioning
- @ Internet access
- 📶 Wi-fi access
- 🏊 Swimming pool

- 🚌 Bus
- ⛴ Ferry
- 🚊 Tram
- 🚆 Train
- 📖 English-language menu
- 🌱 Vegetarian selection
- 👪 Family-friendly

Find your best experiences with these Great For... icons.

 Art & Culture

🏖 Beaches

💳 Budget

☕ Cafe/Coffee

🚲 Cycling

🗺 Detour

 Drinking

 Entertainment

 Events

 Family Travel

🍽 Food & Drink

📖 History

💬 Local Life

🐦 Nature & Wildlife

📷 Photo Op

🔭 Scenery

🛍 Shopping

🧳 Short Trip

🏀 Sport

🥾 Walking

❄ Winter Travel

Sights

- Beach
- Bird Sanctuary
- Buddhist
- Castle/Palace
- Christian
- Confucian
- Hindu
- Islamic
- Jain
- Jewish
- Monument
- Museum/Gallery/ Historic Building
- Ruin
- Shinto
- Sikh
- Taoist
- Winery/Vineyard
- Zoo/Wildlife Sanctuary
- Other Sight

Points of Interest

- Bodysurfing
- Camping
- Cafe
- Canoeing/Kayaking
- Course/Tour
- Diving
- Drinking & Nightlife
- Eating
- Entertainment
- Sento Hot Baths/ Onsen
- Shopping
- Skiing
- Sleeping
- Snorkelling
- Surfing
- Swimming/Pool
- Walking
- Windsurfing
- Other Activity

Information

- Bank
- Embassy/Consulate
- Hospital/Medical
- Internet
- Police
- Post Office
- Telephone
- Toilet
- Tourist Information
- Other Information

Geographic

- Beach
- Gate
- Hut/Shelter
- Lighthouse
- Lookout
- Mountain/Volcano
- Oasis
- Park
- Pass
- Picnic Area
- Waterfall

Transport

- Airport
- BART station
- Border crossing
- Boston T station
- Bus
- Cable car/Funicular
- Cycling
- Ferry
- Metro/MRT station
- Monorail
- Parking
- Petrol station
- Subway/S-Bahn/ Skytrain station
- Taxi
- Train station/Railway
- Tram
- Tube Station
- Underground/ U-Bahn station
- Other Transport

Dinah Gardner

Dinah is a freelance writer focusing on travel and politics. Since 2015 she has been happily based in Taiwan, one of Asia's most charming and courteous countries. She's lived in and written about Vietnam, Tibet, China, Hong Kong, Nepal and Bhutan.

Trent Holden

A Geelong-based writer, located just outside Melbourne, Trent has worked for Lonely Planet since 2005. He's covered 30 plus guidebooks across Asia, Africa and Australia. With a penchant for megacities, Trent's in his element when assigned to cover a nation's capital – the more chaotic the better – to unearth cool bars, art, street food and underground subculture. On the flipside he also writes books to idyllic tropical islands across Asia, in between going on safari to national parks in Africa and the subcontinent. When not travelling, Trent works as a freelance editor, reviewer and spending all his money catching live gigs.

Craig McLachlan

Craig has covered destinations all over the globe for Lonely Planet for two decades. Based in Queenstown, New Zealand for half the year, he runs an outdoor activities company and a sake brewery, then moonlights overseas for the other half, leading tours and writing for Lonely Planet. Craig has completed a number of adventures in Japan and his books are available on Amazon. Check out www.craigmclachlan.com.

Rebecca Milner

California-born and living in Tokyo since 2002, Rebecca has co-authored Lonely Planet guides to Tokyo and Japan. She's also a freelance writer covering travel, food and culture. Rebecca has been published in the *Guardian*, the *Independent*, the *Sunday Times Travel Magazine*, the *Japan Times* and more.

Kate Morgan

Having worked for Lonely Planet for over a decade now, Kate has been fortunate enough to cover plenty of ground working as a travel writer on destinations such as Shanghai, Japan, India, Russia, Zimbabwe, the Philippines and Phuket. She has done stints living in London, Paris and Osaka but these days is based in one of her favourite regions in the world – Victoria, Australia. In between travelling

the world and writing about it, Kate enjoys spending time at home working as a freelance editor.

MaSovaida Morgan

MaSovaida is a Lonely Planet writer and multimedia storyteller whose wanderlust has taken her to more than 35 countries across six continents. Prior to freelancing, she was Lonely Planet's Destination Editor for South America for four years and worked as an editor for newspapers and NGOs in the Middle East and United Kingdom. Follow her on Instagram @MaSovaida.

Thomas O'Malley

A British writer based in Beijing, Tom is a world-leading connoisseur of cheap eats, dive bars, dark alleyways and hangovers. He has contributed travel stories to everyone from the BBC to *Playboy*, and reviews hotels for the *Telegraph*. Under another guise, he is a comedy scriptwriter. Follow him by walking behind at a distance.

Simon Richmond

Journalist and photographer Simon Richmond has specialised as a travel writer since the early 1990s and first worked for Lonely Planet in 1999 on its *Central Asia* guide. He's long since stopped counting the number of guidebooks he's researched and written for the company, but countries covered include Australia, China, India, Iran, Japan, Korea, Malaysia, Mongolia, Myanmar (Burma), Russia, Singapore, South Africa and Turkey.

Phillip Tang

Phillip Tang grew up on a typically Australian diet of *pho* and fish'n'chips before moving to Mexico City. A degree in Chinese and Latin American cultures launched him into travel and then writing about it for Lonely Planet's *Canada, China, Japan, Korea, Mexico, Peru* and *Vietnam* guides. Follow his writing at hellophillip.com, photos @mrtangtangtang and tweets @philliptang.

Benedict Walker

A beach baby from Newcastle, Australia, Benedict turned 40 in 2017 and decided to start a new life in Leipzig, Germany. Writing for Lonely Planet was a childhood dream and he has covered big chunks of Australia, Canada, Germany, Japan, USA, Switzerland, Sweden and Japan. Follow him on Instagram @wordsandjourneys.

Our Story

A beat-up old car, a few dollars in the pocket and a sense of adventure. In 1972 that's all Tony and Maureen Wheeler needed for the trip of a lifetime – across Europe and Asia overland to Australia. It took several months, and at the end – broke but inspired – they sat at their kitchen table writing and stapling together their first travel guide, *Across Asia on the Cheap*. Within a week they'd sold 1500 copies. Lonely Planet was born.

Today, Lonely Planet has offices in Franklin, London, Melbourne, Oakland, Dublin, Beijing and Delhi, with more than 600 staff and writers. We share Tony's belief that 'a great guidebook should do three things: inform, educate and amuse'.

Our Writers

Ray Bartlett

Ray Bartlett has been travel writing for nearly two decades, bringing Japan, Korea, Mexico, Tanzania, Guatemala, Indonesia and many parts of the United States to life in rich detail for top-industry publishers, newspapers and magazines. Ray currently divides his time between homes in the USA, Japan and Mexico.

Andrew Bender

Award-winning travel and food writer Andrew Bender has written three dozen Lonely Planet guidebooks (from Amsterdam to Los Angeles, Germany to Taiwan and more than a dozen titles about Japan), plus numerous articles for lonelyplanet.com. Andy also is a tour leader and tour planner for visits to Japan. Follow him on Twitter @wheresandynow.

Jade Bremner

Jade has been a journalist for more than a decade. She has lived in and reported on four different regions. Wherever she goes she finds action sports to try, the weirder the better, and it's no coincidence many of her favourite places have some of the best waves in the world. Jade has edited travel magazines and sections for *Time Out* and *Radio Times* and has contributed to the *Times*, CNN and the *Independent*. She feels privileged to share tales from this wonderful planet we call home and is always looking for the next adventure.

Stephanie d'Arc Taylor

A native Angeleno, Stephanie grew up with the west LA weekend ritual of going for Iranian sweets after *tenzaru soba* in Little Osaka. Later, she quit her PhD to move to Beirut and become a writer. Since then, she has published work with the *New York Times, Guardian, Roads & Kingdoms* and *Kinfolk Magazine*, and co-founded Jaleesa, a venture-capital-funded social impact business in Beirut. Follow her on Instagram @zerodarctaylor.

← More Writers ←

STAY IN TOUCH LONELYPLANET.COM/CONTACT

AUSTRALIA The Malt Store, Level 3, 551 Swanston St, Carlton, Victoria 3053, 03 8379 8000, fax 03 8379 8111

IRELAND Digital Depot, Roe Lane (off Thomas St), Digital Hub, Dublin 8, D08 TCV4, Ireland

USA 124 Linden Street, Oakland, CA 94607, 510 250 6400, toll free 800 275 8555, fax 510 893 8572

UK 240 Blackfriars Road, London SE1 8NW, 020 3771 5100, fax 020 3771 5101

 twitter.com/ lonelyplanet

 facebook.com/ lonelyplanet

 instagram.com/ lonelyplanet

 youtube.com/ lonelyplanet

 lonelyplanet.com/ newsletter